MW01088012

Secrets of Solomon

or

The Art Rabidmadar
(Clavicula Salomonis de Secretis)

A WITCH'S HANDBOOK

FROM THE TRIAL RECORDS OF THE VENETIAN INQUISITION

Critical edition of the Latin text, with translation by
Joseph H. Peterson

First published in 2018 by Twilit Grotto Press

Kasson, MN, USA

ISBN 13: 978-1-387-83949-0 (hardback)

ISBN 13: 978-1720387053 (paperback)

Second impression with corrections.

Image on frontispiece is from *Christoph Wagner's Leben und Thaten*, in Johann Scheible, *Das Kloster*, Bd. 3, Stuttgart, 1846, p. 41.

Cover based on ms DN91, with seal of Vetael from ms GG.

CONTENTS

Introduction   i

Disclaimer   xxi

Acknowledgements   xxi

Malediction   xxi

Abbreviations   xxiii

Correlation of contents between manuscripts   xxiv

Book 1: Concerning the chthonic spirits.   2

Introduction.   2

     Making the seal of protection.   2

Discourse concerning the infernal spirits.   4

Collection of Secrets.

To make it rain.   28

To make it snow.   30

To cause lightning.   30

In order to not be cold.   32

To not be bothered by excessive heat.   34

A wonderful secret for opening all closed things.   34

To win over the love of a young woman.   36

For love making/coupling. An entirely admirable secret.   38

To have coins as often as we please.   40

In order that an enemy will die.   42

To become invisible. A most pleasant secret.   44

In order to hear the sweetest music.   44

In order that a corpse appear living and able to speak.   46

Book 2: Fundamentals of controlling the Amalthai spirits, with instruments, pentacles, and apparitions.   52

Chapter 1. Concerning the fundamentals of the art.   52

Chapter 2. Those things which are to be observed when working in the Art.   54

Chapter 3. The powers of each superior intelligence.   58

Chap. 4. How we can obtain the preceding knowledge, arts, and secrets from the intelligences.   66

Chap. 5. Concerning those things which are necessary for invocations and conjurations of the daemons.   66

Chap. 6. Concerning the circle.   66

Chap. 7. Concerning the great pentacle.   70

Chap. 8. Concerning the sword.   74

Chap. 9. Concerning the consecrated water.   76

Chap 10. Concerning the garment.   76
Chap. 11. Concerning the fire and incenses.   78
Chap. 12. Concerning blood and ink.   80
Chap. 13. Concerning virgin paper.   80
Chap. 14. Concerning the place and time.   80
Chap. 15. Concerning the invocations and conjurations of spirits.   82
Chap. 16. Concerning the experiments.   90
    Concerning the pentacles of Orifiel (Primum Mobile).   92
    Pentacles of Magriel (Firmament).   98
    Pentacles of Uriel (Saturn).   100
    Pentacles of Pamechiel (Jupiter).   102
    Pentacles of Pomeriel (Mars).   106
    Pentacles of Sabriel (The Sun).   108
    Pentacles of Uchariel (Venus).   112
    Pentacles of Charariel (Mercury).   114
    Pentacles of Pantheriel (The Moon).   116
    Pentacles of Araton (Fire).   120
    Pentacles of Agiaton (Air).   122
    Pentacles of Begud (Water).   124
    Pentacles of Tainor (Earth).   126

Book Three. The Planetary Intelligences and their subordinates   130
    Introduction.   130
    The names of the Intelligences of the Sun and the Moon.   136
    Concerning the Intelligence of the Sun, named Michael.   138
    Concerning the Intelligence of the Moon, named Gabriel.   138
    Concerning the Intelligence of Mars, named Samael.   140
    Concerning the Intelligence of Mercury, named Raphael.   144
    Concerning the Intelligence of Jupiter, named Sachiel.   148
    Concerning the Intelligence of Venus, named Anael.   150
    Concerning the Intelligence of Saturn, named Cassiel.   152
    Concerning the intermediate spirits or the officers of the highest.   154
    The Solar Spirits.   156
    The Lunar Spirits.   160
    The Martial Spirits.   162
    The Mercurial spirits.   164
    The Spirits of Jupiter.   166
    The Spirits of Venus.   168
    The Spirits of Saturn.   170

Book 4. Concerning the stone.   174
    Concerning the preparation of the stone.   174

Concerning the purification of the stone.   176
Concerning the consecration of the stone.   178
The baptism of the stone.   180
The practice and procedure of consecration, and first concerning the Pentacle.
     180

Appendix. Additional spirits from W983   195
Bibliography   198
Index of spirits   204
General Index   210

INTRODUCTION

Spread of magic from the Venetian Inquisition to Gerald Gardner's private library

n spite of intense efforts by authorities to suppress them, manuals of magic spread with amazing speed throughout early modern Europe. Our story of this particular text could start in **Venice, 1636.** Leonardo Longo and Francesco Viola are tried for witchcraft (*Stregheria* in Italian) by the Inquisition. Their grimoire, or handbook of magic, was confiscated and carefully preserved in the Archivio di Stato di Venezia (ASV).[1] The Latin title reads *Clavicula Salomonis de Secretis* ("The little key of Solomon concerning the Secrets"), which I will abbreviate CSDS.

After decades of searching for this elusive text, I now have the pleasure of presenting and translating it here for the first time. It contains their secret techniques for dealing with the more dangerous spirits or daemons, intentionally scattered and hidden within a collection of "secrets" comprising many detailed examples. Together these provide enough clues to enable practitioners to create their own spells for working with all the spirits cataloged.

It is clear that this book was not just a curiosity, but put to practical use. According to eyewitnesses, Longo, a former Dominican monk from Naples, but perhaps a native of Rhodes, was never without it: "He used to recite it and read it out loud without hesitation, and he would always have it on him."[2] Clients would engage him for various things described in the text, such as winning at gambling. They also testified that he used the techniques described in the book, such as preparing "superstitious symbols" with the juice of certain herbs, observation of the planetary hours, and drawing magic circles in the ground.[3] Inquisition records show that this

---

1   The Venetian Inquisition was originally started in 1547 primarily to address protestant reform. It turned more of its attention to prosecuting practitioners of magic in the 1580s. See Barbierato 2002 p. 159.

2   ASV Sant'Uffizio.b.93, June 10, 1636 case against Francesco Viola and Leonardo Longo. Barbierato 2002 p. 164 (his translation of the testimony).

3   Testimony dated June 4, 1636. The popular gambling game of basset is specifically

and other magic texts were circulating widely and "used on a daily basis and at a popular level."[1]

It is clear that the network of monasteries was a chief conduit for the transmission of magical texts such as this,[2] so Longo may have been the actual scribe involved here. However, it was apparently not too difficult to procure such prohibited material from certain bookshops, *botteghe* (studios), or private copyists.[3]

This text is remarkable in many ways. To some extent it bridges the gaps between folklore, witch trial records, and practical and theoretical magic. Likewise it fills a gap between medieval magic and Wicca. It relies on developing a close relationship with the spirits, many of which are said to be subordinates of undisguised evil spirit masters, such as Lucifer and Belzebuth.

Unusual too is the fact that it is explicitly directed to both male and female practitioners, has spells for fertility issues. The chief spirits are referred to as the "Governesses" (*Gubernatrices*). It is tempting to link the epithet to Amalthea (Greek "Tender Goddess"), since the spirits being invoked are referred to as the *Amalthai*.[4]

The methods are much simpler than those found in texts such as the *Key of Solomon* proper, the *Sworn Book of Honorius*, or the *Sacred Magic of Abramelin the Mage*. It also relies heavily on natural ingredients that have sympathetic properties with the goals sought. The charms (i.e. incantations or chants – Latin *carmina*) are generally a few simple words, easy to memorize, and evidently sung. In many ways they are reminiscent of those in the charming and popular grimoire *Le Poule Noire* (*Black Pullet*).

My hunt for this book was lengthy and circuitous. I knew something like this must exist from many clues found in the wildly popular *Grimorium*

---

mentioned.

1   Barbierato 2002 p. 159.

2   Barbierato 2002 p. 162 et passim.

3   Barbierato 2017 p. 274.

4   On the use of Gubernatrix, see Duggan 2002 p. 209. The epithet was also used of the Roman goddesses Bona Dea and Fortuna, as well as Isis: See Brouwer 1989 p. 393. Agrippa lists Gubernatrix as one of the magical epithets of the Moon (OP2.59). Giordano Bruno calls the Moon *manium gubernatrix, dea noctis* ("Governess of the gods of the Lower World, Goddess of the Night") *(Cantus Circaeus*, Paris, 1582, p. 2.) Note, the author of CSDS was familiar with the writings of Cicero (see below), who wrote about wanting to build a shrine to Amalthea.

Verum (GV). Like others, I found that text fascinating. I resolved to track down its sources, in order to clear up many puzzling aspects raised there. Influential occultist A.E. Waite pointed out some of the problems in his *Book of Ceremonial Magic*: missing drawings, passages in garbled Latin which make no sense, and inclusion of plates which have no reference to the text. Waite suggested that the Italian editions of *Grimorium Verum* supplied some of the deficiencies, but that did not prove to be the case: Upon investigation, it became apparent they merely covered them up.[1]

My first breakthrough was finding excerpts in a 1921 German book on Faust by Kiesewetter. It was clear at once that these quotes were from some Latin equivalent to the beginning of GV. Kiesewetter had in turn taken these from a 1788 encyclopedic manual by pioneer of psychiatry, Johann Christoph Adelung.[2] They provided tantalizing clues for identifying additional exemplars, including the title and opening words (*incipit*).

It was still some years before I finally found a mostly complete manuscript, when the Biblioteka Narodowa digitized theirs, making it available on the *polona.pl* website. Unfortunately, that manuscript omitted much of the artwork. Soon afterwards, the Universitätsbibliothek Leipzig published photographs of a manuscript in their collection – a most valuable text, but also incomplete. Scottish artist and author Adam McLean provided some valuable hints which led me to a French manuscript in the Wellcome library; this supplied nearly all the missing figures, albeit misplaced.[3]

While trying to reconstruct the complete text and figures, I came across a brief catalog entry from the library of Gerald Gardner, the father of the modern Wicca movement. The title read *Clavicula Regis Salomonis de Secretis Secretorum,* which included several words I had been searching for. After some time I was able to identify the current owners, and arrange to see and photograph this precious manuscript. Finally I had the complete text with all the missing artwork, to resolve many of the issues that the disparate manuscripts had raised.

---

1   See Waite 1911, pp. 97-99; Peterson 2007, pp. vi-vii. For another edition, with a great deal of practical advice, see Stratton-Kent, 2010.

2   Kiesewetter 1921, pp. 68-73; Adelung 1788, pp. 347-353. Will-Erich Peuckert also quotes Adelung's excerpts in *Pansophie* Bld. II Berlin: E. Schmidt, 1956, pp. 155-156.

3   *http://www.levity.com/alchemy/clav_fr3.html* retrieved Nov 8, 2011. It is incorrectly grouped with Abognazar exemplars.

Equally exciting was identifying a valuable manuscript in the ASV, based on Dr. Barbierato's comments (cited above). I was able to arrange for photo-graphs of the text as well as all the legal records associated with it.

Since then, other manuscripts were brought to my attention by research-ers, each adding valuable information, and allowing for a critical reconstruc-tion of the urtext.

Survey of the text

Despite the title, the text should not be considered a sub-class of the many varieties of *Clavicula Salomonis* (" *The Key of Solomon"*) texts, largely known from the 1889 edition by S. L. Mathers.[1] Instead, it distinguishes it-self as a supplemental *Clavicula* or "little key", focused on chthonic spirits in-stead of aerial spirits.

The manuscripts are remarkably consistent with each other, not exhibit-ing the fluidity often seen in the genre.[2] The four books or parts are comple-mentary in many ways, if not always conforming in style.

Date

A reasonable *terminus post quem* for our text is 1559, given the fact that it quotes from pseudo-Agrippa's *liber quartus*. Given its wide geographic dis-persal and complicated nature of their interrelations,[3] the *terminus ante quem* must be at least several years before the trial events of 1636.

Author

The text provides very few clues about the author. He or she was obvi-ously well educated. The Latin is sophisticated, including obscure vocabulary, such as *scenobata* and *titubantes*. The spells for love and sex are written from the point of view of a male seeking a female, but this may be more an indica-tion of the clientele than the author's gender. The unusual use of English for *voces magicae* (magic words of power) in Book 4 indicates the author was not English, but might have had access to some English magic text or oral

---

1 See Mathiesen, 2007. Skinner, Stephen and David Rankine, 2008, pp. 28-32, 412-414; Skinner, 2015, pp. 92-93, 296-334. This doesn't include the Hebrew or Greek manuscripts, and also includes texts that are unrelated except for name, including the Abognazar group.

2 On this subject, see Klaassen 2013.

3 On which see below.

tradition. According to Barbierato, "the words 'braccio sinistro' indicate that the text was originally Italian."[1] Some of the ingredients used, such as agnocasto, are native to the Mediterranean region. The association of Gog-Magog with invisibility in Book 2 may be evidence of an Arabic influence, corroborating a southern European origin.

Other passages point to the author's higher education: In particular, the author mentions the theory of humors, legends of Achilles, and Cicero's Milo declamation. He or she also expounds the "Great chain of being" theory; this derived from Plato through the neo-Platonists, and was developed further in the Middle Ages. Likewise, Book 3 expounds the popular medieval doctrine of universals and particulars – see Boethius and a whole host of writers on this subject. Similarly, the author demonstrates knowledge of the widely-held doctrine of cosmic motor intelligences.

This higher education could have been monastic, especially given their role in transmitting magical manuscripts.

Contents

Book 1 deals with chthonic spirits (including infernal, earthly, and aquatic spirits), which are all said to communicate visibly. There are three groups of these, divided geographically and headed by a separate chief demon. These spirits and their hierarchy closely parallel those in *Grimorium Verum,* but here their offices are enumerated in greater detail and clarity. Their physical appearance is sometimes given, again indicating they can be expected to appear physically. These spirits are described as earthly, or inhabiting the depths of the earth. Their nature is reminiscent of the spirits described in Book 4 of the *Sworn Book of Honorius.* They are very dangerous, and can inflict great physical harm or death. Many of their offices deal with water and earth, and the other two classes of elemental spirits – fire and air – are explicitly excluded from use in this book. It does add the interesting details that the aerial spirits only communicate invisibly, and can be carried about with the magician in a magical ring.

This is followed by a collection of magical secrets for things such as love, money, and invisibility. These are said to be examples, sufficient to allow the magician to work out how to employ all these spirits. Curiously, none of these secrets are found in GV.

---

1   2002 p. 166.

Book 2 deals with the "Amalthai" spirits. The name is probably related to the goddess Amalthea. There are thirteen orders of these spirits, associated with the four elements (earth, water, air, and fire), and the nine "movable spheres" – namely, the seven classical planets plus the Primum Mobile and the Starry Heavens. They may appear in a frightening form unless ordered otherwise. Detailed instructions for working with these spirits are given, which are reminiscent of those in the *Key of Solomon* proper, such as preparing a protective lamen, a ritual sword, and a magic circle, but details differ.

Book 3 is written in a distinctly more modern and eloquent Latin. It deals with the seven "planetary intelligences," and spirits under them. It also uses the term *genius* – usually defined as a guardian spirit (or deity) of a person. The various angels or spirits enumerated are closely related to those in the *Heptameron*, and the *Sworn Book of Honorius*[1] but more details are added from the "sayings of the astrologers" (*planetariis dictę*) – an unidentified astrological text. The primary intelligences of each planet are all identical to those in *Heptameron*, and their seals are generally similar in appearance. However, the list of intermediate[2] intelligences in the present text is shorter, with name variants. The ruling angels are said to appear in human form, but their subservients appear in animal form.

The ruling angel of Mercury here is Raphael, which agrees with *Heptameron*, Cardanus, and Michael Scotus, but differs from Honorius, who has Michael.[3] But the descriptions of the planetary angels are closer to those in Honorius, although much more elaborate here. The help of these spirits is obtained by the use of various pentacles or seals – these seals are mentioned in the *Sworn Book of Honorius*, but no longer extant there.

Book 4 gives instructions for preparing a magic "stone," a representation of the macrocosm or great Universe. It is said to strengthen your soul, and is a basic prerequisite for all magic operations. It is actually made of clay shaped like a human. It includes additional instructions on consecrations, apparently drawn from pseudo-Agrippa. The image is symbolically birthed, baptized, and named for the spirit which dominates the hour of its baptism. The names are not included, however, but are probably the same as those found in

---

1   These spirits are also closely related to those in *Raziel*; see Peterson 2016 pp. 19-20.
2   Or "middle" – Lat. *medium*.
3   Peterson 2016 p. 21.

the *Heptameron.*[1]

The figures: Some of the figures have very obvious symbolism, such as books (Humeth), cards and dice (Miel), phases of the Moon (Madiel), and rain (Ianiel), so it is quite possible the rest have less obvious symbolism.

Requirements for the magician

Gender: One of the remarkable things about this text is that it is clear it was intended for both men and women. The opening paragraph states that King Solomon composed it for teaching his children. Since the Bible identifies his children as one son and two daughters, the use of the plural must mean that both genders were intended. This is confirmed by the fact that separate instructions are sometimes included for male and female practitioners.

Zeal (alacrity): "For all magic operations there is need for faith, and for the soul to be prepared with zeal for everything which must be accomplished."

Conduct: The text mentions the need to avoid disreputable companions, plus the need for moderation, seclusion, and secrecy.

Outline of the methods

Sacred names. Books 1 and 2 both open with an invocation to Adonai Tetragrammaton, and other names. The spells likewise call on these and other names of God to compel the spirits. The magic circle includes the names Adonai and AGLA.

As mentioned above, some of the techniques differ depending on the class of spirits being called upon. The magic requires some creativity, but abundant examples are given to permit practitioners to create their own spells for other purposes.

Chthonic spirits (infernal, earthly, and aquatic). Most of the instructions for employing these spirits are intentionally scattered throughout the experiments (or "secrets"), but can be summarized in a few paragraphs. Besides some prerequisites, the basic concept is to use some **natural ingredients** which relate sympathetically to the desired end, the names of the spirit, their

---

1   W4667 pp. 414 ff in fact includes such a list from *Heptameron*. See also Kieckhefer 1998
    pp. 182-183.

superior, and a very short (sung) incantation. Properly selected natural ingredients attract the spirits to us because of their affinity, and it also gives the spirits the ability to act on physical things.[1]

The first prerequisite is the lamen, or sigil of protection. The preferred material for the lamen is bloodstone, which Ficino associates with the planet Mars, but Agrippa associates with the Sun.[2] According to Damigeron's classic lapidary (4th ce), it "preserves a person's life and keeps him unharmed, and all kinds of bogey." (i.e. bugbears, Lat. *Terriculas*). "He who wears this stone will never be deceived."[3]

The **lamen** seems to serve somewhat like a badge, indicating that your authority has been vetted. It must be customized with the practitioner's initials.

The cooperation of these spirits requires that you previously enter into an agreement or "**pact**" (*pactus* or *foedus*), namely some pledge of loyalty or friendship to the spirits, using their characters. The term pact I think has misleading connotations in this context, given all the depictions in book and film of a "pact with the devil." The perennial obsessions of the witch hunters – renunciation of God and pledging of one's soul – are not involved. The description in the text is intentionally vague, but includes writing out a specific character, as well as the intention. It becomes more clear when one studies the examples provided later in the book. The spirit hierarchy is important, because specific subordinate spirits should be provoked or "motivated" (Lat. *lacessantur*) using the character (or seal) of their superior. Their own character is also needed to invoke them. When listing the spirits under Satanachi, namely Sergurth etc., it says "the pentacles are very necessary" as spoken of in Book 2.

Moreover, suffumigations, **offerings** or gifts, or sacrifices are to be employed. The text doesn't elaborate much, but the *Key of Solomon* enjoins food and drink, including bread, water, wine, and the meat of certain animals. It also recommends burning an appropriate wood.[4] *Pseudomonarchia*

---

1 See Book 2, chapter 4.
2 Book III chap. 2, Ficino, (tr. Kaske), 2006, p. 249. Agrippa OP1.23, following William of Auvergne, *De universo*.
3 Damigeron, tr. P. Tahil, 2005, p. 6.
4 Mathers 1889 revised layout 2016 pp.127-128. Aub24 reads, "juniper or brambles for the spirits of Saturn; bay-laurel for those of the Sun; oak or boxwood for those of Jupiter; willow for those of the Moon; cherry (or horn, Lat. *corneae*) for those of Mars; myrtle for those of Venus; hazel for those of Mercury. There are countless other woods attributed to

Daemonum recommends leaving a vessel of wine for the spirit Bileth.[1] In the folklore of Northern Europe, spirit and fairy offerings frequently take the form of food and drink, such as bread and milk (or beer) left for them overnight.[2] The *Sworn Book of Honorius* likewise mentions the need for a "small gift" (Lat. *munusculum*) – evidently the "pleasing suffumigations" mentioned elsewhere in the text.[3] The fifteenth century Munich "Necromancer's Handbook" specifies offerings of incense, milk and honey, or a sacrificial bird or animal in various experiments.[4]

Other essential elements are scattered throughout the examples, including putting on "suitable garments", **music** (including both singing the *incantations*, as well as playing the lyre and whistle), magic circles, and calling on the spirits to appear using the names of God. Invocation is generally done facing north. Sympathetic magic is woven into each spell, ritually enacting the desired effect using representative stones, herbs, and other elements.

In some cases a magic wand is needed, but no special preparation is given. GV includes instructions for its preparation, based on the *Key of Solomon* proper. In one experiment, two wands are needed. Some of the experiments have other requisites such as black candles, an altar, and a copper vessel.

The first example, for rain, starts by drawing a simple circle on the ground. It doesn't specify whether this is done with the wand, sword, or knife, but a wand seems intended, since the spirit seal is drawn with that. Next, place in the center of the circle a heliotrope (aka bloodstone), a semi-precious gem with a long history of magical uses. The name *heliotrope* means "turns towards the sun." According to Damigeron (loc. cit.), "this stone turns to the sun, even if it is covered in cloud; therefore this stone calls forth rain." Then, with the magic wand, draw the seal of the spirits whose office is sought – in this case Elelogaphatel, who commands the waters, and Beschard, who causes storms and snow. The astrological symbol for the Sun is also drawn, near the top of the circle. The circle is sprinkled with sea water. Finally, say the words "Aerlea Helelagafaton" (perhaps garbled Greek?) reminiscent of

---

the planets, which can be discovered elsewhere, as in our book where we mention cedar of lebanon and hyssop."

1 Peterson 2001 p. 234.
2 Wilby 2010 pp. 95-96.
3 Peterson 2016, pp 39, CXIV.7, CXV.16-17, 35, 41, CXVIII.24,.
4 Kieckhefer 1998 pp. 50, 53, 60, 98, 157. At one point (p. 121) the master offers the Devil the sleeves of his surplus.

the name Elelogaphatel and *helios* ("the Sun"). This is clearly a magical enactment on a small scale of what you are asking the spirits to do on a larger scale. The spell for snow is similar, but uses Lucifer and Beschard as the operative spirits.

The third example, for lightning, uses lightning stone (fulgurite), the herb lunaria, and an oil lamp as sympathetic elements, and calls on the spirits Beschard, Lucifer, and Syrach, to attend. The form of the invocation given here (page 27) uses the names of God Adonay Tetragrammaton, and is likely a model for other spells; this also seems to be hinted at on 15r/page 32. Following the invocation, you must observe silence, then proceed by lighting the lamp and addressing the spirits with a short chant.

The next two examples, to be insensitive to heat or cold, use the characters of the spirit Frimodth, suffumigated with incense, and placed into fire or ice.

The spell to unlock anything uses the seal of Surgath, whose office is to unlock things, along with lunaria, lodestone, and iron filings. The ritual vicariously represents the moving of the iron bolt or latch of a lock.

The next spell is for love. It also uses a magic circle. The sympathetic magic ingredients used are the stone chrysolite[1] and mandrake, both of which are said to attract love. Another ingredient is milk. An interesting addition is the use of love knots, very rarely seen in grimoires. The spirit Frimodth is again the operative here.

A more erotic spell calls on the same spirit, using a circle drawn on an altar. It also employs animal privates, black candles, and a drawing of genitalia. In addition, a vessel of copper (associated with Venus) is used, no doubt representing a vulva in this operation.

For attracting money, you draw the denomination of coins you want, and invoke the spirit Claunth, again using a circle and his seal. Here an interesting clue is added: The Latin term *carmen*, which I translate as *incantation*, can also mean song, and we are directed to actually sing the words to the lyre, recalling how Psalms were traditionally sung. The spell to evoke music adds the element that the sung words should be interspersed with moans or sighs (Lat. *gemitus*).

---

1   Probably meaning peridot.

Also interesting is the instruction to dismiss the goal from your mind for a time, by sleeping or observing silence.

The spell for invisibility uses the skin of a chameleon or cuttlefish as a sympathetic element.

Observation of times: The introduction for the work promises that this subject will be covered in Book 2. There we find the observation of planetary hours as seen in other grimoires, plus other celestial events such as eclipses, and frequently the feast days of various saints.

Amalthai spirits: Book 2 gives instructions for working with the thirteen classes of these spirits. These require use of conjurations, invocations, and exorcisms. These in turn require preparation and consecration of the following: Holy water, ritual garments (priestly), virgin parchment or vellum, fire and incense, blood or ink for writing, a magic sword, a whistle,[1] and a "great" pentacle. This pentacle, or lamen of protection, is made from an amalgam of seven metals – presumably those that represent the seven planets. It should be kept covered with fine linen, and is customized for each class of spirits. Preparations include a seven-day fast, accompanied by prayers.

Next, a magic circle must be prepared, wherein the master and any assistants will stand. The design of the circle is the same as that prescribed in *Grimorium Verum,*[2] aside from the fact that the GV also specifies four characters be written outside each of the four sides.[3]

We are again instructed that the proper time and place must be observed for magical operations.

Psalms and the Litany of Saints[4] are recited, along with the 72 names extracted from Exodus,[5] and other invocations and conjurations. These perhaps might be viewed as a trance-inducing technique – cultivating a form of "mo-

---

1   The *Sworn Book of Honorius* also employs a whistle to call spirits, and includes detailed instructions for its preparation (Peterson, 2016 pp. 38, 277, 297). *Heptameron* likewise employs a whistle, although the translation by Robert Turner leaves the passage untranslated, and Francis Barrett in his 1801 book *The Magus* mistranslates *sibilet* ("he should whistle") as "there will be hissings," completely missing the point.
2   Minus the printer's errors, in Alibeck's edition, as evident by comparing with W983 p. 53.
3   Peterson 2007, plate between pp. 12 and 13; W983 p. 30.
4   Published in the *Roman Gradual.*
5   On which, see below.

notonous focus."[1]

A large number of pentacles are then given, each providing a specific benefit, such as for acquiring prophecy, or invisibility. The time and date for preparing each is generally specified, often the feast day of a specific saint. Instructions often include having a mass performed over the pentacle being prepared. Some of them include Hebrew words (written in Roman letters), such as *Shem ha-Mephorash*, *hosanna*, and the names of letters *mem*, *nun*, *ain*, and *tau*, but most seem to have no semantic content. The mere possession of the pentacles is generally all that is needed to obtain the desired effect.

Planetary intelligences: Book 3 gives instructions for working with the seven classes of planetary intelligences or genii, to "activate" the "energy of Nature itself." The ruling spirit of Jupiter, Sachiel, is of particular interest: "Before you can be initiated into the magical arts, you should devote yourself to this (intelligence), for you will make great progress in these matters if Jupiter inspires you with the intermediate virtue of his influence." Like the other spirits, they are employed through the use of sigils or pentacles. Likewise you must first enter into an agreement with them, or have promised "loyalty or obedience to the spirits with the characters. Moreover, suffumigations, offerings, and sacrifices are to be employed."

The magic stone: Fasting is enjoined in Book 4, to better prepare one for prayer. The "stone" is composed of clay, oil, salt, wine, and uses a chalice[2] in the preparation, along with another short incantation and prayer. This time the *voces magicae* are in English – evidently a strange and magical language to the author! The incantation should be accompanied by beating your chest three times. The consecration uses a ritual knife, rooster, and holy water. Garments, stole, and wand are also needed, and their consecration is drawn from pseudo-Agrippa.

Establishing a critical edition, and relation of the textual sources

None of the primary exemplars consulted here can be a direct descendant of another, since they each exhibit independent patterns of deviations or errors. This is perhaps not surprising, given their wide geographic diversity. I will provide some examples here only, leaving the details in the footnotes.

ASV (Venice): Only manuscript ASV contains the complete text and

---

1   Wilby 2010 p. 177.

2   A symbolic womb?

figures. There are a number of occasions where ASV alone appears to have the better reading. For example, 16r *coque* vs. *quoque;* 33r: *pręponemus* vs. P *proponemus*; DN91 *pręponebimus*. Reading of the English *voces magicae* is better such as the word divisions, "all the" vs "allthe". ASV also has a large number of errors, especially omitted words.[1] These can thankfully be supplied from the other manuscripts -- indicated with [+...] in the text.

The scribe of ASV, perhaps Longo himself, seems to correct flaws in his source manuscript, e.g. double consonants and punctuation have been sup-plied: e.g. *bacculo* vs *baculo, Iuppiter* vs *Iupiter, immo* vs. *imo.* Likewise ASV uses *characteres* consistently vs *caracteres*. In one case (53r) the *h* is written *supra linea*, evidence that the scribe was responsible for these differences.[2] ASV often uses the accusative case where P uses D/Abl: e.g. *in ignem* ("into the fire") vs *in igne* ("in the fire").

In spite of it being carefully preserved in the ASV, the ms. does show some evidence of active use – as witnesses attest – mostly stains and tears, but no marginalia or corrections are evident.

DN91 (Dresden): Contains the complete text, and only two drawings are missing. Drawings are carefully executed. However, I only find two occasions where DN91 alone seems to have the better reading: p. 76 reads *truculentos Thraso, non Tyrannos, Turbulentos* vs. ASV (53v): *truculentos*, and P: *turbulentos*. The second is that DN91 alone accurately quotes OP4: *in se inuicem*; P: *et in sese inuicem*; ASV: *sese inuicem*.

On the other hand there are many instances[3] where DN91 has errors not found in any of the other manuscripts: For a few examples, p. 26 omits the line "**Surgath** *et circa circulum 4 ramos lunarię ut supra diximus, et hęc uerba pronuntia facite prę manibus lapidem* tenens." P. 55: *God* [sic], *et magog* vs. *Gog et magog;* P. 62: *bubonis* vs. *bufonis;* P. 62 omits 9 words. This ms. has some additional material appended. Like ASV, it shows signs of use, including passages underscored, and asterisks in the margins.

L (Leipzig): Although L omits much of the text and drawings found in other manuscripts, I only find three occasions where it seems to err against the other mss: L p. 71: *superiortām tam ipso* vs. ASV 49v et al: *superior:*

---

1   I count 34.
2   Dr. Barbierato p. 171 observed the same sort of corrections in another manuscript in the case file.
3   I count 37.

tamen ipso; genus vs. *genius;* L p. 32: *indesignente* vs. ASV, 50r, P: *indesinente;* DN91: *indesinenti.*

BNF (Paris): Drawings again are carefully done. I find only one occasion where BNF alone has the better reading: BNF 13v: *ligna hilecis* (with accompanying figure); DN91: *ligna filicis;* P: *signa, scilicet;* ASV 19v: *ligna.* On the other hand, there are many occasions (26) where BNF alone has errors not found in the other manuscripts: A few examples: *(28r) appetissimos* (!) vs. *appetentissimos; obseruatissimos* vs. *obseruantissimos; uarietatibus* vs. *uanitatibus;* (29r) *insinuendas* vs. *infundendas;* (30r) *indutos* vs. *imbutos; asimes* vs. *asinus;* (33r) *stragore* (!) vs. *fragore;* (35r) *susarro* (!) vs. *susurro.*

Another characteristic of BNF is that it frequently skips material, especially in the middle of paragraphs, including key instructions, not just superfluous rhetoric or pleonasms. I conclude that the manuscript was a copy for hire, and the copyist cheated on his work in a way that would be hard to detect.

P (Warsaw, Poland): This manuscript is very carefully executed, but unfortunately many drawings were left unfinished. In the text, I find one occasion where P alone has the better reading: P p. 8 reads *ornatus cum sericis* vs ASV 9r et al: *ornatus cum sociis.* I counted 54 errors not found in any of the other manuscripts. This includes many instances where the scribe demonstrates limited grasp of Latin, e.g. P *sub luce* (!) vs *sub muscae; ulxe* vs. *Ulnae; getibus* and *ietibus* vs *ictibus; sciet* vs. *ciet; pentalis* vs. *pentaculis; exeticorum* vs. *exoticorum; calicitus* vs. *calicisue.; canis* vs. *cunie; ventrem* vs. *veretrum.* I conclude that this manuscript was also a copy for hire.

P2 (Warsaw, Poland): This manuscript is in Polish, is carefully executed, and is also missing many drawings. It does not appear to be a direct descendant of P, because it doesn't propagate errors in the former (such as those in the list of 72 names – see below), but introduces others not seen elsewhere.

GG (Toronto): In a few instances, GG alone seems to preserve the best reading: e.g. p. 27: *ab hoc circulo* vs. *ab hoc spiritu.* The former reading makes much more sense in the context, and is further supported by French manuscript W4669. GG often rephrases the text, including scriptural passages, such as Psalm 118. Usually the changes are very minor, such as "et" vs. "ac," and "Deus" vs "Dominus." In copying one of the more sinister spells, this manuscript stops after the first two words.

Other possible relationships between manuscripts are even more complex: There are many cases where two manuscripts agree against all the others:

- ASV and BNF, ASV and DN91, ASV and L

- BNF and P, BNF and DN91, BNF and L, BNF and W4667

- P and GG

- DN91 and P, DN91 and GG, DN91 and L

- P and L occasionally agree against ASV

- DN91 and L include the line "*omnes autem digitos unguibus instructus habet*" lost from ASV, P, GG, and BNF due to the repeated word *habet*. This is a common scribal phenomenon known as *homeoteleuton*.

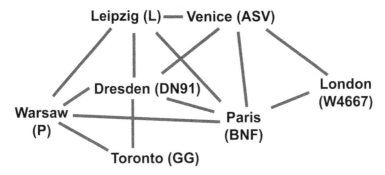

There are also cases where three manuscripts agree against the rest: Where ASV, L, and DN91 agree, but others have different readings. Similarly, DN91, BNF, and GG[1] have the words "+turpi morte interimet. **Abumalith** quemcunque" lost from ASV and P through homeoteleuton.

---

1   DN91 p. 88, BNF 37r, and GG p. 58.

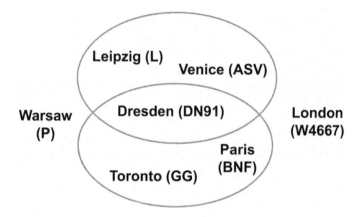

Analysis of the material excerpted from OP4

The final section of the text is clearly derived from pseudo-Agrippa's *De Occulta Philosophia liber 4* (or "OP4").[1] Thus deviations from OP4 clearly represent errors or innovations that can be used to test whether manuscripts depend on each other, directly or indirectly. For example, OP4, ASV, DN91 all read *euentibus*, while P reads *accidentibus*. OP4: *exercitum Pharaonis, in Mari rubro: & si quae alia maledictio in sacris literis reperitur, et sic de similibus. Ita deprecando contra pericula Aquarum, recordemur salutis Noe, in Diluuio: Transitus filiorum Israel, in mari rubro: & meminerimus Christum, siccis pedibus.* Thus at some point a common ancestor of all these manuscripts dropped a line from OP4, due to the repeated phrase *in mari rubio* (homeoteleuton). Another example occurs only in P, where it omits the line *diuinorumque nominum impositione cum sacrorum*. Aside from these examples, the nature of the differences doesn't provide enough evidence of interrelations between the manuscripts currently known.

72 Shem ha-Meforash Angels

One section of the text is the list of seventy-two angels ultimately derived from the Bible. The method is to arrange the Hebrew letters of Exodus 14:19-21 into three parallel columns, then read across. To those are added the divine name EL or IAH, so that "each one bears the great name of God."[2] The details are found in Agrippa OP3.25, who took it from Reuchlin's *de arte cabalistica libri tres* (1517), LV v ff, which I will refer to as "R".

---

1   ASV fol. 68v ff.

2   The only Hebrew letter not appearing in these verses is *gimel.*

According to Reuchlin, each name must always be pronounced with three syllables, and "must be pronounced thus in fear and trembling through invocations of the angels."[1]

The Hebrew in Reuchlin's text is accurate, so can be used as a basis for comparison. Reuchlin distinguishes *Heth* from *He* in his transcription by using an h with a longer tail (ꜧ) for the former. Further, his transcription into Roman letters introduced 2 errors not found in the Hebrew: Name 6: Ielahel should read *Lelahel, and name 66: Mauakel should read *Manakel. Agrippa's printer failed to recognize the distinction between *He* and *Heth*, and prints 'h' throughout. He also introduces additional errors in names 17, 29, 63, 64, and 66. He does however correct name 6. J.F's 1651 English translation introduced additional errors.

Where Agrippa deviates from Reuchlin, manuscripts generally follow Reuchlin, indicating Agrippa was not the direct source.

P has the most accurate list.

GG has 2 names correct that are wrong in all other manuscripts: Louiah and Mauakel.

ASV is missing 13 names, displaces another, and has a large number of errors, often substituting n for u, ending names in *ias* instead of *iah* (it is the only exemplar to exhibit this).

L and BNF omit the list of names entirely.

DN91 has quite a few errors too, but occasionally differs from errors in other mss; thus DN91 incorrectly reads name 31 as Lecalel against all other exemplars, but correctly reads name 34 as Lehahiah against all other manuscripts.

P2 has many errors in common with P, but occasionally has better readings, such as name 8, Cahethel, against P and all the other mss. This is more evidence that P2 and P descended from a common ancestor. It also has errors not found in any of the others, such as 1 Vehujach, 36 Menadel, and 46 Chariel.

Conclusions: Given the lack of consistent error patterns, a stemma is not possible with the manuscripts known thus far, aside from P and P2 probably having a common ancestor.

---

1   Reuchlin 1983, p. 273.

Sources

It is clear that a large part of the underlying fabric of this text is Christian, and specifically Catholicism. Its magic draws on Catholic prayers, rituals, and practices, even if they are stretched to the point of heterodoxy. Thus we find the use of priestly vestments, holy water, the celebration of the Mass, and observation of traditional feast days of various saints. Also used is the Litany of Saints, which can be found in a number of other magical texts, including the *Book of Oberon* and the *Enchiridion of Pope Leo*.[1] Nevertheless the use of these elements was clearly heterodox and radical.

The text also seems to draw on folk magic traditions, including the need to give offerings of some sort to the spirits, and use of natural ingredients and sympathetic magic.

As suggested above, the *Key of Solomon* proper seems to have been more of an inspiration than a source. The author was apparently aware of its methods, such as the use of a magic circle, wand, and sword, but the resemblance is superficial, and could have derived from oral transmission. Similarly, although various catalogs of spirits are found in older magical and demonological texts, the specifics found here appear to be almost entirely original. The exceptions are the few spirits taken from the well-known *Heptameron*, but these have been greatly augmented, based partly on some unidentified astrological texts.

The final section is clearly derived from *Liber quartus de Occulta Philosophia* (*The fourth book of the Occult Philosophy*) of pseudo-Agrippa. Surprisingly though, the seventy-two names used to invoke the Amalthai spirits (pp. 75-76) seem to derive from Reuchlin (1517) directly, rather than Agrippa's *Liber tertius de Occulta Philosophia* (OP3.25). Further evidence that Agrippa proper was not known to the compiler is the fact that none of the other spirits listed by Agrippa are included here, such as Zachariel, Malchidael, and Geniel mentioned in OP3.24.

Influence and legacy

Given its wide geographic dispersal and complicated textual tradition, it is clear that this text became very popular very quickly. This popularity continued unabated into nineteenth-century France through the publication of

---

1   The Litany of Saints is found in the Book of Hours. For *Book of Oberon* see Harms, Clark, Peterson, 2015, pp. 91, 250. For *Enchiridion* see Cecchetelli, 2011, p. 177.

its extraordinarily popular descendant *Grimorium Verum*, and its Italian derivatives. Various composite manuscripts derived material from it, such as Lans. 1202, Wellcome 4669, BNF Arsenal 2349, and Cleveland BF1601 C5313 1834 (associated with George Graham).[1] The *Grimoire of Armadel* has "characters" of Lucifer and Belzebut which seem to be based on CSDS, and the sigil of protection appears to be an embellished version of that here.[2] Other Grimoires drew on it as well, probably via *Grimorium Verum*, including the *Grimoire of Pope Honorius* and *Red Dragon:* Both include spirits ultimately derived from the present text, such as Frimost, Silcharde, Bechard, Guland, and Surgat.[3]

As mentioned earlier, one of the primary manuscripts was from the personal library of Gerald Gardner (1884-1964), a key figure in the modern witchcraft movement. The label on the spine reads "Clavicula," and it contains both CSDS and *Clavicula Salomonis* proper, separately paginated, but in the same hand. It is possible he got this manuscript from Gerald Yorke (1901-1983), who wrote regarding Gardner's *High Magic's Aid* that Gardner "takes his magic from a MS *Clavicula* which I gave him and his witchcraft from a secret society dealing with witchcraft of which he is a member." I don't see any evidence however that he drew directly from this manuscript in any of his writings.[4]

Relationship with *Grimorium Verum*

As mentioned above the *Grimoirium Verum* has proven to be extraordinarily popular, outselling other grimoires by a wide margin. It has been widely put into practice to judge from discussion forums and wide availability of talismans and pendants based on it. Idries Shah made similar observations in his *Secret Lore of Magic*.[5] I thought it therefore of interest to summarize my

---

1 Translation of Wellcome 4669 by Paul Harry Barron published in Skinner and Rankine 2008 pp. 372-405. Graham ms pp. 29-33: http://cplorg.cdmhost.com/digital/collection/p4014coll9/id/930 retrieved June 3, 2018.
2 A translation by S. L. Mathers was published in 1980. Reprint Keith 2001. A new edition was recently published by editionsdumonolithe.com, based on manuscript sources.
3 Cecchetelli 2011, pp. 22-33.
4 http://geraldgardner.com/Gardner46-49.PDF retrieved June 2, 2018. The excerpts from *Clavicula* that Gardner used follow the Mathers edition much closer than this manuscript. This ms reads (p. B76) *arthanus* where older mss read *artavus*, so is not the source of Gardner's *athame*.
5 Shah, Idries, *The Secret Lore of Magic*, New York: Citadel Press, 1970, pp. 79 ff.

observations on the exact relationship between the two texts.

The first part of the French text seems to be based closely on the Latin text. Unexpectedly, however, the Latin passages in GV do not match equivalent text in CSDS, and in fact seem to be inserted randomly in the text of GV, perhaps to add to the mystique.

The French translation is more terse than the Latin, and in some cases garbled. As an example, CSDS reads "Lucifer has the shape of a boy, of very fine appearance, greater than can be described. His eyes flash like the image of the sun, and when he gets angry, they are flooded with redness", while GV reads simply: "Lucifer appears in the form of a handsome boy; when angry he appears reddish."

The seals of Lucifer resemble those in GV, but unlike GV, there is no equivalent to "his proper circle."

The instructions in part two are reminiscent of those in the *Key of Solomon*, but differ in detail. GV seems to have drawn elements from both. For example, the magic circle in GV seems to be a corruption of the magic circle in CSDS, not KSol, and the text in the middle should read "ADONAY."

Curiously, a key spirit in GV – Scrylin – does not appear in CSDS. Another puzzle is the extra spirits cataloged in GV that are omitted from CSDS (see Appendix).

Although both texts include collections of experiments (or "secrets"), they do not correspond at all. The omission is a shortcoming of GV, since they are intended as examples for how to work with the chthonic spirits. The collection of "secrets" in GV does not fulfill the same purpose.

This edition

This edition is based primarily on the manuscript in the Archivio di Stato di Venezia, cataloged as *Sant'Uffizio*, b.93 ("ASV"), with original foliation noted in []. Corrections are indicated by [*...], and omissions by [+...]. Other differences are indicated in footnotes.

Drawings are likewise based on ASV, with a few corrections included in the English translation variants, as noted.

DISCLAIMER

I will take this opportunity to repeat the disclaimer I included in my edition of *Grimorium Verum*. Part of the fascination of this text is no doubt due to the many grotesque elements, such as using blood. **These should in no way be regarded in any other way than horror fiction, and should not be attempted literally. I strongly condemn mistreating animals in any way.**

If you are still determined to attempt any of the spells, Jake Stratton-Kent in particular has written extensively on working with magic of this type.[1] Substitutes for some of the more gruesome ingredients may be found in various places.

ACKNOWLEDGMENTS

I owe thanks to many for their help in bringing this text to print, but especially the following:

Richard and Tamarra James, Toronto, Wiccan Church of Canada, for allowing me to study and photograph their unique and beautiful manuscript, and for other insights.

Dr. Federico Barbierato, Università di Verona, for identifying the ASV manuscript, and for generously sharing details about the Longo/Viola witchcraft trial.

Dott. Raffaele Santoro and Salvatore Toscano, Archivio di Stato di Venezia, for their help photographing the ASV manuscript and related Venetian Inquisition trial records.

QiRui Huo for calling my attention to ms BNF18511.

Paweł Kr for calling my attention to ms P2, and other valuable observations on the text.

MALEDICTION

I will likewise take this opportunity to repeat the **curse** previously used in my edition of *Grimorium Verum*. If you are downloading or distributing a

---

1   Stratton-Kent 2010. For magical properties of plants, animals, and stones, see Ficino and
     Agrippa. See also Skinner, 2012.

PDF version of this text, you are cheating me! If someone asks you where they can get a free copy, tell them to do the right thing and buy a legitimate copy. It should be apparent that considerable effort and expense went into preparing this book. Unfortunately, copyright violators are daily making such ventures more and more impractical. So I will repeat the words of Pseudo-Albertus:

> Inasmuch as, at this juncture, all looks so gloomy in society, the writer of this expects that no pirate of books will wrongfully seize this work and reprint the same, if such an one does not wish to incur the eternal curse, and even condemnation from such an act. While we recommend it to the protection of God and the Holy Trinity, that they may be watching the same, and set the Angel Michael as watch and guard over the undertaking, so that no pirate may rob the real and legal owner of the means of deriving his daily bread from the sale of this publication, and cheat him of his property by the peril of losing his blessedness, such a being would never find rest nor quiet, by day or night, neither here below nor in the hereafter, by seeking to defraud the publisher of his own. This would God the Father, Son, and Holy Spirit grant.
>
> Mirathe saepi Satonich petanish Pistan ytmye higarin ygcirion temgaron-aycon, dunseas cafliacias satas clacius Jacony haslhaja yeynine Stephatitas beaae lud Doneny eya hideu reu vialta cyc vahaspa Saya Salna bebia euci yaya Elenche na vena Serna.[1]

I will add that special dishonor belongs to certain evil and loathsome IP trolls, who try to boost their egos by populating their websites with material pilfered from the hard work of others. May the devils continue to punish them until they finally carry them away to hell.

---

1 Albertus Magnus' *bewährte und approbirte sympathetische und natürliche Egyptische Geheimnisse für Menschen und Vieh*. Zweiter Theil. Allentown, 1869, p. 2.

ABBREVIATIONS

_	Underscoring is used to highlight differences between source texts
[...]	Original foliation
[*...]	Correction
[+...]	Words added by editor
<...>	An error in the text that can be disregarded
ASV	Ms in Archivio di Stato di Venezia *Sant'Uffizio*, b.93
BNF	Ms in Paris: Bibliothèque nationale de France, Latin ms 18511
BoO	*Book of Oberon,* Harms, Clark, and Peterson, 2015
CSDS	*Clavicula Salomonis de Secretis* (text edited and translated here)
DN91	Ms in Dresden: The Saxon State and University Library, N.91
GG	Toronto: Private collection, catalog number B134
GV	*Grimorium Verum. See* Peterson 2007
KJV	King James version of Bible
KSol	*Key of Solomon.* Book and chapter designations as Mathers
L	Ms in Leipzig: Cod. mag. 136
LIH	*Liber Iuratus Honorii: Sworn Book of Honorius*, ed. Peterson
Mathers	*Mathers, S. L.,* 1889. Reprint: 2016
Ms, Mss	manuscript, manuscripts
OP	Heinrich Agrippa, *de occulta philosophia*
P	Ms in National Library of Poland, catalog number Rps 3352 II
P2	Ms in National Library of Poland, catalog number Rps 6698 II
Ps.	Psalm
R	Reuchlin, 1517
r	*recto*
v	*verso*
W	Ms 4667 in the Wellcome Library

Correlation of contents between manuscripts

	Capitulum	ASV	BNF	DN	L	P	GG	P2	W
I.1	Incipit	4r	2r	1	5	1	1	127	1
I.2	De spiritibus Diatribe	5r	2v	3	5	2	2	128	3
I.3	De secretis secretissimis [Pars Prima / De Arcanis]	12r	6v	20	11	13	14	135	
I.4	Ut pluat	12r	7r	21	–	13	14	136	
I.5	Ut ningat	13r	7v	22	–	14	15	137	
I.6	Ut fulguret	13v	7v	24	–	15	15	137	19
I.7	Ut non frigeamus	14r	8r	25	–	16	16	138	401
I.8	Ut nimius Calor nos non Infestet	14v	8v	26	–	17	16	138	401
I.9	Ad Aperiendas clauaturas Secretum mirabile	14v	8v	26	–	17	16	138	402
I.10	Ad Amorem Puellae Conciliandum	15r	9r	26	–	17	17	138	403
I.11	Concubitu Potiendum	16r	10r	28	–	19	18	139	404
I.12	Vt nummos quoties libuerit habeamus	16v	10v	29	–	20	19	140	405
I.13	Ut Inimicus Emoriatur	17r	11r	30	–	21	20	140	407
I.14	Ut simus Inuisibiles	17v	11v	31	–	21	–	140	408
I.15	Ut musica Dulcissima audiatur	18r	12r	32	–	22	–	141	409
I.16	Ut demortui uiui appareant nobis et loquantur	18v	12v	32	–	22	–	141	410
	Finis secretorum	19v	14r	33	–	24	–	141	412
II	Liber secundus De Pentaculis siue Apparationibus	20r	15r	34	11	24	–	141	20
II.1	Cap. 1: De institutione artis	20r	–	34	11	25	–	142	21
II.2	Cap. 2: Quae operanti In Arte Cognoscenda sunt	20v	15r	35	12	26	21	142	23
II.3	Cap. 3: De Potestate Superiorum Intelligentiarum	22r	16r	37	13	28	22	143	27
II.4	Cap. 4: Quomodo obtinere possimus Ab Intelligentiis praedictas Scientias, artes, Et secreta.	26r	–	42	18	32	25	145	32

	Capitulum	ASV	BNF	DN	L	P	GG	P2	W
II.5	Cap. 5. De his quae sunt necessaria ad Inuocationes, Et Coniurationes Daemonum.	26v	–	42	19	33	25	146	34
II.6	Cap. 6. De circulo.	27r	16v	43	20	34	26	146	34
II.7	Cap. 7. De Pentaculo.	28r	16v	44	21	35	27	147	37
II.8	Cap. 8. De gladio.	30r	17r	48	24	38	30	148	42
II.9	Cap. 9. De Aqua benedicta.	30v	–	48	24	38	30	148	43
II.10	Cap. 10. De Veste.	31r	–	48	24	39	31	148	43
II.11	Cap. 11. De Igne et Suffumigiis.	31r	17v	49	25	39	31	149	44
II.12	Cap. 12. De Sanguine et Atramento.	32r	–	50	25	40	32	149	45
II.13	Cap. 13. De charta virginea.	32r	–	50	26	41	32	149	46
II.14	Cap. 14. De Loco et Tempore.	32v	–	51	26	41	33	149	46bis
II.15	Cap. 15. De Inuocationibus et Coniurationibus Spirituum..	33r	–	51	27	41	33	150	46bis
II.16	Cap. 16. De Experimentis.	36v	–	56	–	46	39	152	
II.17	De Pentaculis.	37r	17v	57	–	47	39	152	57
II.17.1	- Orifielis.	37r	17v	57	–	47	39	152	58
II.17.2	- Magrielis	38v	19r	59	–	50		153	
II.17.3	- Urielis	39v	19v	60	–	51	42	154	64
II.17.4	- Pamechiel	40r	20r	61	–	53	43	154	65
II.17.5	- Pomerielis	41r	20v	62	–	54	43	155	67
II.17.6	- Sabrielis	42r	21r	63	–	56	44	155	68
II.17.7	- Ucharielis	43r	22v	64	–	58	45	156	72
II.17.8	- Charielis	43v	23r	65	–	60	45	156	73
II.17.9	- Pantheriel	44v	23v	66	–	61	46	157	74
II.17.10	- Araton	45v	24r	67	–	62	48	157	79
II.17.11	- Agiaton	46r	24v	67	–	63	48	157	80
II.17.12	- Begud	46v	24v	68	–	64	49	158	80
II.17.13	- Tainor	47v	25r	69	–	65	50	158	82

	Capitulum	ASV	BNF	DN	L	P	GG	P2	W
III	Liber Tertius	48r	27r	70	30	65	–	159	83
III.1	Incipit	48r	27r	70	30	65	–	159	83
III.2	Nomina Intelligentiarum Solis et Lunae	51r	27v	74	–	69	50	162	94
III.3	De Intelligentia Solis nomen Michael	51v	27v	74	–	70		162	94
III.4	De Intelligentia Lunae nomen Gabriel	52r	28r	75	–	70		162	95
III.5	De Intelligentia Martis nomen Samael	53r	28v	75	–	71		163	96
III.6	De Intelligentia Mercurii nomen Raphael	54r	29r	77	–	72		163	97
III.7	De Intelligentia Iouis nomen Sachiel	55r	29r	78	–	74		164	98
III.8	De Intelligentia Veneris nomen Anael	56r	29v	80	–	75		165	100
III.9	De Intelligentia Saturni nomen Cassiel	57r	30r	80	–	76	53	165	101
III.10	De spiritibus mediis siue Satellitibus Supremorum	57v	30r	81	–	77		166	102
III.11	Spiritus Solares	58r	30v	82	–	77	53	166	
III.12	Spiritus Lunares	59v	31v	83	–	79	53	166	
III.13	Spiritus Martiales	60v	33r	84	–	80	56	168	
III.14	Spiritus Mercurii	61v	34r	85	–	81	54	168	
III.15	Spiritus Iouis	62v	35r	86	–	82	55	168	
III.16	Spiritus Veneris	63v	36r	87	–	84	57	168	
III.17	Spiritus Saturni	64v	37r	88	–	85	58	169	
IV	De Lapide	65v	39r	89	33	87	–	170	–
IV.1	[Incipit]	65v	39r	89	33	87	–	170	–
IV.2	De confectione lapidis	66r	39v	89	34	87	–	170	–
IV.3	De purgatione lapidis	67r	39v	90	35	88	–	171	–
IV.4	De consecratione lapidis	68r	40r	91	36	89	–	172	–
IV.5	Baptismus lapidis	68r	40v	92	36	89	–	172	–
IV.6	Praxis Et Ordo Consecrationis Et Primo De Pentaculis	68v	(app ends OP4)	92	–	89	–	172	–

[2r] CLAUICULA SALOMONIS
AD
SCIENDUM SECRETA SECRETORUM[1]

[4r] CLAUICULA SALOMONIS
DE SECRETIS.

In nomine **Adonai Tetragrammaton Apyruch Exbranor.**

ncipit Clauicula Salomonis, quam olim composuit ipse sapientissimus Salomon filius[2] Dauidis, ut filios suos instrueret[3] in arte **Rabidmadar.** Continet autem in prima parte utilissima[4] ad omnes euentus secreta secretissima, quorum Catalogum in ipsius fronte perspicies.

In secunda[5] [+pentaculorum][6] uarias docet dispositiones secundum locum, diem, horam, mensem, annum, ut talis qualis opus fuerit ueniat spiritus, qui de quibuslibet rebus interrogatus siue politicis, siue philosophicis, siue [4v] quibuscunque aliis ad unguem, et doctissime sine errore respondebit,[7] sed antequam legas uolo te instructum hoc caractere

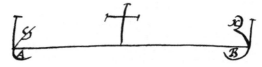

---

1   L, DN91, P omit this title page. GG has a beautiful title page reading *Clavicula regis Salomonis / de secretis secretorum.* Below that is an angel with a quill pen writing "Accipe Fili Mi Roboam."

2   DN91: *filii.*

3   So ASV, BNF, L, GG. P, DN91: institueret ("he might prepare.")

4   L adds "quodam."

5   L adds *parte.*

6   So DN91, BNF, P, GG.

7   DN91: *sine errore rationem rendebit* [sic]; GG: *sine errore responsum tribuet* ("he will present the answer without error"). L omits the last sentence of this paragraph, and the figure, and text up to "De spiritibus."

1

THE KEY OF SOLOMON
FOR
KNOWING THE SECRETS OF THE SECRETS[1]

THE KEY OF SOLOMON
CONCERNING THE SECRETS

In the name of **Adonay, Tetragrammaton, Apyruch,**[2] **Exbranor.**

ere begins the Key of Solomon, which was composed by the most wise Solomon himself, the son of David, in order that he might teach[3] his children[4] in the art **Rabidmadar.**[5] Moreover, it contains in the first part the most secret secrets, most useful for all outcomes, as you will see enumerated in the table of contents at the beginning of it.[6]

The second part teaches about the different [+pentacles], secondly the arrangement of the place, hour, day, month, year, in order to accomplish such work from the spirits, regarding anything you may ask, whether political, or philosophical, or whatever else, precisely, and it will answer most learnedly, without error. But before you may learn that, I wish to teach you to construct this character.

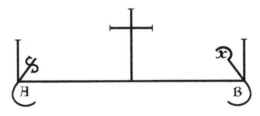

---

1   The wording of the title page and incipit varies in each of the manuscripts. See the references.

2   Apyruch: So ASV, DN91, P, P2. L: Appruch; Ar: Abiruch; W 4667: aspiruche. GG omits this phrase.

3   L, GG: instruct.

4   It is significant that this is in the plural: According to the Bible, Solomon had three children: One son and two daughters.

5   Rabidmadar is described below as the secretary of Sigambach.

6   Namely, to make it rain, snow, etc. For the table of contents mentioned, see below, p. 28.

Hoc si masculus in pera dextera geras tecum in pergamo[1] sanguine tuo, aut testudinis[2] maris scriptum in semicirculis A B tuum nomen, et cognomen, primas scilicet litteras pone nomen in semicirculo A, loco litterę A, cognomen in semicirculo B, loco litterę B. Si uelis ac melius hoc[3] caractere in iaspide uiridi, aut helitropio excudere iubebis, utrunque enim maximam habet cum spiritibus <orientalibus>[4] simpathiam, solaribus pręcipue, qui reliquis [5r] sunt sapientiores et meliores.

Si sis foemina in pera sinistra[5] geres,[6] aut inter mammillas appendes, tanquam periapta,[7] reliqua, que[8] de masculo dicta sunt obseruabis, pręterquam sanguine nomen tuum scribes die ♂.

Explicit pręludium.

In sequentibus pauca de spiritibus enodantur ad totius libri intelligentiam omnino necessaria,[9] et scitu dignissima.

De spiritibus Diatribe.[10]

Spiritus sunt occultę quędam potentię,[11] quę non nisi confœderatis, et ui pacti unitis mediante certo[12] quodam caractere ex **Sigambach** aut eius secretarii **Rabidmadar** uoluntate[13] descripto seruiunt.[14] Hoc autem character nihil[15] aliud est pręter insigne, ut Amici ab inimicis distinguantur. Tanti enim sunt utrique, ut non nisi [5v] signo aliquo distingui, et dignosci queant, ut Amicis uocantibus ipsi opitulentur spiritus, ipsi autem non opitulabuntur

---

1   So too BNF, P; DN91, GG: *pergameno*.
2   BNF: *testitudinis*.
3   BNF adds *ce*.
4   DN91, BNF, P, L, and GG all omit the word *orientalibus* ("with eastern").
5   BNF: *dextra*.
6   P: *geras*.
7   BNF: *percepta*.
8   BNF: *quæ*; P: *quod*.
9   DN91: *nomina*; BNF: *memoria*.
10   L: De spiritibus. GG omits the chapter heading.
11   BNF: *personæ*.
12   So ASV, DN91, L, BNF. Deest P.
13   BNF: *volente*.
14   BNF skips ahead to "*Pactum duplex est.*"
15   DN91: *nisi*.

If you are male, you should carry this with you in your right pocket, writ-ten on parchment in your own blood, or that of a sea tortoise. In the semi-circles A and B, write the first letters of your name and surname: Namely, place the first letter of your name in place of A, and the first letter of your surname (or family name) in place of B. It is better still, if you wish, to have it fashioned from green jasper or heliotrope (bloodstone), for those (stones) indeed have the greatest sympathy with <eastern>[1] spirits, of the solar order, which are wiser and better than the others.

If you are a woman, carry it in your left pocket or hung between your breasts, like a relic periapt,[2] observing the other instructions given for a male (above), except you should write your name with blood on the day of Mars.

End of the introduction.

In the following section, a few of the spirits are explained which are abso-lutely necessary for understanding the whole book, and deemed most appropriate.

Discourse concerning the spirits.

The spirits are certain hidden forces, who will not willingly serve unless you make an alliance and unite with the strength of an agreement (or pact), by means of a certain specific character from **Sigambach**, or his secretary **Rabidmadar** with the intention spelled out. Nevertheless this character is nothing else but an emblem, in order that friends can be distinguished from enemies; so great indeed are they, that the spirits will not aid you unless they

---

1   Only ms ASV includes the word *orientalibus* ("with eastern"). This association of the spirits of the East with the Sun may simply be intuitive, but is found in the *Sworn Book of Honorius* as well.

2   Periapt: Charm or amulet.

nisi te prius insigni quadam declaratione [*demonstratione],[1] quale [*qualis][2] est pactum inter te, et ipsuminitum eius Amicum, et iustum[3] donum[4] ostenderis. Iustum Amicum intellige, quiipso uolente spiritu in ipsam dominacionem accipit.[5]

Qua autem ratione pactizare debeamus ex sequentibus non cum paruo studio dignosces. Res enim est plane obscura, et clara nimis, si a quodam explicetur, hoc autem[6] explicari non opportet iussu ipsius **Rabidmadar**, nisi magno antea auri pondere, utpote Cathena spiritibus orientalibus oblata, thure accenso suffumigata, et sanguine proprio aspersa [*respersa][7] cum certis quibusdam inuocationibus.

Hoc ne uulgatum fiat expressis uerbis tibi declarare nolui, satis est quod totum negotium in hoc libello inclusum est si bene animaduerteris.

[6r] Pactum dupplex est, spiritus autem[8] sunt quamplures,[9] quidam superiores, quidam Inferiores: Superiores sunt: Imperator, Princeps, Comes: nomina sunt

Lucifer, Belzebuth, Elestor.[10]

Inferiores sunt[11] subditi **Lucifero**, et tales Europam et Asiam incolunt, uel subditi **Belzebuth**, et tales Africam incolunt. Tandem subditi **Elestor**, et tales Americam incolunt.

Et omnes habent duos duces, qui subditis imperant, quę Imperator, Princeps uel Comes decreuerunt. Hi enim tres omnimodam sibi uendicant potentiam, de toto orbe deliberant, et quęcunque facienda sunt ducibus pręcipiunt, subditis enim, et inferioribus non apparent propria forma, nec

---

1 So DN91, P, GG. L has an abbreviation which is unclear.
2 Following L, DN91. P, GG: *quale.*
3 L: tuum.
4 Abbreviated *dñū* in ASV, but spelled out in DN91 and GG. L: *dñ.* P misreads *dominum.*
5 P: *Accepit.*
6 L: à.
7 DN91, P, L: *respersa.* GG omits.
8 P omits.
9 So also L, DN91, BNF. P, GG: *complures* ("many").
10 BNF skips ahead to *Luciferi figura talis est....*
11 So also DN91, L; P, GG: *scilicet.*

can distinguish and discern by some sign, that it is one of his friends calling for help. Moreover, they will not aid unless you have shown some kind of conspicuous declaration beforehand, such as an agreement or pact that was entered into between you and itself – clearly indicating you as his friend, and you should show a suitable offering.[1] Understand, a trusted friend is one whom the spirit himself has willingly accepted mastery.

Therefore, you will not be able to discern the manner of making the pact from the following without a little study; for indeed the matter is kept quite obscure, but would be abundantly clear if explained in one particular place. Nevertheless this must not be explained by the order of the same **Rabidmadar**, unless previously, with a great weight of gold, as a bond offered to the spirits of the East,[2] fumigated with kindled frankincense and sprinkled with your own blood, with certain specific invocations.

Let this not become generally known; I have not been willing to declare everything expressly; it is enough that the whole matter has been included in this little book, if you notice it carefully.

A pact is twofold, the spirits however are very many, some of which are superiors, and some inferiors.

The names of the Emperor, the Prince, and the Count are **Lucifer, Belzebuth**, and **Elestor**.

The inferiors who are subordinate to **Lucifer** inhabit Europe and Asia; those subordinate to **Belzebuth** inhabit Africa; lastly, those subordinate to **Elestor** inhabit America.

And each of those has two dukes who rule over the subordinates, as the emperor, prince, or count has determined. For these three sorts claim power for themselves, they decide for the whole world, and whatever things are to be done, the dukes (for example) order their subjects; and they do not appear

---

1   P: *amicum et iustum dominum ostenderis* ("clearly indicating you as his friend and lawful master"). Instead of *iustum donum* ("suitable gift"), L reads *tuum dñ.* ("your gift").

2   W4667: *ayent pralablement offert un grand poid d'ors comme estant la chaine du a l'esprit orienteaux.*

alicui alteri,[1] sed modo formam equi in circo ambulantis modo formam[2] lupi cum cornibus, modo, et saepius formam hirci cum ingenti proboscide.[3] Ducibus autem propria tantum figura se se offerunt, ut de negotiis pręsentibus ipsos instruant.[4]

[6v] **Luciferi** figura talis est, puer est [*et] formosissimus, quantum dici non potest, eius[5] oculi solis instar coruscant, et dum irascitur[6] rubore suffunduntur. Tandem, Lucifer nihil[7] habet stupendum in sua figura.

Belzebuth Imperator spirituum,[8] qui Africam incolunt sępius sub muscę[9] paulo grandioris figura[10] Duces alloquitur, aliquando dum magni ponderis res agitur sub forma uituli sed portentosa[11] apparet, humanis scilicet pedibus, pręterquam quod unum ex posterioribus ceruinum habet, [+omnes autem digitos unguibus instructus habet][12] leonis, aut harpię, non longe dissimilibus, dum irascitur flammam[13] uomit, et ululat instar lupi.

Elestor alatus est, et niger usque ad umbilicum, reliquum uersus inferius parte dextra album, sinistra roseum est[14] Proboscis illius tamen uiridis est ad ulnę[15] fere magnitudinem extensa, et dura, quam instar zonę circa uentrem obuolutam[16] nodo sistit: hac autem suos subditos ad ea, quę sunt facienda desides [7r] prouocat, et quamplures ex Americanis eius ictibus[17] necat, si non necat moribundos[18] prosternit. Scio quod sub asini figura saepius uisus est.

Et hi dęmones sunt terrestres, eorum characteres tales sunt.

---

1   So too GG, P; DN91, L: *alio.*
2   P omits.
3   P: *Proboside.*
4   DN91: *instruat*; GG: *instruunt*; L omits this sentence.
5   DN91: *cuius.*
6   P, GG add "in."
7   P: *nil.*
8   BNF: *... imperat Eos Spiritus qui....*
9   So also DN91, L, BNF; P: *sub luce.* GG: *sub lupi.*
10 So also DN91, L, BNF, but GG and P omit.
11 So too DN91, BNF, GG; P: *portentesa*; L: *portentosi.*
12 BNF, P, and GG are also missing the line through *homeoteleuton,* but so DN91, L.
13 BNF: *flammas.*
14 BNF skips ahead to *scio quod sub asini....*
15 So L, DN91, GG; P: *ulxe.*
16 So L, GG; DN91: *abuolutam*; P: *obuolutans.*
17 So also L, DN91. P: *getibus*; GG: *ciuibus.* W4667: *habittans delamerique.*
18 DN91: *moribundis.*

to their inferiors in their own form, nor to anyone else, but with the manner and form of a horse walking in a circle, or with the manner and form of a wolf with horns, or most often, with the manner and form of a he-goat with a huge snout. But to their dukes they show themselves in their own true forms, so that they can instruct them regarding the business at hand.

Lucifer has the shape of a boy, of very fine appearance, greater than can be described. His eyes flash like the image of the sun, and when he gets angry, they are flooded with redness.[1] Nevertheless, Lucifer has nothing startling about his form.

Belzebuth is emperor of the spirits who inhabit Africa; he often speaks to more senior leaders in the form of a fly, sometimes when conducting matters of great weight, in the form of a calf, but with unnatural (or monstrous) appearance, namely with human feet, except with hind quarters of a deer, [+but equipped with claws] not unlike those of a lion or harpy. When angry he vomits flame, and howls like a wolf.

Elestor[2] is winged and black all the way to the navel; below the navel, on the right side he is white, but red on the left side, his snout however is green and hard, and extends almost a yard in length, like a belt around his belly, tied up with a knot; moreover, he uses this to provoke his own subordinates to act when they are lazy, and he kills many of the Americans that he hits with it, or if he does not kill them, they are knocked down dying. I know that he is most often seen in the form of an ass.

And these demons are earthly, and their characters are these:[3]

---

1   The Bible describes angels as having eyes that shine like fire. See Dan. 10:6, Rev. 1:14, Rev. 19:12. Compare also Matt. 28:3.
2   W4669: Elector. W4667: Clestor. In place of Elestor, GV has Astaroth.
3   Compare seal of Lucifer within composite seal on pp. 29-30.

Lucifer in Europa   Vel sit in Asia

Belzebuth

Elestor sit.

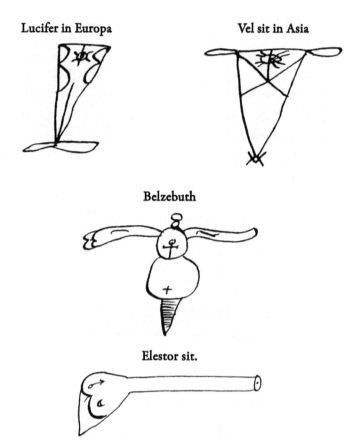

Nota quod quando aliquid ex his dependens[1] obtinere uolueris ipsos primum suo charactere lacessere [7v] debes aliter si ipsis oblitis sacrificares, irrita esset oblatio, et apud Americanos te **Elestor** pene ictibus[2] obrueret.[3]

Ad inferiores partes descendamus.

1   DN91: *ab uno ex his dependet*. P: *ab his dependens*; GG: *ab his dependes*.
2   P: *Ietibus* (!)
3   BNF omits this paragraph.

Lucifer in Europe.   or in Asia

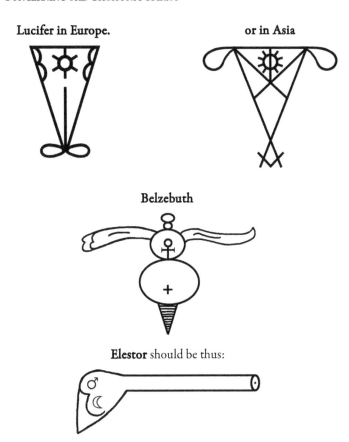

Belzebuth

Elestor should be thus:

Note that when you wish to obtain anything from these subordinates, you must first provoke them with his character, otherwise if you forget to sacrifice to them, the offering might be ineffective, and in America **Elestor** could nearly overwhelm you with his blows.

We now descend to the lower regions.

Duces Luciferi sunt

Scyrach [*Syrach]¹ apud Europęos   **vel Apud Afros**

Satanachi

Duces Belzebuth sunt **Agaleraptarkimath** et **Ftheruthi**

Agaleraptarkimath   **Ftheruthi**

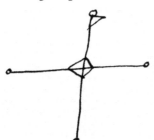   

[8r] Duces Elestor sunt Serphgathana et Resbiroth.

Serphgathana.   **Resbiroth.**

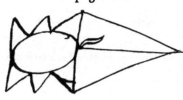   

Alii sunt dęmones pręcipui pręter supradictos sub duce Syrach sunt 18.

---

1   Also spelled Scyrach on fol. 7v, but Syrach on fol. 8r , 15v,, 16r, and 18r. DN91, P, P2, and
     W4667 all read Syrach/Sirach.

Lucifer's dukes are Syrach and Satanachi:

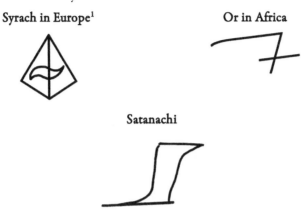

Syrach in Europe[1]

Or in Africa

Satanachi

Belzebuth's dukes are **Agaleraptarkimath** and **Ftheruthi**.

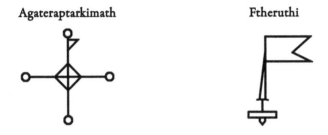

Agateraptarkimath

Ftheruthi

Elestor's dukes are Serphgathana and Resbiroth.

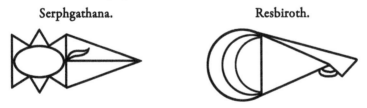

Serphgathana.

Resbiroth.

There are other particular daemons besides those mentioned above, under the duke **Syrach.** They total 18:

---

1   Compare seal of Syrach within composite seal on page 30.

1. Claunth.	10. Hepath.
2. Reschin.	11. Segol.
3. Beschard.	12. Humeth.
4. Frimodth.	13. Frulthiel.
5. Klepoth.	14. Galand.
6. Klio.	15. Surgath.
7. Merfiel.	16. Menail.
8. Glithrel.	17. Fruthmerl.
9. Sirkael.	18. Hurchetmigarot.

Reliqui sub hoc duce sunt nihil,[1] quippe qui nullam habent potentiam, quod nulla habuerint [8v] in[2] factis merita: isti autem has[3] habent potentias, et inter omnes tam Europęos, Africanos, quam Asiaticos, et Americos.[4]

Tales eorum sunt potentię

1. **Claunth** in diuitias quas dare, et tollere potest.

2. **Reschin** in scientias quas hominibus infundere,[5] et auferre potest:[6] item ad omnia quę in regnis, et rebus publicis, geruntur[7] scienda est accommodatus, quippe qui omnia interroganti declaret quouis modo id fieri expostulet.

3. **Beschard** in uentos, tempestates, pruinas, hyemes,[8] fulmina, niues, grandines, pluuias omnismodi siue cum[9] bufonibus[10] siue cum sanguine, siue cum lapidibus ciendas,[11] uel compescendas imperium habet.

---

1 So too GG; P, DN91: *nihili.*
2 P, DN91, GG: *ex.*
3 P: *hos.*
4 BNF omits this paragraph.
5 So too L, DN91, BNF; P, GG: *fundere.*
6 BNF omits the rest of this paragraph, and most of the following paragraphs on spirit powers.
7 So too L; DN91: *et rebus pergeruntur.* GG just has *in regnis geruntur.*
8 P: *Ruinas, Ignes.*
9 P omits.
10 P: *battonibus.*
11 P: *sciendos.*

1.	Claunth.	10.	Hepath.
2.	Reschin.	11.	Segol.
3.	Beschard.	12.	Humeth.
4.	Frimodth.	13.	Frulthiel.
5.	Klepoth.	14.	Galand.
6.	Klio.	15.	Surgath.
7.	Merfiel.	16.	Menail.
8.	Glithrel.	17.	Fruthmerl.
9.	Sirkael.	18.	Hurchetmigarot.

The rest under this duke are of no importance, since they have no power, because there is no merit from their deeds. Nevertheless, they all have these same powers among all of them, whether Europeans, African, or Asiatic and Americans.

Their powers are these:

1. **Claunth** is able to give wealth, and to take it away.

2. **Reschin** can infuse knowledge into people, and he can also remove it. Likewise he can disclose knowledge of everything involving the interests of kingdoms and public affairs anywhere.

3. **Beschard** provokes winds, storms, hoarfrost, winters, lightning, snow, hail, rains of various kinds, such as with toads or blood, or moving stones, or he can command them to be stopped.

4. **Frimodth** in mulieres imperium habet, in amorem, et omnes humanas partes [*passiones, siue]¹ cohercere, siue excitare lubeat, amorem quippe amatę puellę restinguere, uel augere usque [9r] ad coitum uolet, mulierem grauidare, grauidam abhorrere [*aborire]² sępius cogit.³

5. **Klepoth** mille ciet ludibria spectatoribus,⁴ si iubeas aliquid, modo choręas si lubeat [+excitabit]⁵ cum suis comitibus uestibus ad id accommodatus ornatus cum sociis [*sericis].⁶ Musicam cuiuslibet generis audientibus affingit,⁷ ut uera quis⁸ credere posset. Vidi quandoque eum⁹ alapham prętereunti infligentem,¹⁰ ita ut affectus unde proueniret ignoraret, quod si ludendo cartas eius qui tecum ludit scire uolueris tibi in aure suggeret.

6. **Klio**. terremotus ciet¹¹ in urbes et domos imperium habet.

7. **Merfiel** te subito in alienam¹² regionem, aut locum alterum qualemcunque transportabit, et qualemcumque rem uolueris ex aliena regione in pręsentem transferre¹³ unico fere instanti.

8. **Glithrel** diem, et tenebras ut lubebit¹⁴ spectatoribus sentire facit.

[9v] 9. **Sirchael** [*Sirkael¹⁵], cuiuslibet generis animalia tibi proponet¹⁶ in qualibet actione placuerit, uel saltantia, uel ambulantia, uel saeuientia suis armis¹⁷ naturalibus scilicet.

---

1   So DN91, P, GG, L.
2   So DN91, P, GG, L.
3   P: facit.
4   P omits this word.
5   So DN91, P, GG, L.
6   As P, which fits better with *ornatus*. L, DN91 also read *"cum Sociis"* ("with servants"). GG omits.
7   L, DN91: *effinget*; P, GG: *affinget*.
8   P: *qui*.
9   P, GG: *cum*.
10 So too DN91, L; P, GG: *infigentium*.
11 P: *sciet*.
12 So also L, DN91, BNF; P, GG: *aliam* ("another").
13 P: *presentia transferet*.
14 DN91: *iubebit*
15 So above.
16 DN91 omits the last 2 words.
17 DN91: *armibus*.

4. **Frimodth** has command over women in love, and all human passions, either to curb or to arouse it, as you please; for he can extinguish or increase the love of young women, up to the point where she wishes to couple. He can also make women pregnant, or cause a pregnancy to disappear if desired.

5. **Klepoth** can [+provoke] a thousand hecklers if you order it, somewhat like a choir[1] if it pleases you, with his companions suitably adorned with silk garments; he will provide the audience with any type of music, which all will believe to be true. I have also seen him inflict a blow in passing, such that the victim is unaware of the source.

But if playing cards, if you wish to know, he can reveal in your ear the cards of the person playing with you.

6. **Klio** has command of earthquakes in cities and houses.

7. **Merfiel** can instantly transport you to a foreign land, or location of whatever kind, and can transfer anything you wish from a foreign place to your present location, almost instantly.

8. **Glithrel** can make spectators think it is daytime or darkness as desired.

9. **Sirkael** can display any kind of animal to you, doing any action he wants, such as prancing or walking, or raging in their normal way.

---

1   Latin *chorea* could also mean "dance" or "circle dance," and this is clearly how the French translator interpreted it, but that doesn't seem to fit the context as well.

10. **Hepath** homines in longinquis regionibus habitantes tibi pręsentes efficit,[1] siue exercitum, siue Imperatorem, siue tuam puellam, amicamque expostulaueris.

11. **Segol** formidanda, et prodigiosa monstra effingere ualet, et illiusmodi [*cuiusmodi] excogitaueris[2] chimeras tibi effinget.

12. **Humeth** quoslibet[3] libros uolueris afferet.[4]

13. **Frulthiel** mortuos tibi, uel cuilibet uiuos adducet, ut Ciceronem quandoque adduxit, suam Milonianam declamantem et Cęsarem adstantem.

14. **Galand** quoslibet mortuos [*morbos][5] excitat, luem ueneream, cancros, etc.[6] uel etiam curat.

15. **Surgath** ad aperiendas clauaturas est idoneus.

[10r] 16. **Menail** inuisibilem reddit ita ut domum inuades quin te aliquis uiderit.[7]

17. **Fruthmerl**. cuiuslibet generis conuiuia apparabit, item uina meliora apponet, et cibos delicatiores utpote perdices, lepores turdos cuniculos, soleas etc. immo[8] et fructus meliores.

18. **Hurchetmigaroth** somnia, et uigiliam unicuique excitabit.

Ut autem his spiritibus utamur eorum characteres sciendi sunt quibus[9] inuocantur.

---

1 DN91, BNF: *efficiet.*
2 GG, L, DN91: *cuiusmodi excogitaueris*; P: *cuiusmodi excitaueris.*
3 DN91: *quolibet.*
4 DN91 adds *statim* ("immediately").
5 So DN91, BNF, P, L, GG.
6 Instead of etc. DN91 reads *si uelit* ("if he wishes"). GG: ... *morbos excitat et etiam curat.*
7 P omits *ita ut domum inuades quin te aliquis uiderit.* GG substitutes *totaliter* ("completely").
8 P omits *utpote ... immo.*
9 BNF: ... *eorum characteres faciendi sunt quibus....* P: *Caracteres scire oportet quibus.*

10. **Hepath** can make people appear to you that you urgently call for, whether they are in a remote place, or an army, or the emperor, or your sweetheart.

11. **Segol** has the power to fashion fearsome and freakish monsters, and will fashion all kinds of chimeras that you can think up.[1]

12. **Humeth** will bring to anyone whatever books you wish.

13. **Frulthiel** will bring to you anyone living or dead,[2] such as when Cicero once argued his Milo declamation, and assisted Caesar.

14. **Galand** can infect anyone with sickness, venereal disease, crabs, and *cantera*,[3] or he can also cure it.

15. **Surgath**, can serve for opening locked things.

16. **Menail**. He makes you invisible when you enter into a house, so that no one can see you.

17. **Fruthmerl** will prepare any kind of feast. Likewise, he will set out fine wines and delicacies, such as partridge, hares, thrushes, rabbits, sole, etc. and the finest fruits.

18. **Hurchetmigaroth** makes anyone sleep, or vigilant.[4]

Moreover, in order for you to enjoy the employment of these spirits, you should know their characters, by which they should be invoked. They are as follows:

---

1   P: that you wish to call up.
2   The last part of this sentence is not found in GG. The reference to Caesar does not occur in P2.
3   *Cantera:* Unknown. L omits this word. GG: galant quoslibet morbos excitat et etiam curat ("Galant can induce any sickness, and also cure any.").
4   L skips ahead to "Sequitur 1ª pars de secretis secretissimis."

Character Claunth est[1]

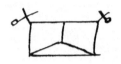

2. Res.

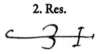

3. Bes.

4. Fri.

5. Kle.

6. Khl.

7. Mer.

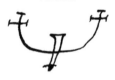

8. Gli.

9. Sir.

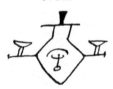

10. Hep.

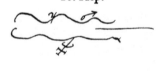

---

1   DN91: *Characteres ptorum sunt in ordine numerorum incipiendo primum a Claunth.*
GG: *Horum spirituum Characteres sic oportet habere a quibus Inuocantur et sunt
sequentes.*

The character of Claunth is:[1]

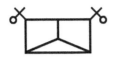

2. Reschin

3. Beschard[2]

4. Frimodth[3]

5. Klepoth[4]

6. Klio

7. Merfiel

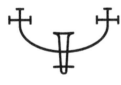

8. Glithrel

9. Sirkael

10. Hepath

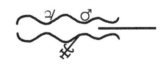

---

1   Compare seal of Claunth [sic] on composite seal on p. 37, which is slightly more complex.

2   Compare seals of Beschard on pp. 25 and 29.

3   ASV has a cross at top here, but not later in the manuscript; none of the othe mss have this, so I removed it from my version. Compare seals of Frimodth in composite seals below, pp. 33 and 35.

4   Compare seal of Klepoth on page 41.

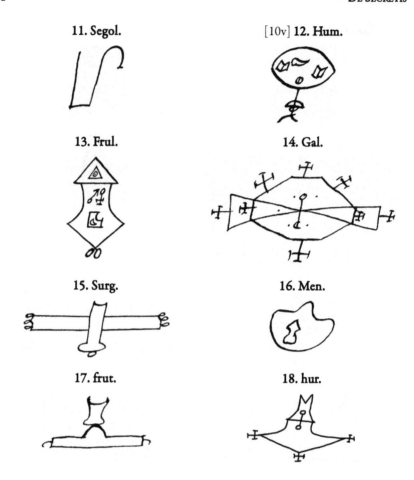

11. Segol.

[10v] **12. Hum.**

13. Frul.

14. Gal.

15. Surg.

16. Men.

17. frut.

18. hur.

Alia et perplurima sunt dęmonia, quę etiam sunt pręcipua sub duce **Satanachi** sunt 54 quorum 4 sunt principaliora, et magis nobis accommoda, reliquos tacebimus, nihil enim refert[1] inutilia explicare, ipsa quattuor sunt **Sergurth, Heramael, Irmasliel, et Suffugruel**, et ad pentacula sunt pernecessaria,[2] ideo [11r] de iis in 2a parte dicemus.

---

1   DN91: *res est.*
2   P, GG: *supernecessaria.*

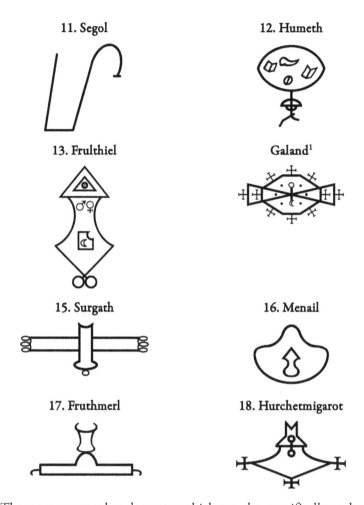

11. Segol

12. Humeth

13. Frulthiel

Galand[1]

15. Surgath

16. Menail

17. Fruthmerl

18. Hurchetmigarot

There are many other daemons, which are also specifically under duke **Satanachi.** There are 54, of which four are the principal ones, and the magic can be adapted by us; we will remain silent about the rest, because they would be pointless to expound. Those four however are: (1) **Sergurth**, (2) **Heramael**, (3) **Irmasliel,** and (4) **Suffugruel**, and for which the pentacles are very necessary [+for them to appear promptly and easily]; therefore we will speak about them in the second part.[2]

---

1 Compare seals of Galand on composite seal below (p. 39), which have extra rectangles in center, but that is not found in other manuscripts.

2 The text in [+...] per W983. These four are in fact not mentioned again, but see GV pp. 17-18. See also appendix.

Sub duce **Agaleraptarchimath**, unus est ex principalioribus[1] maxime notandus, scilicet **Elelogaphatel**, qui undis, et aquis omnino[2] imperat. Sub duce **Resbiroth** duo sunt pręcipui, **hael** et **Sergulaf.**

Hael quascunque litteras scribere docet, et quaslibet linguas loqui subito nos facit, immo et epistolas secretissime scriptas aperire, et in uerum sensum reducere ualet.[3]

Sergulas [*Sergulaf] quęlibet instrumenta ad faciendum aliquid idonea suppeditat, ut cultrum &c. item machinas omnis generis ostendit.

Horum tres[4] characteres sunt.

1. Elelogaphatel

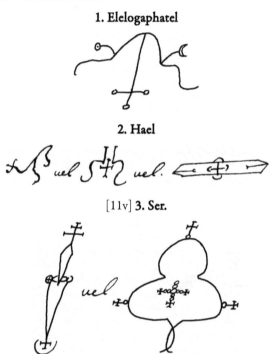

2. Hael

[11v] **3. Ser.**

---

1   BNF: *primatibus.*
2   P omits.
3   DN91 adds *in instanti.*
4   BNF, P, DN91: *trium.*

One of the chiefs under duke **Agaleraptarchimath**[1] is especially to be noted, namely **Elelogaphatel**, who commands the waves and the waters entirely. Under duke **Resbiroth** there are two in particular: **Hael** and **Sergulaf**.

Hael teaches how to write any kind of letters, and indeed can make anyone speak any language instantly, and can reveal the most difficult secret writing, and is able to deduce the true meaning thereof.

Sergulaf supplies any kind of tool needed to make anything, such as a knife, etc. Likewise he reveals machines of all types.

The three characters of these are:

1. Elelogaphatel[2]

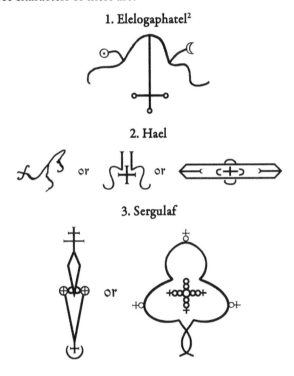

2. Hael

3. Sergulaf

---

1   Spelled Agaleraptarkimath earlier and in other mss. "Kymat" actually starts a separate paragraph in P, but it is clear from earlier text (p. 6) and other manuscripts that it belongs with Agaleraptor. Compare GV, p. 17 ("Agalierapta, Tarchimache/ Tarihimal"). L1202: Agateraptor, Himacth.

2   Compare seal of Elelogaphatel below, p. 25.

Alii etiam sunt spiritus aerei, sed nullius in hoc libello sunt usus. de iis[1] scriptus est libellus quidam: alii sunt ignei qui etiam nullius sunt usus, tandem igitur ut finem[2] huic capitulo[3] imponamus spiritus uel sese uisibiliter [+nobis][4] comunicant, uel inuisibiliter, qui se comunicant uisibiliter sunt terrestres, qui inuisibiliter sunt aerei: nos hoc libello de iis qui sese uisibiliter comunicant agimus,[5] alium enim scripsimus de inuisibilibus, qui etiam Clauicula inscribitur.[6] Inuisibiles [12r] autem tantos non producunt effectus; hoc autem habent opportunitatis, quod in anulo secum geri queant.[7]

Hęc dicta sunt[8] de spiritibus, ut melius sequentia intelligantur.

Sequitur prima pars de secretis secretissimis quorum catalogus hic est, quem promisimus in pręludio huius libelli.

Ut pluat,

ut ningat,

ut fulguret,

ut non frigeamus,

ut non[9] nimio calore torqueamur,

[+ut aperiamus clauaturas,][10]

ut amorem puellę conciliemus,

ut amatę puellę concubitu potiamur,

ut nummos quoties libuerit habeamus,

ut simus inuisibiles,

ut inimicus emoriatur,

ut musica audiatur dulcissima,

ut demortui uiui appareant nobis, et eloquantur.

---

1   DN91, GG: *his.*
2   DN91: *in finem.*
3   DN91, P, GG: *capiti*
4   So DN91, P, and GG.
5   DN91 omits.
6   P: *scribitur.*
7   BNF omits this paragraph.
8   DN91: *sint.*
9   DN91 omits *non.*
10 So DN91, BNF, P, GG, L. See also below.

There are also other spirits of the air, but their uses are not written in this booklet. Others are fiery, which are also not used.[1]

Finally, therefore, in order to bring this chapter to a conclusion, the spirits can communicate [+with us] either visibly in person, or invisibly. Those who communicate visibly are terrestrial, while those who communicate invisibly are aerial. We share this little book with those who are dealing with those who communicate visibly. We have written elsewhere about the invisible ones, for which a little key (*Clavicula*) is also written. However, the invisible ones do not accomplish such great effects; moreover, they have this convenience, that they are able to be carried with him in a ring.

This much has been said concerning the spirits, in order that the following will be better understood. The first part concerning the most secret of secrets follows, the enumeration of which is what we promised in the introduction of this booklet:

- To cause rain
- To cause snow
- To cause lightning
- To not be cold
- To not be hurt by great heat
- [+To open closed things]
- To win the love of a young woman
- To couple with a beloved young woman
- To have as many coins as desired
- To become invisible
- In order that an enemy dies
- To hear the sweetest music
- That the deceased may appear living and speak with us.

---

1   GV gives names, offices, and some of the seals for spirits who are under Hael and Sergulath: See appendix for details.

Ut pluat.

Accipe aquam marinam, uel marina[ta]m,[1] ut postea [12v] docebo conficies artifialiter,[2] hac ablue circulum in terra descriptum, in medio[3] circuli pone heliotropium lapidem, in dextra parte sculpe (baculo scilicet magico, cuius constructionem pauci norunt, [+et alibi descripsi][4]) character **Beschard**, et in sinistra parte **Elelogaphatel**, et supra baculum insistens hęc uerba pronuntia [+**Aerlea**] **Helelogaphaton**,[5] et uidebis cęlum nubibus densatum in aquam resolui.

Talis debet esse circulus in terra[6] designatus.

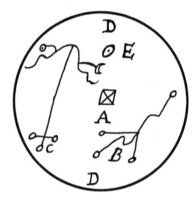

D. D. Circulus est. A. Eliotropium, B. character **Beschard**, C. character **Elelogaphatel.** E signum siue figura solis.

[13r] Ut fiat aqua marina artificialiter, Accipe aquam fluminis, et sale contempera, cum lutoque buliendam trade igni per quadrantem horę, iniice parum per pulueris pumicis, et erit factum, quod faciendum erat.[7]

---

1   P: *marinam uel marinatam*. ASV and DN91 both read *marinam uel marinam*. GG perhaps has the best reading: *marinam uel naturalem uel artificialem*.

2   BNF omits *uel marinam ... artifialiter.*

3   BNF and P add *ipsius*; DN91adds *illius.*

4   So DN91, BNF, P.

5   DN91: Helelugaphatel; BNF: Helelugaphraten; GG: Aerlea Helelagafaton fortiter; L1202: Eliogaphatel.

6   P omits *in terra.*

7   DN91, GG omit the last 3 words.

To make it rain.

Take sea water, or *marinata*, which I will teach you to make artificially afterwards. Sprinkle this on a circle which you have drawn on the ground, and in the middle of this circle place a stone of heliotrope (bloodstone). Then, with the wand, namely the magic one, whose construction few know [+which I have described elsewhere], draw on the right hand side the character of **Beschard**, and on the left side **Elelogaphatel**, and standing over the wand, recite these words: "[+**Aerlea**] **Helelogaphaton**" and you will see clouds fill the sky, and be released as water.[1]

The designated circle should be like this:[2]

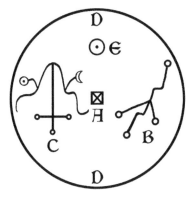

D D is the circle. A is the heliotrope; B is the character of **Beschard**; C is the character of **Elelogaphatel**; E is the symbol or sign of the Sun.

In order to make artificial sea water, take river water and salt mixed with clay, and boil for a quarter hour over a fire on which you have thrown a little ground pumice. And so is done that which was to be accomplished.

---

1 GG seems to have the best reading here: you recite "'Aerlea Helelagafaton' strongly, and you will see the sky thickened with clouds, to be released as water." According to L1202, you recite "*Eliogaphatel*, the sky is composed of clouds, may they resolve into water."

2 Compare seals of Beschard and Elelogaphatel above.

Ut ningat.

Fac ut superius, non utere uero[1] charactere **elelogaphatel**, sed pone loco illius character **Luciferi**.[2]

Nota obiter quod dum de niue[3] loquimur non alienum erit loqui de glacie, quę naturaliter[4] fieri potest [+etiam][5] in calidissimis ęstatis diebus sic.

Accipe phialam uitream, imple aqua calida, [+mediocriter, hanc deinde phialam][6] in puteum ad fundum usque [+cum corda][7] suspende per horam,[8] et aqua quę erat in phiala fiet[9] glacies, quod omnes qui uidebunt mirabuntur.

Ex niue etiam candela fieri potest hoc modo. habe camphoram in longum productam admodum elicnii,[10] [13v] et niue circunuolue, ita ut candela niuea uideatur tam colore quam materia, deinde accende elychneum, et comburetur,[11] et flammabit, et mirabile uidebitur iis, qui nescient potentiam[12] camphorę putantes niuem comburi.

Ut fulguret.[13]

Habe herbam uocatam lunariam, serua per 15 dies[14] in uentre bouis, deinde hoc sic utere dum uolueris fulgetra[15] emicare:[16] hanc inuocationem pronuncia priusquam aliquid aliud feceris,[17] debes autem[18] esse indutus

---

1   P omits.
2   BNF omits the rest of the chapter.
3   DN91: *uere*.
4   Instead of *naturaliter,* DN91 has *nam aliter.*
5   So DN91, P.
6   DN91 adds *quamdiu aqua est calida* ("as long as the water is warm").
7   Words in [+] per P, DN91. Instead of *cum corda* DN91 reads *eum corda*. GG simplifies the paragraph even more.
8   P adds *unam* ("one").
9   P: *erit.*
10 P: *elichnei.*
11 P: *comburatur.*
12 DN91: *prędictam.*
13 BNF: *fulgeat.*
14 P adds *eam.*
15 DN91: *fulgura.*
16 BNF: *micare.* The ms then skips ahead to *accendes lucernam....*
17 P omits *hanc inuocationem pronuncia priusquam aliquid aliud feceris.*
18 P: *enim.*

To make it snow.

Do as above, but instead of using the character of **Elelogaphatel**, use the character of **Lucifer**.

Note by the way, that since we are speaking about snow, it is not out of place to speak here about ice, which can be made naturally [+even] on a hot summer's day, as follows:

Take a drinking glass,[1] and fill [+it with lukewarm water, then suspend] this glass at the bottom of a well, suspended [+from a cord] for an hour, and the water which was in the glass will be ice, which all who see it will be amazed.

A candle can also be made from snow in the following way. Have camphor stretched out into a very long wick, and wrap snow around it, so that it looks like a candle made of snow, then light the wick, and it should burn, and it will seem to be a miracle by those who don't know the power of camphor, thinking that snow is being burned up.

To cause lightning.[2]

Take the herb called *lunaria,*[3] and preserve it in the stomach of an ox for fifteen days. Then use it when you wish to cause lightning to burst out. Pronounce this invocation before anything else is done. However, you should

---

1   The next two paragraphs are not found in GG.
2   GG omits everything after "use it when you wish."
3   Common name is "honesty."

uestibus ad hęc idoneis, et baculum magicum sub pedibus tenere, Inuocatio talis est.

> Per nomen **Adonay Tetragrammaton** uos coniuro spiritus Comites **Beschard**, et te **Luciferum, et Syrach,** ut eis iubeas ad carmen accedere, et eorum potentiam mihi ministrare.

Deinde sile per semihoram,[1] postea accendes lucernam cuius [14r] elychnium[2] sit ex lunaria confectum,[3] et hęc uerba pronunciabis

Errath abacam Cebathalater fermuth.[4]

Mox ex lapide fulminis puluerem confectam[5] in lampadem immittes, et circulum describes bacculo magico, in medio lampadem pones, et supra lampadem character **Beschard** describes, infra character **Luciferi**, à dextris character **Syrach**, et omnia deinde arena cooperies, et fulgurabit, talis est circulus.

Ut non frigeamus.

Ne frigeamus[6] describe character **frimodth** in pergamo,[7] et myrra suffumiga non thure: [14v] deinde bacculo magico arrepto ipsum pergam-

---

1   DN91 omits the last 6 words.
2   BNF: *Elichricum.*
3   BNF skip ahead to *mox....*
4   DN91: Enathabatum, Cebathalather, fermurth; BNF: Errath, abacam, cebathalathar, fermurdth; P: Errathabacam, Cebathalater, Termuth; P2: Errata-Bacam – Cebat – Halatir – <u>Termuth</u>. GG amd W4667 truncate the instructions.
5   P: *puluere confectum.*
6   DN91, GG omit *ne frigeamus.*
7   BNF adds *virgineo* here and in the next chapter.

have on suitable garments for this, and then hold the magic wand down under your feet, and invoke thus:

> Through the name **Adonay Tetragrammaton**, I conjure you O spirit Count **Beschard**, and you **Lucifer** and **Syrach**,[1] that you order them to approach this incantation, and force them to attend to me.

Then observe silence for half an hour. Afterwards kindle an oil lamp, whose wick should be made of *lunaria*, and then recite these words:

Errath abacam, Cebathalater fermuth.

Then take powder made from lightning stone,[2] put it into the lamp, and draw a magic circle with the magic wand, placing the lamp in the middle, and over the lamp draw the character of **Beschard**, below the character of **Lucifer**, on the right side the character of **Syrach**, and then cover everything completely with sand, and it will cause lightning. The circle is thus:[3]

In order to not be cold.

To not be cold, copy the character of **Frimodth** on parchment, and fumigate it with myrrh, not with frankincense. And afterwards, fumigate it again

---

1   See below. The same as Scyrach mentioned earlier as one of Lucifer's dukes.
2   I.e. fulgurite.
3   DN91, BNF, P, and W4667 all show wavy lines above the lamp not found in ASV, which I have added to my version. Compare seals of Beschard, Syrach, and Lucifer above.

[en]um in ignem[1] coniice, postquam autem myrrha suffumigatus es[t][2] aluminis aqua cum oui albumine[3] distemperata<m>,[4] ungi debes[5] mane autem ante ignem donec pergam[en]um sit ustum, et non frigebis.

Ut non nimius calor nos infestet.

Describe character **frimodth** in pergamo, et thure suffumiga non myrrha,[6] deinde bacculo magico arrepto pergamum supra[7] glaciem proiice, nec nimius calor te infestabit.

Ad aperiendas clauaturas secretum[8] admirabile.[9]

Accipe magnetem, et supra ipsum lapidem magnetis fac ter signum[10] crucis Sancti Andreę uel duos bacculos magicos decussatim[11] impone, et circa magnetem describe circulum: [+et][12] in circulo inscribe quadratum [15r] et in singulas lunulas[13] pone character[14] **Surgath** et circa circulum 4 ramos lunarię[15] ut supra diximus, et hęc uerba pronuntia facite prę manibus lampadem [*lapidem][16] tenens.

Rechat, surgat Menail Remicheal Raga damor Eschirtmuth.[17]

---

1 P: *igne.*

2 DN91, BNF: *suffumigatus est*; P: *suffumigatus ex.* GG: *suffumigatus erit.*

3 BNF: *albumino.*

4 DN91, GG: *distemperata*; P: *distempera.*

5 P: *debet.*

6 DN91 omits *non myrrha.* GG: *cum myrrha suffumiga, non autem thure .*

7 So too DN91; P, GG: super.

8 DN91, GG: *arcanum.*

9 P: *mirabile.*

10 BNF: *signos.*

11 BNF: *decustatim.*

12 So P, GG.

13 DN91 and BNF also read *lunulas*; P: *lienulas*; GG: *lunales.*

14 DN91 omits approximately 2 lines of text here, jumping to *surgat menail.*

15 BNF skips ahead to *deinde omnia....*

16 So GG, L1202, and W4669 p. 84. P: *lampadem.*

17 DN91: Surgat menail, Remicheal, Ragadamor eschutmut. P: Rechath, Surgath, Menail, Remicheal, Ragadamor, Eschetmuth; GG: Raehat, Sargath, Manail, Remicheal, Regadamos, Eschertmath. P2: Rechath, Surgath Menaier, Remicheal, Ragadamor, Eshetmuth; W4667: Raoth, Surgath, menael, Bermichael, Ragadamor, Escharmuth.

with myrrh, and anoint it with water of alum, tempered with an egg white. Then with the magic wand, pick up the parchment and put it into the fire. Until the fire has burned out in the morning, and the parchment is consumed, you will not be cold.

To not be bothered by excessive heat.

Copy out the character of **Frimodth** onto parchment, and fumigate with frankincense, but not myrrh, then pick up the parchment with the magic wand, and throw it down onto ice, and excessive heat will not bother you.

A wonderful secret for opening all closed things.

Take a lodestone, and above it make the sign of Saint Andrew's cross three times, or else make the cross by placing two magic wands crosswise above it. Inscribe a circle around the lodestone, [+and] in the circle inscribe a square, and inside each crescent-shaped space put the character of **Surgath**. Surround the circle with four branches of *lunaria* as mentioned above, and pronounce these words, holding a lamp [*the stone][1] before you in your hands.

Rechat, surgat Menail Remicheal Raga damor Eschirtmuth.

---

1   Reading *lapidem,* as GG, L1202, and W4669 p. 84. W4667 p. 402: et autour du cercle quatre rameaux de lorrier comme nous auons dit sy dessus, et dit ses parolle tous bas tenans la lempe En les mains....

Deinde omnia limatura ferri obrue, et si magnetem tecum feras, et ante clauaturas ponas aperientur sine dubio.

Ad amorem puellę conciliandum.

Accipe Chrisolitum lapidem, et herbam dictam mandragoram, et hęc duo in puluerem minutissimum redige, et serua ad usum, debes autem habere Cyatum ligneum ad agnocasto, et in tundo [*fundo],[1] uel intus ubicunque uolueris scribere character **frimoth** [*frimodth] et tres lunas circa cyatum, deinde[2] cum infundas lac in Cyatum hęc uerba pronuntia.

Segaloth [15v] frimodth eligalath Errethin Elemh, Seriuthrath.[3]

Sunt autem carmina,[4] et uersus simul. Postquam uero infuderis[5] lac puluerem supradictum in Cyatum insperge, et pone cyatum in medio circuli, et in circulo[6] describe triangulum, in anguloque trianguli describe character **frimodth,** in lunulis[7] autem tribus A B C scribe nomen, et cognomen puellę eius qua potiri cupis litteris hębraeis, aut Syriacis, et circa circulum, ubi trianguli anguli desinunt scribe tuo sanguine amoris signum hoc

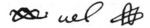

et supra[8] circulum sic confectum dormi per semihoram, et amor puellę in te conciliabitur.[9]

---

1   So DN91, BNF, P, GG.
2   BNF skips ahead to *puluerem supradictum....*
3   DN91: Segaloth <u>frimath</u>, elegalath enethin elemh, seriuth rath; P: Segaloth, frimodth, <u>Eligulath, Erechim</u>, Elemh, Seriuthrath. GG gives only a single magic word: <u>Sagaloth.</u> P2 reads: Segaloth <u>Frimoth,</u> Eligulath, Erechim, Elemh, <u>Sereuthrath.</u>
4   P: *termina.*
5   DN91: *infunderis.*
6   P in cyato.
7   DN91: *in lunibus.*
8   P omits.
9   In ASV the word "vel" ("or") is written between the two types of love knots, indicating either can be used.

Then cover everything over with iron filings, and if you bring the lodestone with you, and place it before anything that is closed, it will open without doubt.

To win over the love of a young woman.

Take the stone chrysolite (peridot), and the herb that is called mandrake; reduce these two into a fine powder, and preserve it for use later. Next, you should have a ladle of agnocasto wood, and on the bottom or inside, wherever you wish, write the character of **Frimodth** and three moons around the ladle. Then while pouring milk into the ladle, pronounce these words:

Segaloth frimodth eligalath Errethin Elemh, Seriuthrath.

There are also incantations and verses at the same time.[1] After you have finished pouring the milk, sprinkle the powder mentioned above onto the ladle, and place the ladle in the middle of the circle. Within the circle draw a triangle, and in each angle of the triangle draw the character of Frimodth. Within the crescent-shaped spaces labelled A B C, write the name and surname of the girl that you wish to have, in Hebrew or Syriac letters. Around the circle, where the three corners end, write with your blood, this sign of love:

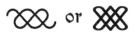

And thus completed, sleep over the circle for half an hour, and the young woman will be united in love with you.[2]

---

1   Probably meaning you should adapt the invocation found on 15r/p. 28. This sentence is not found in GG or W4667. P2: są zas terminy i razem wiersze, po którym.

2   Love knots. As explained in the description, and from the word *uel* ("or") here, only 3 knots are to be used in this spell, but they can be either design shown. Compare seal of Frimodth on pg. 10 above.

[16r] Ad amatę puellę¹ concubitu potiendum secretum omnino² admirabile.

Accipe ueretrum³ lupi uel leonis, et igne coque⁴ in ueru scilicet aut patina, et alicui ex animalibus⁵ domesticis eiusquam cupis⁶ comedendum trade, post tres deinde dies sacrifica simiam **frimodth**; altare autem instrues⁷ 14 candelis [+cereis,]⁸ cera autem debet esse nigra: supra autem altare circulum facies puta baculo ad ignem usto in extremitate: in ipso⁹ formam cunie¹⁰ inscribes, in medio character **frimodth** scribes cretha rubra, quam rubricam¹¹ uocant,¹² et supra hunc circulum occide simiam cultro in pectus demisso, et sanguinem recipe¹³ in uase aeneo,¹⁴ et quoties libuerit amica potieris,¹⁵ ipsa ab initio parumper renuente sed in fine annuente.

---

1   In P these two words are the label of the figure above, not part of the chapter title.
2   BNF omits this word.
3   So too DN91, BNF. P: ventrem; which is also reflected in W4667: *le ventre.*
4   So too BNF; DN91, P: *quoque.*
5   P: *animantibus.*
6   BNF: *domesticis quam cupis puellæ ejus ....*
7   DN91: *institues.*
8   So DN91, BNF, P.
9   P omits *in ipso.*
10 Presumably *cunnus/cunni.* DN91: *cunui.* BNF: *cuniei*; P: *canis* ("of a dog") (!).
11 DN91: *rubea, quam rubicam.*
12 BNF skips the last 6 words.
13 P: *accipe.*
14 DN91: *in sanguine* [sic] *ęneo.* P: *in uase aereo.*
15 DN91: *potiri poteris.*

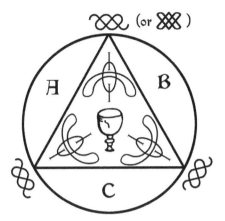

For the love of a young woman.

For love making/coupling. An entirely admirable secret.[1]

Take the penis[2] of a wolf or a lion, and roast it on a spit or pan, and feed it to any domestic animal you wish. After three days, sacrifice a monkey to **Frimodth**. Then construct an altar with fourteen [+wax] candles, which must be black. Moreover, upon the altar you must make a circle, for example with the tip of a stick that has been burned in the fire. On the outermost part draw the shape of a vulva,[3] and in the middle the character of **Frimodth,** written with red, which they call red ocre. Over this circle kill a monkey with a knife thrust into the chest. Collect the blood into a copper vessel, and as often as you please you can have liberties with a female friend. She will refuse at first, but in the end she will agree.

---

1 Compare W4667 pp 404-405, which has the title in cipher. GG p. 18 has only "Accipe ne ---" and keeps the rest of the secret.

2 P reads *ventrem* ("stomach").

3 P: *canis* ("of a dog"), no doubt a mistake, the word being similar to *cunie*.

[16v]

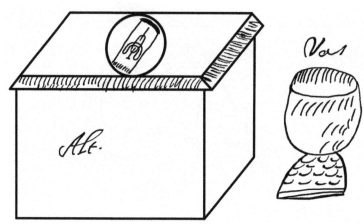

Vt nummos quoties libuerit habeamus.

Quot nummos habere uolueris siue cupreos, siue aereos,[1] siue argenteos,
siue aureos, tot circulos rotundos seca ex pergameno dupplicato, et simul
conglutinato, et in utraque parte signum describe monetę quam cupis, fac
deinde circulum supra tabulam, et tot fac characteres **Claunth**, quot sunt
nummi quos[2] habere cupis, et deinde omnes pergammicos [*pergamenicos][3]
nummos in altum tanquam Cylindrum erige[4] et hoc carmen pronuntia.

[17r] **Claunth feras catelam**
Pignuth nemtheranot agan
Securma ferunt erithren
Clebanot nechin Trebren.[5]

---

1   DN91, BNF, P also read *aereos* but that is synonymous with *cupreos*. GG omits. Perhaps
    aeneos ("bronze") is intended. BNF skips *siue argenteos siue aureos*.
2   BNF: *quot*.
3   So DN91; P: *pergameos*.
4   BNF omits the rest.
5   DN91: Claunth feras catebam / Pignugth nemtheranot agan / Serurma ferunt erithren /
    Clebanoth nechin Trebren. P: Claunth <u>seras catebam</u> / <u>Sygnugth</u> nemth Eranot <u>agam</u> /
    <u>Serurma serunt erithrim</u> / <u>Clibanot</u> nechin <u>Irebren</u>; GG: Claunt seras <u>catabam Signuth</u>
    <u>memtheranot agam Serruma ferunt arithem</u> Clibanot <u>hec</u> hin Irebren. P2: <u>Chaunt,</u> Seras,
    <u>Cateban</u> (2) <u>Sygnuath, Nemith, Eranoth</u> Agam (3) Serurma, Serunt, <u>Crithim</u> (4)
    <u>Clibonoth,</u> Nechin, Irebren.

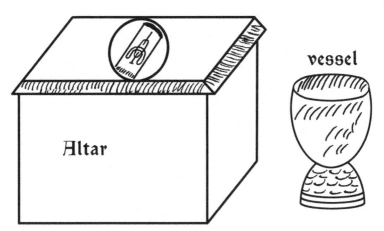

vessel

Altar

To have coins as often as we please.[1]

To have as many coins as you wish, whether copper, or gold, or silver, or bronze, cut circles of parchment of the same size as the desired coins, and also glue them together so they are the right thickness, and on each piece copy the image of the money which you desire. Then make a circle upon the table, and make as many characters of **Claunth** as the coins you wish to have, and then place all the parchment coins into a stack, and recite this incantation:

> **Claunth feras catelam**
> **Pignuth nemtheranot agan**
> **Securma ferunt erithren**
> **Clebanot nechin Trebren.**

---

1 Compare W4667 pp. 405-406; L1202; GV pp. 87, 155; W4669 p. 85. Note the French translations have misunderstood the instructions.

Deinde hęc iterum cane ad lyram ter, et dormi per horam supra lecto[1] de nummis non cogitans, et post horam loco nummorum pergamm[en]icorum inuenies nummos tot quales uolueris, hoc ex sequenti figura percipies.

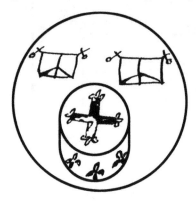

Ut inimicus emoriatur.

Accipe cor galli in mense martio nati, et pone in circulo, in quo sint tres characteres **Galand**, et pone supra hos characteres tres[2] lucernas ex [17v] oleo amygdalę[3] uel sulphuris, et hęc uerba pronuntia.

Remanor adhuch
Calemturis archalh
Elestor.[4]

Deinde eneca[5] tres lucernas, et cor galli acu transfige[6] et inimicus emorietur sine dubbio. talis est figura circuli.[7]

---

1   P *supra lectum* would be more correct (or *in lecto*).

2   DN91 omits.

3   DN91, P: *amigdalarum*.

4   DN91: Remanor adhuc, Calemtuch, Archalth elestor; BNF: Remanor aduch Calemturoh archalth Elestor; P: Remaner adhuch / Calemturis archalth / Elestor; GG: Remaneraduch, Calemturch, Arcalth, Elestor; P2: Remanet, Adhuh (2) Calemturch, Archadh (3) Elestor.

5   So too DN91, BNF; P: *intra* ("between"); GG: *infra* ("beneath"). The inclusion of the word *et* also suggests the missing verb.

6   BNF: *ha~as, fige....*

7   P omits.

Then sing these words again three times to the lyre, and sleep for an hour on the bed, not thinking about the coins, and after an hour in place of the parchment coins, you will discover as many coins as wished. See the following figure:[1]

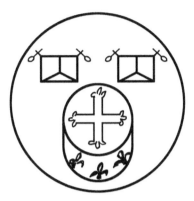

In order that an enemy will die.

Take the heart of a cock in the month of March, and place it in a circle in which should be three characters of **Galand**, and place over those characters three oil lamps, fueled with almond oil or sulfur, and pronounce these words:

**Remanor adhuch
Calemturis archalh
Elestor.**

Then extinguish the three oil lamps, and pierce the heart of the cock with a needle, and the enemy will die without doubt. The figure of the circle is thus:[2]

---

1   ASV shows Clahunt figure with vertical line extending to bottom of box (compare above), but none of the other examples show it, so I have not included it in my version. The coin in the drawing may resemble a 16th century Venetian gold scudo della croce.

2   Compare seal of Galand on page 11.

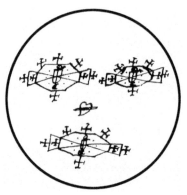

Ut simus inuisibiles
secretum iucundissimum.[1]

Habe peram uel crumenam[2] ex pelle chamaleontis, [18r] uel polypodis,[3] intus pone tres characteres unum **menail**, alterum **Syrach**, alterum **Luciferi**, utrosque ex sanguine Chamalientis uel Polypodis:[4] Character autem **Menail** debet esse in charta triangulari scriptum, **Syrach** in quadrangulari et **Luciferi** signum in pergamo pentagonaliter scisso: hęc tria signa deinde sacrifica cum chameleonte, et XI candelis ex rosina [*resina],[5] et pice confectis, et quoties hos characteres tecum attuleris, si dicas **Harets, Menail, Bathusam**[6] eris inuisibilis.

Ut musica dulcissima audiatur.

Musicam quam audire uolueris in circulo pone supra character **Elepoth** [*Klepoth], et canens per interiectos gemitus hęc uerba 12 pronuntia.

---

1 GG skips rest of experiments.
2 DN91 omits *uel crumenam*.
3 So also DN91; P omits *vel polypodis* ("or an octopus or cuttlefish"), here, but see below. This is also supported by W4667 p. 408: *ou de polipode*. Latin *pulypus* could includes both octopus and cuttlefish, and like the chameleon, they can both alter their skin pigmentation to hide.
4 BNF skips to *characteres hos sacrifica cum chamæleonte et xi....*
5 So DN91, BNF, P.
6 DN91: Hareths, Menail, Bathalano; BNF: Harets menail <u>bathasam</u>; P: harith, Menail, Bathalam; P2: <u>Haryth,</u> Menail, Bathalam; W4667: Harith, Manael, bathalam.

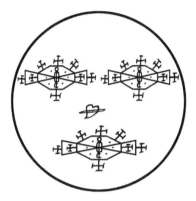

To become invisible. A most pleasant secret.

Have a satchel or pouch made from the skin of a chameleon, or an octo-pus (or cuttlefish), place within three characters: One of **Menail**, another of **Syrach**, and another of **Lucifer**, each drawn with the blood of a chameleon, or an octopus, or a cuttlefish. Moreover, the character of **Menail** must be written on a triangular parchment, that of **Syrach** on a square of parchment, and the sign of **Lucifer** on a parchment cut into a pentagonal shape. Then sacrifice these three signs with the chameleon, and with eleven candles made out of resin and pitch, and as often as you bring these characters with, if you say **Harets, Menail, Bathusam,** you will be invisible.

In order to hear the sweetest music.

When you wish to hear music, place in the circle the above character of **Klepoth**, and pronounce in song these twelve words,[1] interspersed between moans:

---

1   It could mean utter the words 12 times, or simply utter the twelve words. Only ASV has
    12 words however. W4667 says to "pronounce these twelve words two times."

[18v] **Ador, Clepoth, Chelath, Micaratabot, filma, Syrath, Seruchel, Uriel, Mystertsh, Chybenoth, Rstemaron, furcolsten,**[1]

et immediate post audies musicam[2] dulcissime decantatam. talis est circulus.

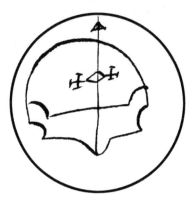

Ut demortui uiui appareant nobis et eloquantur[3] secretum stupendum et admirabile.

Scribe nomen illius, quem videre cupis in corio canino sanguine draconis, debet autem esse corium in formam stelle[4] sic.

---

1   DN91: Sador, Clepoth, Micaracaboth, Chibenoth, Rhtemaron, furcolton; BNF: *hæc verba decem pronuntiata,* Ador Clepoth <u>Cheluth</u> <u>Micaracabot</u> filma, Syrath <u>Serachel</u> Vriel <u>mystheoth</u> Chibenoth <u>Rthemaron</u> <u>furcolten</u>; P: Ador, Clepoth, Chelath, Micara, Cabot, Silma, Scirach, Seruchela, Rhtemaron, Surcolten; Compare P2 p. 141, which gives the number of repetitions as ten: Ador, <u>Klepoth,</u> Chelath, Mikara, <u>Kaboth,</u> Sylma, Scyrach, <u>Seruhela,</u> Rhtemaron, <u>Surkolten.. compare also</u> W4667 p. 409: Ador, <u>Elepoth,</u> Micara, Cabot, Silma, <u>Sirach, Sinuch, la Retimara, Surcolon.</u> W4669 has twelve as follows: Ador, Elepoth, Cheluth, Migareth, Cubot, Sylma, Sirath, Fernechel, Rotromaron, Surcollen, Agra, Seron. Compare GV pp. 87, 155, where the "eleven" words are: Ador, Klepoth, Chelath, Migaroth, Pooch, Silma, Sirath, Sernichiel, Rotho, Maron, Collen.
2   BNF: *misicam* (!).
3   DN91, P: loquantur.
4   DN91, P: *in forma stellae.* BNF: *in fora (!) stellæ.*

Ador, Clepoth, Chelath, Micaratabot, filma, Syrath, Seruchel, Uriel, Mystertsh, Chybenoth, Rstemaron, furcolsten.

And immediately thereafter, you will hear the most sweetly chanted music. The circle is thus:[1]

In order that a corpse appear living and able to speak. An astounding and admirable secret.

Write the name of the one you wish to see on the skin of a dog with the blood of a serpent. Moreover, the skin should be in the shape of a star, like this:

---

1   Compare seal of Klepoth above.

Vel[1] si non habeas corium caninum supra corium [19r] uaccinum [+paratum][2] figuram quam uides,[3] talis est figura corii uaccini.[4]

Vel ex pergameno, sed figura facienda est difficilior[5] admodum[6] sic.

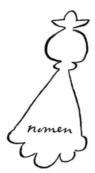

---

1   BNF, P add: *etiam.*
2   So DN91, BNF, P.
3   P adds *facies.*
4   DN91 omits these 5 words.
5   DN91, P: *difficilis.*
6   BNF, P omit *admodum.*

However, if you don't have the skin of a dog, you can use the prepared skin of a cow, made into the shape shown. This is the shape of the cow skin:

Or, it can be made from parchment, but the shape to make is much more difficult, thus:

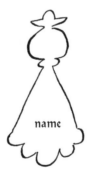

Deinde suffumiga tale nomen ter thure, et myrrha, et bitumine, et cum
uersibus sequentibus ter recitabis

[19v] **frulthiel**

**frulthiel gelopsa courth
Hebeiuin Irach adonay
Reschit hogma behours
Elchut mirai Chebaietai.**[1]

Deinde concinnabis multa ligna [+helicis],[2] aut onobrichis, aut linguę
serpentinę, et cumulum efficies in medio circuli cum charactere **frulthiel.** In
capite deinde accendes et ueniet **frulthiel** in forma<m>[3] hominis sine
manibus nigri in capite, et nudi, cui dabis nomen illius, quemuis resuscitare
per horam et non magis,[4] et ille dentibus arripiet;[5] animaduerte ne digitos
amputet[6] dentibus, sepius stantes momordit, et dormientes in circulo, et post
horam ueniet homo quem desiderabas.[7]

finis secretorum[8]

---

1   DN91: <u>Furcthiel</u> <u>furcthiel</u> <u>Galapha</u> courth / <u>Hebeiuin</u> Irach adonay /Reschit hogma
    Behours / <u>Elchuth</u> mirai Chebaietai; BNF: frulthiel / frulthiel <u>gelopha</u> <u>Courh</u> / hebeiuin
    Irach adonay / Reschit hogma behours / <u>Eschuth</u> mirai Chebaietai; P: <u>Fructhiel.</u> /
    <u>fructhiel gelapha</u> / <u>hebiruin</u> Irach Adonay /Reschit <u>ogma</u> / <u>Elchuth</u> mirai Chebaietai.
    Note the three variations of the spirit's name in P, including "Frulthiel" on pages 7 and 9.
    P2 reads: <u>Fruchthiel</u> <u>Fruchthiel,</u> <u>Gielapho,</u> <u>Hebirum,</u> <u>Iiach,</u> Adonay, <u>Reshit,</u> Ogma
    Elchuth, Mirai Chebaietai. The magic words in W4667 are only "feruothiel, feruthiel" (p.
    411). The equivalent spirit in GV is Frucissiere.
2   BNF seems to point us to the solution to this bizarre passage: *ligna hilecis [sic *helicis]*,
    supported by the accompanying figure. This is also supported by W4667: tu ammasseras
    bien promptement force bois se <u>saul</u>, ou de langue serpentenne ("pile up willow wood, or
    adder's tongue."). DN91: *ligna filicis* ("woods of the fern") (!); P: *signa, scilicet* (!).
3   ASN91, P: *in forma.*
4   P: *amplius.*
5   So too DN91; P: *arripies.*
6   So too DN91; P: *amputes* (!).
7   DN91: *desiderabis.*
8   DN91: *finis libri primi.*

Then fumigate the name three times with frankincense, myrrh, and bitumen and recite aloud three times the following words:

frulthiel

> **frulthiel gelopsa courth**
> **Hebeiuin Irach adonay**
> **Reschit hogma behours**
> **Elchut mirai Chebaietai.**

Then you should prepare much wood [+of slender willow wands], or of onobrychis, or adder's tongue,[1] and make a heap in the middle of the circle with the character of **Frulthiel** at the top, then kindle it, and **Frulthiel** will come in the form of a man without hands, with a black head, and nude, to whom you should give the name of the one you wish to resuscitate, for an hour and no longer, and he will seize it with his teeth, but beware that he does not bite off your fingers with his teeth, for he has often bitten those standing or sleeping in the circle. And after an hour the man will come, whom you desire to see.[2]

End of the secrets.

---

1 Besides the proposed *hilecis* = **helice* ("slender willow"), the plants mentioned are herbs, not wood, so some other wood is needed to burn everything.

2 BNF is the only manuscript which includes this figure.

SEQUITUR LIBER SECUNDUS DE PENTACULIS SIUE APPARATIONIBUS.

In nomine Adonay Elohim Tetragrammaton aliorum[que][1] nominum Altissimi.

equitur *Clauicula Salomonis* seu[2] apertura secretorum, quę nemin[i] mortalium reuelanda nisi filiis diuinę scientię initiatis,[3] quam Dominus[4] seruo suo soli Salomoni[5] reuelauit, amulsaaco abenarar [*a me Isaaco Abenarach][6] in celeberrimo C. T.[7] professore ex haebraica lingua in latinam conuersa fideliterque recognita, et in lucem characteribus manuscriptis mandata filiis in arte tantummodo tradita, a qua olim magnus Pas[8] aliique complures doctrinam suam sunt mutuati.

De institutione artis. Caput 1.[9]

In omnibus tuis operationibus[10] inuoca altissimi nomen ineffabile, a quo omnia tam terrena, quam cęlestia dependent, quem spiritus tam boni, quam mali colunt, uelimque scias tibi doctrinę [20v] hanc artem traditam esse non ad contemptum Dei, illique seruientium, sed ad illius honorem, et gloriam, ad proximi tui utilitatem, et ad proprium usum quando necessitas requirit: uelimque pręterea eam secreto serues, neminique nisi filiis sapientię reueles, iisque maxime, qui timent dominum, qui secreto secreta custodire sciunt, qui corde, et mente puri sunt, uentri non indulgentes nullique corporis uoluptati dediti, qui ab omni hominum societate nisi sapientum se alienare cupiunt,

---

1 So DN91, BNF, P.
2 P: *siue.*
3 P: *initentis.*
4 Instead of *quam Dominus*, BNF has *quatenus.*
5 BNF: *Salomini* (!). The rest of this paragraph is not found in L.
6 So DN91, BNF. P: *a me Isaaco aAbenarot*; P2: Izaak A Benarot. W4667: Isac abanarol.
7 DN91, BNF, P: *C.S.* W4667: *dans la celebre huniuersité C. H.* ("the famous University of C. H.") Apparently it wasn't all that famous, since everyone read the initials differently.
8 Unknown. So too DN91, BNF; P: *Las.* L omits the end of this paragraph.
9 DN91: *De Instructione Artis Cap. Primum*, but the manuscript later cites the chapter as *de Institutione Artis*. BNF skips this chapter.
10 So ASV, L. P, DN91: operibus. W4667 p. 21: tes action. P2 follows P more closely: We wszystkich Twoich Dziełach....

HERE FOLLOWS THE SECOND BOOK, CONCERNING THE PENTACLES, OR APPARITIONS.

In the name of **Adonay, Elohim, Tetragrammaton**, and of the other names of the Most High.

ere follows the *Key of Solomon*, or the revealing of the secrets, which no human being should be shown, except the children initiated into the divine knowledge, which the Lord revealed only to his servant Solomon, and translated by me, Isaac Abenarach, a celebrated C. T. professor, from the Hebrew language into Latin, and faithfully edited, and handwritten in clear characters, and bequeathed solely to the children entrusted in the art, from which formerly the great Pas--, and many others have obtained their education.

Chapter 1. Concerning the fundamentals of the art.

In all your works call upon the ineffable name of the Most High, on whom all things in heaven and on earth depend, which all spirits honor, whether good or evil. And I want you to know that this art has been handed down not to scorn God, and those who serve him, but for his honor and glory, for helping your neighbors, and for one's own use when necessity requires,[1] and I wish further that you protect those secrets, and reveal them to none but the children of wisdom, and especially to those who fear the Lord, who know how to guard the secrets with a secret, whose heart and mind are pure, who are not given to indulging their bellies with bodily pleasures, those who are willing to alienate themselves from all human society aside from the wise, and finally those who, in your judgment, are most suited

---

1   This is highly reminiscent of *Arbatel* aphorism 2. See Peterson 2009 p. 13.

illisque denique, qui iudicio suo [*tuo]¹ huic arti sunt aptissimi, quę² nisi obserues omnia opera tua, arsque propria damno, et periculosa tibi erit.

Quę operanti³ in arte cognoscenda sunt. Caput 2ᵐ.

Sciendum est totam artem dependere a⁴ causis cęlestibus, siue intelligentiis post deum orbem mouentibus, ipsisque⁵ Principibus regionum cęlestium et elementarium a quibus dependent.⁶ Cęteras [21r] omnes inferiores paratę⁷ ad exigendum uoluntatem superiorum pro filiis sapientię, quorum⁸ numerus non superat numerum orbium cęlestium, et elementarium: Cętereuero inferiores [+pene]⁹ sunt inter ritę [*infinitę]¹⁰ addictę non tantum quibuslibet speciebus rerum¹¹ huiusce mundi [*huiuscemodi],¹² sed etiam cuilibet indiuiduo uocanturque¹³ **amalthai** quasi seruientes spiritus parati ad obedientiam superiorum,¹⁴ quos non inuocabis, nisi inuocaueris superiores intelligentias, quę tot sunt, ut dixi quot [+sunt]¹⁵ coeli, et elementa uocaturque.¹⁶

1 Orifiel, 2 Magriel, 3 Uriel, 4 Pamechiel, 5 Pomeriel, 6 Tabriel [*Sabriel],¹⁷ 7 Vchariel, 8 Charariel, 9 Pantheriel, 10 Araton, 11 Agiaton, 12 Begud, 13 Tainor.

---

1   L, P, DN91: *tuo.*
2   So too L, but P had *quod.*
3   DN91: *querenti.*
4   L: *ea.*
5   L: *issisque.*
6   DN91: *dependet.*
7   So too L, BNF, but P reads *partes.* DN91 omits.
8   L, DN91, P, BNF: *quarum.*
9   So L, DN91, P. BNF: *inferiores paratae pene sunt infinitae....*
10 L, DN91, P: *infinitę.*
11 So too DN91, L, BNF; P omits.
12 DN91, L, P: *huiuscemodi.*
13 DN91, BNF: *uocaturque.*
14 BNF skips these 4 words.
15 ASV omits *sunt* but so L, P, DN91, BNF.
16 DN91 adds: *Oriphiel, et prout in suo loco scripti inferius uides* ("... Oriphiel, and as you will see, where it is written in its place below."). Then follows the figure, whereupon it jumps to *nullumque nomen* etc.
17 So all the other manuscripts, plus below.

to this art, because unless you observe all your works and art, it will be dangerous to you, and lead to their own damnation.

Chapter 2. Those things which are to be observed when working in the Art.

It must be understood that the whole art depends, after God, on celestial influences or intelligences, the movements of the spheres themselves, with the rulers of the heavenly regions, and elementary ones, on which all inferior parts depend, for enforcing the will of the superior ones, on behalf of the children of wisdom, which number only as many as the celestial spheres and the elements. The other inferiors are [+nearly] infinite, and devoted not only to any species of this sort, but also to any individual, and they are called the **Amalthai**, since the subservient spirits are prepared to obey the superior ones; you should not invoke them, unless you have called upon the superior Intelligences, which as I have said, number as many as the Heavens and the elements,[1] and [+are] named as follows:

1 **Orifiel**, 2 **Magriel**, 3 **Uriel**, 4 **Pamechiel**, 5 **Pomeriel**, 6 **Sabriel**, 7 **Uchariel**, 8 **Charariel**, 9 **Pantheriel**, 10 **Araton**, 11 **Agiaton**, 12 **Begud**, 13 **Tainor.**

---

1   Namely, nine heavens plus four elements, totalling thirteen intelligences.

Quarum ordo, et domicilium ut facilius tibi innotescat subsequenti figura declarabitur.[1]

[21v]

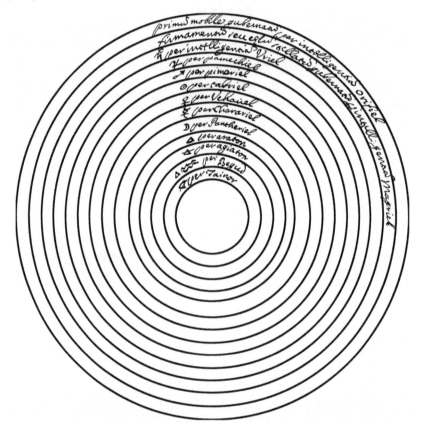

Primum mobile per intelligentiam gubernatur quę Orifiel, firmamentum per intelligentiam Magriel. ♄ Saturnus per Vriel. ♃ Juppiter per Pamechiel. ♂ Mars per Pomeriel. ☉ [Sol] Per Sabriel ♀. Venus per [22r] Vchariel ☿ Mercurius per Charariel. ☾ Luna per Pantheriel. △ Ignis per Araton. ♎ Aer per Agiaton. ▽ <♒> Aqua per Begud. ▽ Terra per Tainor a quibus ut dixi cęteri spiritus tam boni quam mali dependent, suntque parati mandatoque superiorem, nullumque nomen proprium nisi Amalthai, habent, et suos proprios habent Principes, quibus iussu Altissimi obedire debent.

---

1   P: *declarabimus. uides sequenti pagina.* BNF skips the rest of this chapter.

We will show the order and position of which in the following figure, in order that you may understand it more easily.

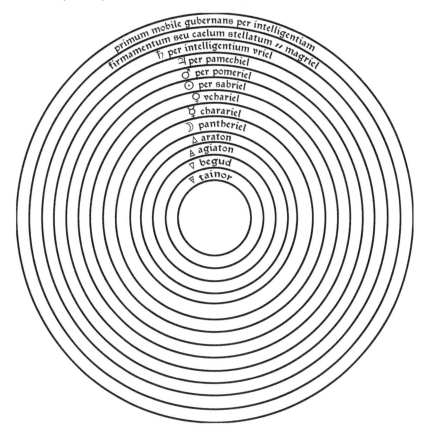

The Primum Mobile is governed through the intelligence Orifiel. The Firmament is governed through the intelligence Magriel. ♄ Saturn through Uriel. ♃ Jupiter through Pamechiel. ♂ Mars through Pomeriel. ☉ The Sun through Sabriel. ♀ Venus through Uchariel. ☿ Mercury through Charariel. ☾ The Moon through Pantheriel. △ Fire through Araton. ♎ The Air through Agiaton. ▽ Water through Begud. ▽ The Earth through Tainor. As I have said, the other spirits, both good and evil, depend on these, and are prepared to obey the orders of their superiors, and they don't have any name of their own, except "the Amalthai," and they have their own princes, to whom they must obey the orders from on high.

Orifiel habet sub se decem millia[1] spirituum.[2] Magriel 9100. Uriel 5000. Pamechiel 4040. Pomeriel 3100. Sabriel 2000. Vchariel 1500. Charariel 500. Panteriel [*Pantheriel] 200. Araton 150. Agiaton 130. Begud 105. Tainor 100.

De Potestate Superiorum Intelligentiarum Cap. 3.

In precedentibus capitibus[3] diximus de institutione artis, dequo[4] numero, ordine, dignitate cuiuslibet [22v] intelligentię quemlibet orbem proprium mouentis[5] dicendum est, iam nobis[6] de earum potestate, quam Altissimus illis tribuit, quę supra humanę gentis[7] captum fertur, pro cuius notione sciendum[8] est, omnes res huiusce mundi[9] tam naturales, quam diuinas iussu altissimi illis esse subditas, maximeque scientias, artes, secretaque omnia, quę humana mens excogitare potest, quę ut cognoscas faciemus amplam diuisionem scientiarum, artium, et secretorum quę habet unaquaque sub se.[10]

Primumque de potestate **Orifielis**, quę quia[11] est prope domicilium diuinum, et est Princeps omnium post Deum, ideoquęque diuina sunt habet sub se iussu altissimi, scientiasque diuinas, habet igitur Theologiam, Metaphisicam, Mysticam scripturam, Religionem, prophetiam: potest facere, ut duo corpora sint in uno, et eodem loco [23r] et idem corpus[12] possit esse semel[13] et in instanti in pluribus locis, ut corpus reddatur inuisibile, idque subito, habet pręsentia, pręterita, et futura, homines illi seruientes reddit, deoque beneuolos,[14] docetque illos per suos Amalthai supradictas scientias, artes, et secreta.

---

1   P: 1000.
2   P, DN91: *spiritus*. L omits this paragraph.
3   DN91: *capitulis*.
4   DN91, P: deque; L: de.
5   So too L; DN91, P: *mouentes*.
6   DN91 omits.
7   So too DN91, L, but P reads *mentis* ("of the mind").
8   So too DN91, L, but P reads: *dicendum*.
9   DN91: *huiuscemodi*.
10 BNF skips this paragraph, and reduces the catalog of spirits to a few words each, then jumps to *De Circulo*.
11 So too L, BNF; P: *primumque ... quae qod*; DN91: *1 usque de presemti / Oriphielisque, quam*; GG: Orifiel quia est proprium domicilium diuinum.
12 DN91: *... loco etiam id corpus*.
13 BNF, P: simul.
14 L, DN91: *Deo beneuolos*; P: *Deo beneuoles*.

Orifiel has under him 10000 spirits, Magriel 9100, Uriel 5000, Pamechiel 4040, Pomeriel 3100, Sabriel 2000, Uchariel 1500, Charariel 500, Pantheriel 200, Araton 150, Agiaton 130, Begud 105, and Tainor 100.

Chapter 3. The power of the superior intelligences.

In the preceding chapters we have spoken about the fundamentals of the Art, and about the number, order, and authority of any intelligence which moves in their own particular orbit; we will now speak about their power, which the Most High grants to them, which is beyond the capacity of humankind to comprehend. According to the inquiry of which, it must be known that all things of this world, both natural and divine, by the order of the Most High, are subordinate to those, and especially the knowledge, arts, and all secrets which the human mind is able to comprehend, which in order that you learn, we will make a major division of knowledge, arts, and secrets which each has under itself.[1]

And first concerning the power of **Orifiel**,[2] who is nearest the divine abode, and is prince of all things after God, and therefore he has under him all things which are divine, by the command of the Most High, and he has divine knowledge, therefore theology, metaphysics, mystical writings, religion, and prophecy. He can make it possible for two bodies to be in the same place at the same time, and to be present in many places, such that the body is returned invisibly, and instantly; he has[3] the present, past, and future, he returns all those serving him kindly to God,[4] and he teaches them the aforesaid knowledge, arts, and secrets, through his Amalthai.

---

1   This paragraph is only found in ASV, P, P2, and L.
2   This catalog of spirits is greatly abridged in GG; and the French mss W4667, W4669, and L1202.
3   W4667: et de rendre toute les chose passez presente et a venire ("he makes all things past, present, and future to come"). W4669: apprend ... ("he learns ...").
4   This phrase is possibly corrupted. GG, W4669 omit. W4667: il rend aimable a dieu tous les homme qui le serve ("He makes all who serve him agreeable to God.") L1202: il met bien avec Dieu les hommes ("he makes men well with God").

Magriel, quia parum distat a domicilio diuino[1] quasdam scientias diuinas habet, ut sunt astronomia,[2] astrologia, phęnomena cęlestia, artem diui-natricem per aspectus, coniunctiones, et oppositiones syderum, docet com-positionem sygillorum, habet politicam artem, docet secreta regum, Principum, et plebeię gentis, ac omnia quę sunt in hominum intellectu serui-entibus illi patefaciunt,[3] deponit potentes de sede sua, et quos optat erigit.

Vriel habet sub se geometriam aritmeticam perspectiuam,[4] Magicam naturalem, scientiasque [23v] illis subalternantes, dat intelligentiam in instanti harum scientiarum, reddit homines studiosos, reddit uerecundos, uirtuosos, et cuilibet personę amabiles, docet seruientes illi ire inuisibiliter, et uolare per aerem instar uolueris.

Pamechiel phisicam, artem diuinandi per somnia, docet proprietates animalium tam aeris, quam aquę, et terrę, imperat animalibus ut obediant seruientibus illi, stent, ueniant, quando uocantur, discedant data uenia, facit producere in instanti monstrosa,[5] et portentosa animalia, uitam dat animalibus, mortem uero quando uult, [+ad uenationes docet terras,] facit in instanti transmutationem animalium, ita ut mutabit homines in suem, canem, taurum, asinum, et in quodlibet animal transformabit [+quando uolet; Idem, que transmutatus,][6] si cupit, in pristinam formam reuertetur.

Pomeriel [24r] habet sub se Pyrotegniam artem ferrariam, et quamlibet fusoriam, artem bellicam, reddit homines bellicosus, martiales, sine timore pugnantes reddit inuisibiles, facit pugnare [+inuisibiliter, et][7] inuulnerabiliter,[8] redditque homines fortissimos, ita ut solus homo nemine iuuante totum exercitum possit[9] destruere, docet secreta hostium, et

---

1 DN91: *dicto.*
2 BNF: *athonomia* (!).
3 DN91, P, L: *patefaciet.*
4 So too DN91. *Perspectiuam* is also supported by L1202 p. 117, W4669 p. 89, and to fit the context. L: *Pespectiuam.* P: *prospectiuam.*
5 DN91: *monstruosa,*
6 The words in [] supplied from P, DN91, L. W4667 p. 29 also supports the first phrase: Il enseigne a tous le monde la chasse ("He teaches how to hunt all the land").
7 So P, L, DN91.
8 DN91 omits *et inuulnerabiliter.*
9 DN91: *poterit.* Perhaps the word was abbreviated in the urtext, as it is in L, *pōit.*

Magriel, because he stands a short distance from the divine abode, has certain divine knowledge, which includes astronomy, astrology, celestial phenomena, the art of divination by aspects, conjunctions, and oppositions of celestial bodies, he teaches the compositions of sigils. He also has political arts, and teaches the secrets of kings, princes, and of common people, and he will reveal to those serving, everything which is in the comprehension of people. He casts down the mighty from their thrones, and raises up those whom he chooses.

Uriel has under himself geometry, arithmetic, optics, natural magic, and knowledge subordinate to those. He gives the understanding of those sciences in an instant. He can make any person studious, modest, virtuous, and lovable. He teaches those serving to go about invisibly, and also to fly through the air if desired.

Pamechiel teaches the art of physics,[1] divination through dreams, the distinctive properties of animals, such as those of the air, the waters, and the lands; he commands animals that they obey and serve one, such as staying when commanded, or to come when called, or depart when given permission. He can produce monstrous and unnatural animals in an instant. He gives life to animals, or death when you wish. [+He teaches hunting the land.] He can instantly transmute animals, thus he can change a man into a pig, dog, bull, ass, or into whatever animal shape [+he wishes, and likewise, if] he wishes, he will be returned to his former shape.

Pomeriel has under himself pyrotechnics, iron works, the smelting of metals, the art of war, and can make men warlike, martial, and fight without fear. He can make them invisible and fight [+invisibly and] with invulnerability, and he can make men extremely strong, such that one man could demolish a whole army without any help. He can teach the secrets of

---

1　Or natural philosophy.

quidquid[1] illis est[2] in animo, urbes[3] reddit inexpugnabiles, et quando uult oppugnabiles,[4] immo faciles captu, idque in instanti.

Sabriel habet sub se alchimiam, docetque transmutationem metallorum, habet artem lapidariam, sculpturam, docetque secreta, et proprietates metallorum, lapidum, imaginum, ex[5] morte ad uitam homines sepultos euocat idque in instanti, cursum solis impedit, quando uult, meteora mittit deorsum, ut sunt pluuia [24v] nix, grando, Ros,[6] tonitrua, aliudque id genus, arma, [+spectra],[7] exercitus, animalia in aere excitat,[8] redditque homines longęuos, ita ut possint durare perennos[9] in hac uita usque ad 150 annos.

Vchariel, habet grammaticam, Rethoricam,[10] logicam, et medicinam, artesque omnes liberales, et illiberales,[11] herbarum proprietates, quasdamque incognitas docet, nouasque, uiribus quibusdam occultis donatas, quando opus est producit,[12] mortem, et uitam, quando uult, quibuslibet[13] plantis dat, easque, salubres, et insalubres reddit hominibus, sanos facit homines aegro-tosue, idque subito, senectutem aufert, datque iuuentutem, dat uitam, dat mortem.

Charariel docet artem amandi, reddit homines beneuolos, maximeque puellis, et foeminis, [25r] dat pulchram prolem, magnam potestatem super fęminas, et puellas habet, ita ut solo uisu aliciantur, uel aliter, reddit foeminas, et puellas uerecundas, uirtuosas, maritum suum timentes,[14] non secus [*leves][15] ac procliuos ad luxuriam,[16] habet uim soluendi, et dissoluendi

---

1   So also L, DN91; P: *quicquid.*
2   So also L, DN91; P: *et.*
3   P: *uobis.*
4   DN91 omits the last 4 words.
5   Corrected from "*et*". P, DN91: *et.* L has *e, an ambiguous abbreviation* which probably points us again to the urtext.
6   So also L, DN91; P omits.
7   So P, L, DN91.
8   P: *ecitat.*
9   P, L, DN91: *perrenes.*
10 So also L, DN91; P omits.
11 DN91: *inliberales.*
12 So too L, DN91; P: *producet.*
13 So too L, DN91; P: *quibusdam.*
14 DN91: *stimantes* (!)
15 So P.
16 So also L. P: *non leues, ac procliues ac luxuriam.*

enemies, and whatever is in their hearts. He can make cities indestructible, or when he wishes, vulnerable and easily and instantly captured.

Sabriel has under himself alchemy; he teaches the transmutation of metals, lapidary art, and sculpture. He teaches the secrets and distinctive properties of metals, stones, images, and he calls buried men forth from death to life, and this instantly. He can hinder the course of the Sun when he wishes. He can send meteors down like they were rain, snow, hail, dew, thunder, and other things of that sort. He can also call forth weapons, [+specters,] armies, or animals in the air. He restores the aged, so that they are able to live many years, even as much as 150 years.

Uchariel, has grammar, rhetoric, logic, and medicine, all arts, liberal as well as illiberal (common). He teaches the distinctive properties of certain new and unknown herbs, with certain hidden properties. He will produce death and life when needed. Likewise, he can give certain plants which can make a healthy person sick, or an unhealthy person well. And he can remove old age in an instant, and give youth; he can give life and death.

Charariel teaches the art of loving; he can make men greatly favorable, especially to girls and women. He gives beautiful offspring; he has great power over women and girls, so that they are drawn to him by sight alone, or otherwise, he makes women and girls shy and virtuous, respecting (or fearing) their husbands, not fickle or inclined to be extravagant. He has the potestatem genitalem utriusque sexus, dat pulchritudinem, dat foecunditatem, dat amorem, aufertque si uult.

Pantheriel habet artem circulatoriam, mercaturam, artemque nauigandi, facit hominem lucrosum in ludo, et in mercatura,[1] uincula incarceratorum dissoluit, eosque liberat, ad torturam reddit insensibiles, ita ut facile e manu[2] iudicum euadere possint, submersionem nauigantibus impedit.

Araton habet artes tormentarias, impeditque ne homo ab illis, nec ab igne laedatur,[3] [25v] facitque ut homo eat securus absque ullo periculo per flammas, et per ignem, potest urere, ignique submittere quidquid uolet, ut domos, Urbes, Ciuitates integras, immo totum uniuersum, si Deus permitteret.[4]

Agiaton habet artem diuinandi per uolucres, imperatque auibus, aerem[5] reddit hominibus salubrem, uel insalubrem,[6] redditque pestiferum si cupit potest facere ut in nubibus homo feratur idque inuisibiliter.

Begud docet artem diuinandi per [+aquam, ambulandi super] aquas,[7] eundi ad imum maris, retardat naues quando uult, ducitque nauigantes celeriter quo cupiunt, proprietates piscium docet, et thesauros in mari reconditos, docetque pręsentia, preterita, et futura per aquam.

Tainor docet agriculturam, reddit agros fertiles, uel contra[8] infertiles, insecta[9] [26r] animalia producit, et interficit quando uult. Thesauros in terra abditos reuelat, terramque aperit, et urbes integras quando uult ingurgitat, diluuium prouocat, auocat quando uult, motus rerum artificialium ligat, ut sunt horologia, et rerum omnium, quę per aquam, leuitatem, et grauitatem mouentur.

---

1 DN91: *mercantia.*
2 L and GG also read *e manu;* P: *ex manu;* DN91: *est manu.*
3 Note he doesn't use ę here.
4 So also L, DN91; P: *permiserit.*
5 DN91 omits *aerem.*
6 So also L, DN91; P omits. It is perhaps redundant.
7 The words in brackets are only found in DN91, apparently lost elsewhere via homeoteleuton.
8 So also L; P omits.
9 P: *incerta.*

power to free and release the reproductive power of each sex.[1] He gives beauty, fertility, and love, and takes them away if desired.

Pantheriel teaches the art of the juggler, and the art of trade and navigation. He makes a person profitable at gaming and in trade, releases the chains of those who are imprisoned, and frees them. He can make one not feel torture, and thus allowing one to more easily escape the hands of the judges. He also hinders sinking while sailing.

Araton, has the art of firearms, and can prevent a person from being hurt by fire, and he makes it possible for a person to pass safely through any danger from flames and fire, and he is able to burn up and demolish whatever he wishes with fire, such as homes, cities, and whole communities, indeed the whole world if God permits it.

Agiaton has the art of the divination by means of birds, and commanding birds. He brings healthy air to people, or can bring pestilential air. If he wishes, he can make a person be carried away in the clouds, and that invisibly.

Begud teaches the art of divination by means of water, [+walking upon the waters,] and going to the bottom of the sea. He delays or hastens ships when desired. He teaches the distinctive properties of fish, and hidden treasures in the sea, and he teaches the past, present, and future through water.[2]

Tainor teaches agriculture, makes fields fertile or infertile, causes insects to come forth, and kills them when desired. He reveals treasures hidden in the earth, and excavates the earth, and when he is willing will engulf whole cities, bringing forth floods, or diverts them when desired. He binds the movements of artificial things, such as clocks, and all things which move through the water through buoyancy and weight.

---

1   Presumably curing fertility problems.

2   The description in L1202 p. 118 is quite different: Begud intruit dans l'art de deviner, apprend la Chyromancie, se mêle de Magie et sorcellerie, rend les hommes impuissants et les femme stériles. ("Begud intructs in the art of divination, chiromancy, mingles magic and witchcraft, makes men impotent and women sterile.")

Quomodo obtinere possimus ab Intelligentiis prędictas scientias artes et secreta. Cap. 4.

Medium inuestigaturi quo has scientias artes, et secreta, immo spirituum familiaritatem et consortium nobis comparare possimus scire debetis[1] non alio obtineri posse quam per inuocationes, coniurationes, exorcismos, superstitiones, aliaque mysteria diuina, quę tanquam spiritualia [26v] certa quadam sympatia has res, ipsosque spiritus nobis comparant, et quia spiritualia in hoc mundo sublunari nisi ope corporalium operari non possunt, et corporalia nisi ope[2] spiritualium [*spirituum],[3] ideo corporalia cum spiritualibus miscebimus, et quę ad operationes artis erunt necessaria adhibebimus, primumque de corporalibus loquemur, quibus utimur ad spiritualia, quę sunt, ut dixi inuocationes, coniurationes, exorcismi, ac deinde de spiritualibus.

De his, quę sunt necessaria ad Inuocationes, et coniurationes Dęmonum. Cap. 5.

Necessaria sunt ut diximus pręcedenti capite Corporalia quędam ad inuocationes, et coniurationes dęmonum,[4] sine quibus Magister[5] [27r] operari minime potest, sunt igitur necessaria Circulus, pentacula, gladius, aqua benedictam, Vestis, ignis, suffumigia,[6] sanguis, uel atramentum, Charta uirginea, locus, tempus, de quibus seorsim,[7] suisque locis tractabimus, et operantem admonebimus, ut hęc omnia supradicta habeat, eaque pręparata antequam operetur, ex his[8] enim tota ars dependet. Primo igitur de Circulo.

De Circulo Cap. 6.

Operaturus in arte circulum describes in loco electo (quem postea dicemus) cum omnibus his circumstantiis. Magnum circulum describes, intra quadratum, (in quo tu, et alter, uel etiam duo si uelis contineri possitis in

---

1   DN91: *debetur.*
2   So also L; P omits.
3   DN91, P, L: *spirituum.*
4   So too DN91; P, L omit.
5   L: *mago*; DN91: *magus.*
6   DN91: *fumigia.*
7   DN91: *seorsum.* L skips to *haec omnia....*
8   P: *hoc.*

Chap. 4. How we can obtain the preceding knowledge, arts, and secrets from the intelligences.

We must understand that the means of investigating where these sciences, arts, and secrets, indeed the familiarity of the spirits, and their consorting together with us, is only possible to obtain through the invocations, conjurations, exorcisms, superstitions, and other divine mysteries, which as spiritual things have a certain sympathy, and these things themselves bring the spirits together to us, and because the spiritual beings are not able to operate in this sublunar world except by the labor of the corporeal beings, nor the corporeal ones except by the spiritual ones, and therefore we will mix the corporeal with the spiritual, and we will make use of those which are necessary for operations of the art.

And we will speak first about the corporeal things, which we will use to obtain the spiritual, which, as I have said, are conjurations, invocations, exorcisms, and then about the spiritual.

Chap. 5. Concerning those things which are necessary for invocations and conjurations of the daemons.

As we have said in the preceding chapter, certain materials are necessary for the invocations and conjurations of daemons, without which the master[1] will be able to accomplish little. These necessities are therefore the circle, pentacle, the sword, consecrated water, the vestment, the fire, incense, blood or writing ink, virgin paper, the place, the time, which we will discuss separately and in their own places, and we admonish you to prepare all these things mentioned above before working in this art, and on these the whole art depends; therefore we begin with the circle.

Chap. 6. Concerning the circle.

For operating in this art, you should draw out this circle in the chosen place (which we will describe later), with all these particulars. You should copy out a large circle within a square (in which you and another, or even

---

1   L: *mago* (magus or magician).

quorum medio consistas, si sint duo[1]) illumque describes [*diuides][2] in 4 partes equales, 4^r mundi partibus respondentes [27v] intra quem alterum minorum, illique concentritum [*concentricum][3] describes cum hoc ineffabili nomine **Adonay**, et in quolibet angulo supradicti quadrati hoc nomen solum[4] **agla** scribes, pro cuius faciliori intelligentia figuram hanc apponemus.

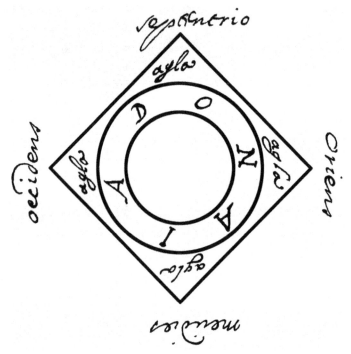

Postquam rite circulum perfeceris, et nomina supradicta [*sancta][5] apposueris, antequam illum ingrediaris aqua benedicta asperges quattuor angulos quadrati[6] dicendo Asperges [+me domine hysopo][7] &c. dicesque cum sociis lytanias sanctorum, et hanc orationem pronunciabis.

---

1   P adds *tecum*.
2   So P, L, DN91. BNF also reads *describes*.
3   So L, P, DN91, BNF.
4   P: *tantum*; L, BNF: *sanctum*.
5   DN91, P, L, GG: *sancta*.
6   P: *quadri*.
7   ASV, L give only *asperges*; GG: *asperges me*; P: *asperges me domine;* DN91: *asperges me domine hysopo.*

two if you wish, can be contained – you should stand in the middle if two are with you) and divide that into four equal parts, corresponding to the four parts of the world.[1] Between the concentric circles, copy this ineffable name: **Adonay**, and in each angle of the square mentioned above write this name only: **Agla**. To facilitate understanding, we are attaching this figure:

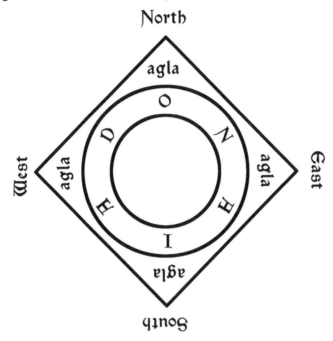

After you have duly completed the circle, and placed the sacred names therein, before entering you should sprinkle the four corners of the square with consecrated water, saying, "Sprinkle [+me, O Lord with hyssop]," etc. You and your associates should also say the Litany of Saints, and recite this prayer:

---

1   I.e. north, south, east, and west.

Domine conditor Cęli, et terrę, qui per tua sacrosancta [28r] mysteria seruis tuis concessisti, ut miracula ederent[1] quando opus esset, exaudi nunc pręces serui tui, et promissionem tuam[2] confirma, omnemque malignum spiritum ab hoc spiritu [*circulo][3] depelle,[4] sitque mihi quęso propugnaculum, ac pręsidium ab omni immunda creatura, sitque tibi laus, honor, et gloria per omnia secula sęculorum Amen.

De Pentaculo. Cap. 7.

Nunc de pentaculo loquemur, quod pręcipuum est instrumentum artis, sine quo magister operari non potest, a quo cętera omnia artis dependent, in quo omnis uirtus, ac potestas ab altissimo posita est, a quo omnes spiritus **Amalthai** tam boni quam mali [+operanti][5] obedire urgentur;[6] cuius descriptio, ac pręparatio, ut facilius tibi patefiat docebimus te dupplex esse pentaculum, quo uti debemus [28v] in arte, unum[7] uniuersale, alterum particulare, siue ut nostri uocant magnum, et paruum; de utroque dic[e]mus, maximeque de Magno, quo nobis iam opus est.

Magno pentaculo utimur ad inuocationes, et coniurationes spirituum **Amalthai** ad impetrandas scientias, artes, et secreta a superioribus spiritibus siue Intelligentiis per spiritus[8] **Amalthai**, qui magno pentaculo coacti iussu superiorum parua pentacula, et characteres nobis distribuunt, ut commodius earum rerum cognitionem habeamus seseque nutu proprio, ac sponte nobis offerunt, ut uoluntatem nostram exequantur, nobisque obediant, uelimque scias pro qualibet Intelligentia opus esse uno tantum pentaculo, eodemque fere modo constructo, ac pręparato ab altero non differente nisi [29r] quod habeat unumquodque nomen Intelligentię, a qua aliquid impetrare desideras,

---

1 So also L, DN91; P reads *Adessent*. W4667: *a dessent*; W4669: *abstrahent* (!).
2 DN91 omits *tuam*.
3 Reading *circulo* as in GG and W4669, which fits the context better. P, L, DN91, and W4667 also read *spiritu*.
4 Soo too L and DN91. P, GG, and W3447: *expelle*; W4669: *repelle*.
5 So DN91, L, P, GG.
6 So too L, DN91; P: *cogentur*; GG: *coguntur*.
7 P adds *esse* here too.
8 L, DN91, GG: *per spiritus*. P: *pro spiritibus*. Abbreviation of the first word in ASV could perhaps be read either way.

O Lord, maker if Heaven and Earth, who through your sacrosanct mysteries have granted your servants to produce miracles in their work; hear now the prayers of your servant, and confirm your promise, and may all evil spirits be expelled from this circle, and may it be my fortress and protection from all impure creatures, and may praise, honor, and glory be yours, through all the ages. Amen.

Chap. 7. Concerning the pentacle.

Now we will speak about the pentacle, which is a special tool of the Art, without which the master[1] is not able to operate, on which all other arts depend, in which all virtue and power from the Most High has been placed, which all **Amalthai** spirits, whether good or evil, will be forced to obey [+the operator]. Its description and preparation can easily be revealed to you. I will teach you about two kinds of pentacles which must be used in the Art: One is universal, and the other is particular, or those which our followers call great, and small. We will speak about each, and especially about the great, which is what is needed now.

We must make use of the great pentacle for invocations and conjurations of the **Amalthai** spirits, for obtaining sciences, arts, and secrets from the superior spirits, or the intelligences through the **Amalthai** spirits, which are compelled by the great pentacle, by order of the superiors, they distribute the lesser pentacles and characters to us, in order that we may have knowledge of those things more conveniently, and which they themselves offer to us of their own free will and accord, in order that they may carry out our wishes and obey us. And I wish you to know that for any kind of intelligence, there is only one pentacle design needed, constructed and prepared in the same

---

1   L: *Magus.*

illudque inscriptum in quolibet angulo alterius quadrati pentaculi: ueluti si
cupis obtinere scientias, artes, et[1] secreta, immo quemdam spiritum **Orifielis**
nomen illius, aut illius intelligentię, a qua aliquid obtinere cupis in prędictis
angulis subsignabis,[2] ut mox patebit in sequenti figura pentaculi, quod ita
compones, ac[3] pręparabis 7 Metallorum partes ęquales habebis, et Cyatum
succi[4] heliotropii, et succi lunarię, miscebisque simul sole intrante in
Cancrum, illaque[5] omnia fundes per ignem exorcisatum hoc modo.

> Exorcizo te Creatura ignis per nomina altissimi **Ilchias**, et
> **Ischirias**,[6] ut omnis immundus, omnisque malignus spiritus a
> te exeat, fiatque [29v] de uoluntate altissimi, qui uiuit, et regnas
> [*regnat][7] per omnia secula seculorum Amen.

Quo exorcizato prędictam mixturam fundes, fusamque ex igne detrahes,
solidamque in modum octanguli parabis, et mane ante ortum solis tempore
caniculę in plenilunio sculpes hoc modo, et hęc uerba dum sculpes dicies
recitabis.

> **Ancor, Maguras, Isichys, Eliphlahum, Alhamdu, Silahi,
> rabil, elaminor, Rachmanio, Ruphalon, Trehiph, Nassabel,
> Phail, muphal, Muphred, gemathon, Caibet, Lametha,
> Vachar.**[8]

---

1   DN91 omits.
2   So ASV, P, L, BNF; DN91, GG: *subsignatis.*
3   P omits *compones, ac.* L: *Ita compones*; GG: *quod ita praeparabis.*
4   So also L; P: *cythum sacri* (!). GG omits. DN91: *et cyatum sac. Heliotropii et succi
    lunarię...*
5   DN91: *aliaque.*
6   So also DN91; Compare below fol. 35v: Ilchios, et Eschirioth. P: Ilschias, et Ilchirias, later
    Ischiros, et Ischirioth. L: Ischias et Ischirias; GG: I̲s̲c̲t̲i̲a̲s̲,̲ ̲I̲l̲c̲h̲i̲a̲s̲,̲ Ilchirias, elsewhere
    Ischir̲i̲o̲s̲, et I̲s̲c̲h̲y̲r̲i̲o̲t̲; P2: Illihias, i Ilchinas; W4667: Ischias, Ilchias; W4669: Iskios et
    Iskivios. Compare conjuration on P p. 45 which gives the names "Ischiros, et Ischirioth". =
    Greek Ischos, Ischyros (ἰσχυς, ἰσχυρός) = "strength, strong/mighty"?
7   So DN91, P, GG. L: *uiuis et regnas.*
8   L: Ancor, m̲a̲g̲a̲r̲a̲s̲, I̲l̲y̲c̲h̲i̲s̲, E̲l̲i̲p̲h̲, Lahum, Alhamdu Silahi, r̲a̲b̲i̲d̲ e̲l̲a̲m̲i̲n̲e̲r̲, r̲a̲c̲h̲m̲a̲n̲i̲r̲
    r̲a̲p̲h̲a̲l̲o̲n̲, T̲r̲o̲h̲i̲p̲h̲, N̲a̲s̲s̲a̲b̲e̲t̲, phail, m̲a̲p̲h̲u̲t̲, m̲a̲p̲h̲r̲e̲d̲ gemathon, Caibet, Lametha
    Vachar; DN91: Ancor, M̲a̲n̲g̲a̲r̲a̲s̲, I̲l̲y̲c̲h̲i̲s̲, e̲l̲i̲p̲h̲, lahum, Alhamdu, Silahi, rabil, e̲l̲a̲m̲i̲n̲e̲r̲,
    Rachmanir, R̲a̲p̲h̲a̲l̲o̲n̲, Trehiph, Nassabel, Phail, M̲u̲p̲h̲u̲l̲, M̲a̲p̲h̲r̲e̲d̲, Gemathon, Caibet,
    Lametha, V̲a̲i̲s̲a̲r̲. P: Ancor, magaras, Ilychys, Eliphlasum, Alhander, Silahirbit, Elamins,
    Rachmanir, Raphalon, Trehiph, Nassabs, Lhail, Maphut, Muphrad, gemathon, Caibet,
    Lamother, Vachar. P2 is almost identical to P: Ancor, magaras, Ilichys, Eliphlasum,
    Alhander, Silahirbit, E̲l̲a̲m̲i̲r̲i̲, Rachmanir, Raphalon, Trehiph, Nassabs, Lhail, Maphut,

way, differing only from one another in that each should have the name of the intelligence that you desire something from, and that should be written on alternate angles of the square in the pentacle. So for example, if you wish to obtain the knowledge, the arts, and the secrets of that spirit named **Orifiel**, or any other intelligence from which you wish to obtain anything, you should inscribe that name in the said angles, as shown in the following figure. The pentacle must be made of equal parts of the seven metals, and a shot[1] of juice of the heliotrope plant, and the juice of lunaria, and furthermore, you should mix them when the Sun enters the sign of Cancer, and pour them all while exorcising fire in this manner:

> I exorcise you O creature of Fire, by the most high names **Ilschias** and **Ischirias** [*Ischos, Ischyros (?)], that all impure and evil spirits depart from you; let it be so according to the will of the Most High, who lives and reigns forever and ever. Amen.

With this exorcised, pour the preceding mixture, and spread out from the fire, so that it solidifies into the shape of an eight-pointed star, and in the morning before sunrise, during the dog-days, when the moon is full, engrave it in this manner, and while engraving it, recite the following words aloud ten times:

> **Ancor, Maguras, Isichys, Eliphlahum, Alhamdu, Silahi, rabil, elaminor, Rachmanio, Ruphalon, Trehiph, Nassabel, Phail, muphal, Muphred, gemathon, Caibet, Lametha, Vachar.**

Muphrad, Gemathon, Caibet, Lamother, Vachar; GG: Ancor, chagaras, Ilychys, Eliphlanum, Albamda, Silahirbit, Elamias, Rachmanit, Raphalon, Trehiph, Nasrabos, Phail, Maphut, Maphrad, gematon, Caibet, Lamotha, Vachar. NOTE: "Alhamdu ... Rachmanio" are the opening words from the *Quran* (thanks to Alexander Eth for this observation.)

1 Cyatum: 1/12 of a pint = 1.3 oz = 39 ml.

[30r] **Pentaculum Magnum.**

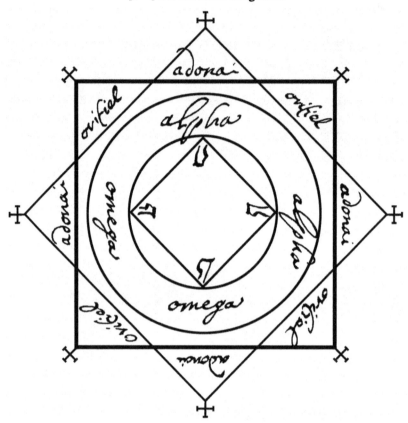

Pentacula parua tot sunt quot scientię, artes, et secreta, immo fere innumera a spiritibus Amalthai nobis dantur non secus,[1] ac characteres ad multa experimenta utiles, quorum erit talis compositio. Cartam uirgineam, eamque pręparatam habebis, quo pentacula,[2] et characteres scribes, ut uidebis in illo tractatu.

De gladio. Cap. 8.

Gladius habeatur ex chalibe confectus longitudine 3 pedum, cuius

---

1   So also L, DN91; P, GG: *leues* ("lightly").
2   P adds *uero.*

The Great Pentacle.[1]

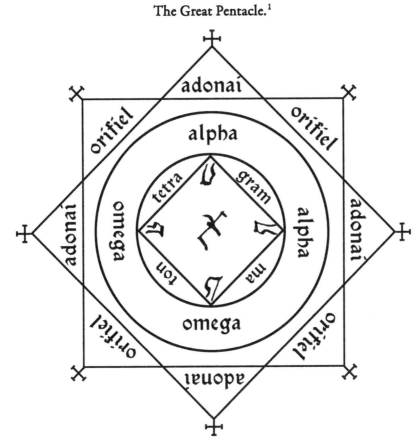

The lesser pentacles are as many as there are sciences, arts, and secrets, and indeed are nearly innumerable. They are not given otherwise to us by the Amalthai spirits, and characters for many useful experiments, the arrangement of which should be as follows. And you should have virgin paper prepared for it, writing the pentacles and characters accurately, as you will see in that treatise.

Chap. 8. Concerning the sword.

The sword should be made of iron, three feet in length. Its haft should be

---

1 ASV, L, DN91, and BNF all have crosses at all 8 points of the diagram, while GG and W4667 have crosses only at the top, bottom, left, and right. W4669 has crosses in all 16 outer angles. P has none. Since both L and DN91 have the extra glyph and "tetra / gram / ma / ton" in center, I have included them in my version.

manubrium sit christallinum hisce characteribus in plenilunio sanguine humano [30v] scriptis insignitum.

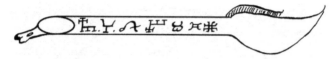

talisque erit descriptio.

Postquam rite eum perfeceris dicetur missa super eo, sicque prǝparatum in sinistra manu tenebis stola sacerdotali coopertum dum[1] scilicet circulum tu[2] ingredieris, et in illo consistes donec uenerint[3] spiritus, coram quibus nudum habebis.

De aqua benedicta. Cap. 9.

Aquam benedictam habebis, illam scilicet, qua sacerdotes utuntur, illa asperges quǝ necessaria sunt ad benedictiones, et aspergendo hunc uersiculum pronuntiabis.

Asperges me Domine hysoppo, et mundabor, lauabis me, et super niuem dealbabor.

[31r] De Veste. Cap. 10.

Vestis sit pontificis, uel sacerdotis, et si fieri potest habeatur uestis illius qui apud Iudǝos, et Marranos dicitur Magnus Magister, uel sacerdos cum omnibus ornamentis sacerdotalibus, quǝ omnia benedicta [*benedices][4] aqua benedicta dicendo. Asperges me domine &c. et antequam tibi induas[5] ueste hanc orationum ter recitabis.

1　DN91 omits *dum*.
2　Added *supra linea*. DN91, P, L, GG omit. The pronoun is superfluous here in any event.
3　So also L, DN91; P: *venerit* ("it comes"). GG: *uenient* ("they will come").
4　So DN91, P, L. GG: *benedicendo.*
5　So also L; DN91: *te induas*; GG: *induas te*; P: *te indas* (!).

made of crystal, with the following characters written on the full moon with human blood.

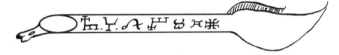

so that it looks like this:

After duly completing it, you should have a Mass dedicated over it, and thus prepared, you should hold it in your left hand, covered with the priestly stole, namely when you enter the circle, and you will stand therein until the spirits have arrived,[1] to whom you must uncover it.[2]

Chap. 9. Concerning the consecrated water.

You should have consecrated water, namely, the same holy water that priests use, and you will use it to sprinkle whatever needs to be blessed, and while sprinkling you should recite this verse:

> Sprinkle me with hyssop, O Lord, and I shall be cleansed; wash with me, and I shall be whiter than snow.[3]

Chap 10. Concerning the garment.

The garment should be that of a bishop or priest, and if possible, it should be the garment of the one which the Jews and *marranos*[4] refer to as the Great Master,[5] or a priest, along with all priestly ornaments, all of which you should bless with consecrated water while saying, "sprinkle me O Lord," etc. And before you put the garment on, you should recite aloud three times:

---

1   ASV, L: until the spirits come.
2   Compare KSol e.g. Aub. 24 72r: "habeat ensem novum nudum in manu." Cp. Mathers II.IX, Aub. 24 72r, Ad10862 124v.
3   Adapted from Psalm 50:9.
4   Spanish Jewish converts (or forced converts) to Christianity, a term dating back to the 15th century.
5   Or, Great Rabbi.

Sacrim, Machibe, Madrus, bursas, Erichay, Curiuran, Sabail, Pameros, grabur, derintay, Stirux, cramin, numonai, staphios, barahum, canigol, Gifdey, Lalugol, Dametay, Magoly, Lahul.[1]

De Igne, et de suffumigiis. Cap. XI.

Ignem habebis exorcisatum eo modo, quo diximus in cap. de Pentaculo, suffumigia uero sic compones, aloes, myrrhę, musci, balsami [31v] naturalis partes ęquales miscebis in cratere benedicto, cuius operculum sit perforatum, illamque compositionem seruabis, et dum[2] opus erit igni exorcisato iniicies, et quę necessaria sunt suffumigabis dicendo hanc orationem.

> Domine iniquos odio habui, et legem tuam dilexi, adiutor, et susceptor meus es tu, et in uerbum tuum semper [*super][3] speraui, declinate[4] a me maligni, et scrutabor mandata Dei mei, suscipe me secundum eloquium tuum et uiuam, et non confundas me ab expectatione mea, adiuua me, et saluus ero, et meditabor in iustificationibus tuis semper.

Sequitur schema crateris.

---

1 DN91: <u>Sarim</u>, <u>Machebe</u>, madrus <u>Bachas</u> erichay, <u>cumrran</u> Sabail <u>Pameres</u> grabur derintay stirux, cramin <u>namonai</u> <u>staphires</u> <u>brahum</u> Canigol Gifdei <u>salugol</u> dametay <u>magolis</u>, Lahul. P: <u>Sarim</u>, <u>machebe</u>, madrus, <u>burchas</u>, Erychai, <u>Curuiram</u>, Sabail, <u>Pameues</u>, grabur, derintay, <u>Styrum</u>, Cramyn, <u>Namonay</u>, <u>Staphies</u>, barahum, <u>Lanigel</u>, gifdey, Lalugol, <u>Damitay</u>, Magoly, Lahul; P2 again has the closest reading to P: Sarim – machebe – madrus – Burchas – Erichai – Curuiram – Sabail – Pameues – grabur – <u>Derintaj</u> – Styrum – Cramyn - Namonay, - Staphies - <u>Barachum</u> – Lanigel – Gifdey – Lalugol - Damitay, - <u>Magolj</u> – Lahul. L: Sarim, machebe <u>maduis</u> <u>barhas</u> erichay <u>curuiran</u> sabail <u>pomeres</u> grabur derintay <u>stirax</u> <u>Cranim</u> namonai staphies barahum <u>Canigol</u> [gifdey Lalugol] <u>dametay</u> magoly Lahul; GG: <u>Satim</u>, <u>Marchebe</u>, Madrus, <u>Barchas</u>, Erichay, <u>Luruiram</u>, Sabail, <u>Pameres</u>, grab<u>ar</u>, Derintay, <u>Hirum</u>, Cramin, Namonai, Staphies, Barahum, Lanigel, gifdej, <u>Salugel</u>, <u>Dametray</u>, Magoly, Lahul.
2 So also L, DN91; P, GG: *cum.*
3 So Vulgate. ASV, DN91, P, and L all misread *semper.* Deest GG, W4669.
4 DN91: *declinant.*

Sacrim, Machibe, Madrus, bursas, Erichay, Curiuran, Sabail, Pameros, grabur, derintay, Stirux, cramin, numonai, staphios, barahum, canigol, Gifdey, Lalugol, Dametay, Magoly, Lahul.

Chap. 11. Concerning the fire and incenses.

You should have fire exorcised as we have said in the chapter on the pentacle. For a good incense, take equal parts of aloe, myrrh, musk, and natural balsam; mix them in a consecrated mixing vessel, the lid of which should be perforated, and when needed for the work, throw it into the exorcised fire, while saying this prayer:

> O Lord I have hated the unjust, and I esteemed your law. You are my helper and my supporter, and I have always [*greatly] trusted in your word. Turn away from me, O spiteful ones, and I will study the commands of my God. Support me according to your pronouncement, and I will live, and don't dash my hopes. Help me and I will be safe, and I will always reflect on your judgments.[1]

The form of the mixing vessel follows:[2]

---

1   Ps. 118 (KJV 119):113-117. W4669 is missing verses 114-115.
2   Mss all have slight variants of the flower-like element on the top half, but it seems unlikely to be critical to its function, otherwise it would probably be pointed out, as with the sword.

[32r] De sanguine, et attramento. Cap. XII.

Sanguis, quo uteris sit hominis[1] biliosi, uel puellę cuius temperamentum sit calidum, et humidum, noctuę, et upubę, scorpionis, galli, et bufonis,[2] quem colliges dum tibi opus erit in uase aeneo fabrefacto[3] tempore coniunctionis Martis, et Saturni. Atramentum uero sit uulgare, cui miscebis parum aquę benedictę, et miscendo dices. Asperges me Domine &c.

De Charta Virginea. Cap. XIII.

Chartam uirgineam sic pręparabis, membranam, seu pergamenum Capreoli habebis gladio nostro, eoque pręparato occisi sub dio[4] radiante luna idque fiat si fieri potest in plenilunio [32v] supra quam membranam, seu pergamenum missa Cantetur[5] die Natiuitatis Christi, et sic pręparatum pergamenum seruabis donec tibi opus fuerit.[6]

De loco, et tempore. Cap. XIIII.

Locum eligas[7] ab omni societate alienum, si fieri potest, ut in cacumine alicuius montis uersus septentrionem appositi, uel in sylua inhabitata, in

---

1   DN91 omits *hominis*.
2   So also L; DN91, P, and GG: *bubonis,* also supported by W4669: *hibou*.
3   DN91: *fabricato.*
4   So also L. DN91, P, GG: *sub die.*
5   DN91: *cantatur.*
6   DN91, P, L: *erit.*
7   DN91, P, L, GG: *eliges.*

Chap. 12. Concerning blood and ink.

The blood that you use should be from a bilious person, or from a girl whose temperament is warm and humid,[1] or from a small owl, hoopoe, scorpion, rooster, or toad.[2] While working, you should collect it in a copper[3] vessel constructed at a time when Mars and Saturn are in conjunction. The writing ink may also be common (ink)[4] which you should mix with a little consecrated water, while reciting "Sprinkle me, O Lord" etc.

Chap. 13. Concerning virgin paper.

Virgin paper should be prepared thus: vellum or parchment, prepared from the skin of a roe-deer,[5] killed with our sword, under the open sky, when the moon is shining, and if possible during the full moon. Over this vellum or parchment you should have sung a Mass of the Nativity of Christ, and thus prepared you should preserve the parchment until needed for the Art.

Chap. 14. Concerning the place and time.[6]

If possible, you should select a place apart from all society, such as at the top of a mountain facing north, or in an uninhabited wood, in the middle of

---

1   Perhaps menstrual blood is intended. The French texts misunderstand. See also the theory of humours.
2   So ASV, L, DN91. P, GG read *bubonis* ("horned-owl"). *W4669: hibou* ("owl").
3   *Aeneus* can mean copper or bronze.
4   GG adds: *nouum tamen* ("yet new").
5   Use of red deer parchment is very traditional in Jewish religion and magic.
6   Compare KSol II.7.

cuius medio sit aliquod[1] pratulum, in quo possis facilius operare,[2] uel si mauuis[3] locum aliquem subterraneum, ut caueam uersus septentrionem perforatam eliges.

Tempus, quo operaturus es in inuocationibus spirituum sit matutinum ante solis ortum, uel si mauuis serotinum, ante solis occasum, idque serenum, temperatum, neque nebulosum si fieri potest; habeasque faciem semper erectam uersus septentrionem.[4] Hoc te tantum admonebimus[5] ut cum in locum [33r] prędictum perueneris[6] illum suffumiges suffumigio nostro recitata oratione.

De Inuocationibus, et Coniurationibus Spirituum. Cap. XV.

Adhibitis hisce omnibus rebus, et rite pręparatis facile ad familiaritatem spirituum deueniemus, fiemusque[7] per illos prędictarum artium, scientiarum, et secretorum possessores, modo illos conuocemus [+et coniuremus][8] hisce sequentibus inuocationibus, quę antequam proferantur pauca pręponemus.[9]

Antequam ad occultas inuocationes, puta ad inuocationes spirituum procedas, debes ieiunare per spatium septem dierum septies recitando in aliquo loco secreto singulis diebus ieiunii septem psalmos Dauidis, et Lytanias[10] Sanctorum cum oratione Dominica, idque facies cum magna humilitate, immo nudo corpore[11] si fieri potest, et hoc facto operaturus in arte ibis in locum designatum cum sociis [33v] adhibitis omnibus, quę necessaria sunt ad operandum, ibique circulum pręparabis eo[12] modo, quo diximus in cap. de circulo, eoque pręparato uestem indues sacerdotalem,

---

1 DN91: *aliquid.*
2 DN91: *facilius poteris operari.*
3 DN91 omits *si mauis.*
4 L omits the rest of this paragraph.
5 So too DN91; P, GG: *monebimus.*
6 So also DN91, GG. P: *proueneris*, perhaps corrected from *perueneris.*
7 P: *erimusque.*
8 So DN91, P. GG only has *coniuremus.*
9 P: *proponemus*; DN91: *pręponebimus.* L omits this paragraph.
10 DN91: *lectanias.*
11 So also DN91, L; P: *pectore* ("chest"). GG: <u>detecto</u> *pectore* ("having the chest uncovered"). W4665 also supports the equivalent: *et vous aures la <u>poitrine</u> descouuerte* ("and you should have your chest uncovered").
12 P: *in.*

which there might be a small meadow in which you may be able to work more easily, or if you prefer some place subterranean, such that the opening faces north.

You should pick a time for performing the invocation of spirits in the early morning before sunrise, or if you prefer it can be deferred to before sunset. The weather should be clear, mild, and not misty if possible, and you should always stand facing north.[1] This we highly advise you, that when you proceed into[2] the before-mentioned place, fumigate it with our incense, while reading the prayer.

Chap. 15. Concerning the invocations and conjurations of spirits.

With all these things accomplished, and duly prepared, we will easily achieve the familiarity of the spirits, and thereby we will possess the knowledge, arts, and secrets spoken of before, calling them forth [+and conjuring them] with the following invocations, which have been revealed to only a very few.

Before you can proceed with the hidden invocations, for example the invocations of the spirits, you must fast for the space of seven days. Each day of the fast, in some secret place, you should recite seven times the seven psalms of David,[3] and the Litany of the Saints, with the Lord's Prayer, and do it with great humility with your body[4] bared if possible, and with this done, go to the designated place with the associates, supplying all things which are necessary for laboring in the art, and there you should prepare the circle in the manner described in the chapter on the circle, and with it prepared, put on the priestly garment with the appropriate ceremonies, as described in

---

1   This is unusual. In many magical texts, different types of spirits are associated with each cardinal direction, and one faces whatever direction is appropriate, and often addresses each in turn. In KSol II.9, the entrance to the circle should be situated toward the north, and perhaps this was the original intent.

2   ASV, GG: arrive at.

3   i.e. The seven penitential Psalms: 6, 31, 37, 50, 101, 129, and 142 (6, 32, 38, 51, 102, 130, and 143 in the Hebrew numbering). These are widely used in magic texts. See GV p. 22; BoO pp. 89, 141. Also used in Abramelin, and by John Dee in his magical workings.

4   So ASV, DN91, and L, but P, GG, W4665 all read "chest."

qualem descripsimus in capite de ueste cum cęremoniis, qua induta munitus
gladio in sinistra manu, ut iam diximus, et in dextera pentaculo sindone
cooperto incedes,[1] et nudo capite circulum ingredieris, et ibi in medio
sociorum consistens flexis genibus hanc orationem pronunciabis, in qua
continentur 72 nomina sacra omnibus scientiis,[2] et mysteriis diuinis initiatis,[3]
ad inuocationes spirituum a Deo concessa.

> Vehuiah, Ieliel, Sitael, <u>Elemhiah</u>, <u>Mahusiah</u>, Ielahel, <u>Achaias</u>,
> Cahetel, haziel, <hakamiah,> aladiah, <u>laniah</u>, <u>hahaias</u>, <u>Isael</u>,
> <u>Mebael</u>, <u>haruel</u>, [hakamiah,] <u>loniah</u>, Caliel, <u>Leuniah</u>, Pahaliah,
> <u>nechael</u>, <u>Ieiasiel</u>, [34r] <u>Melahel</u>, <u>hainias</u>, <u>nithaiah</u>, haaiah,
> <u>Iecatel</u>, <u>Saehiah</u>, <u>Reiasel</u>, Omael, Lecabel, Vasariah, Iehuiah,
> <u>Lelahiah</u>, <u>Chanakias</u>, Manadel, aniel, <u>hahamiah</u>, Rehael, Ieiazel,
> <u>hahael</u>, Michael, <u>Venaliah</u>, Ielahiah, Sealiah, ariel, <u>Ahaliah</u>,
> <u>Michael</u>, Vehuel, Daniel, <u>hahasias</u>, <u>Imumiah</u>, <u>Nanuel</u>, <u>Nichael</u>,
> <u>Melahiah</u>, <u>Priel</u>, <u>nemamias</u>, Ieialel, [Haraħel, Mizrael, Umabel,
> Iahhael, Anauel, Meħiel, Damabiah, *Manakel, Eiael, ħabuiah,
> Roehel, Iabamiah, Haiaiel,] <u>Mumias</u>.

Hac oratione rite, et cum magna deuotione pronuntiata erectus uersus
septentrionem inuocabis primo[4] intelligentias orbium motricos,[5] et illam
precipue nominabis, a qua aliquid impetrare desideras, et sic procedes:

> Inuoco uos Intelligentię totius mundi iussu altissimi
> gubernatrices, per hęc sacrosancta nomina, quę Deus reuelauit
> [34v] seruis suis, ut implorarent auxilium a uobis, tempore
> necessitatis, inuoco uos, et deprecor, per sacrosancta mysteria
> diuinę Trinitatis ut mittatis ad me per seruos uestros **Amalthai,**

---

1   So too DN91; P, GG: *procedas.* L omits.
2   DN91: *hominibus sanctis*; P, L: *sanctis.*
3   So also L, DN91. P: *initiabis.*
4   So too L; P: *eo*; GG: *eas.* DN91 omits.
5   P: *motiuas*; L, DN91, GG: *motrices.*

the chapter on the garment. With this put on, defended with the sword in the left hand as we have just said, and in the right hand the pentacle, covered with fine linen, proceed into the circle with head uncovered. The associates should stand in the middle, while you kneel, and pronounce this prayer, in which is contained 72 sacred names with all knowledge and the divine mysteries that you will initiate, granted by God for the invocations of the spirits.[1]

> Vehuiah, Ieliel, Sitael, Elemiah, Mahasiah, *Lelahel, Achaiah, Cahethel, Haziel, Aladiah, Lauiah, Hahaiah, Iezalel, Mebahel, Hariel, Hakamiah, Louiah, Caliel, Leuuiah, Pahaliah, Nelchael, Ieiaiel, Melahel, ħahuiah, Nithhaiah, Haaiah, Ierathel, Sęehiah, Reiaiel, Omael, Lecabel, Vasariah, Ieħuiah, Lehaħiah, Chauakiah, Manadel, Aniel, ħaamiah, Rehael, Ieiazel, Hahahel, Michael, Veualiah, Ielahiah, Sealiah, Ariel, Asaliah, Mihael, Vehuel, Daniel, Haħasiah, Imamiah, Nanael, Nithael, Mebahiah, Poiel, Nemamiah, Ieialel, Haraħel, Mizrael, Umabel, Iahhael, Anauel, Meħiel, Damabiah, *Manakel, Eiael, ħabuiah, Roehel, Iabamiah, Haiaiel, Mumiah.[2]

With this prayer recited duly, and with great devotion, stand facing north, invoking first from that direction the motor intelligences[3] of the spheres, and especially you should name that one from which you desire to obtain something, and you should commence this way:

> I invoke you O Governess Intelligences of the whole world, by order of the Most High,[4] by these venerable names which God revealed to his servants in order that they might call upon you in times of need, I invoke you and beseech you by the venerable mysteries of the divine Trinity, that you send to me through

---

1   L omits the list of names. See introduction for analysis. This list is derived by arranging the Hebrew letters of Exodus 14:19-21. It is found in Agrippa OP3.25, who took it from Reuchlin *Arte*, LV v ff. According to Reuchlin, each name must always be pronounced with three syllables.

2   Corrected per Reuchlin's Hebrew and the Hebrew Bible, where ħ represents the Hebrew letter *Heth* (ח).

3   On the medieval concept of the cosmic motor intelligences, see the introduction. GG: Intelligentias orbium mo<u>trices</u>.

4   See introduction, p. ii and footnote 2.

a quibus obtineam iussu uestro quod cupio, et dum fient pręsentes impediatis, ne mihi et sociis terrorem incutiant,[1] ueni-
antque, et appareant prediti pulcra, et decenti forma, et figura,
puta humana, uel animalis alicuius non ferocis, et uisui[2]
horribilis, sed mitis, et sociabilis.

Hac dicta inuocatione sacrificabis gallum gladio pręparato in nomine intelligentiae, quam inuocaueris, et sacrificatum igni exorcisato combures, et
cineres colliges, e.t in uino recenti, (cui miscebis parum aquę benedictę) cum
sociis bibas,[3] et dum biberis hęc uerba dices.[4]

Gog Magog capimus, [35r] gog magog bibimus, gog magog
uincimus.[5]

quibus peractis gladium tenebis in sinistra manu coopertum, pentaculum
uero in dextera, et uersus orientem erectus hęc uerba proferes.

Haiah, haiah, uos[6] facti ad imaginem, et similitudinem Dei
altissimi, cui uobis ab ęterno mandatum est obedire, a quo et a
uestris Principibus potestatem, et autoritatem supra uos impe-
trauimus. Coniuramus uos per illum, cui magnum nomen est
tetragrammaton, et per uestros principes, quorum estis
Amalthai, ut fiatis nobis pręsentes, et creaturę uisibiles, absque
tremore,[7] et murmure, et mandatis nostris obediatis. Coniuramus uos ut non moremini per hanc orationem magnę
uirtutis.

Tunc dices orationem pręcedentem, in qua continentur 72 nomina sacra,
illaque peracta in 4 partibus mundi in circulo tuo [35v] denotatis sibilabis,

---

1   So also L, P; DN91: *incutinant*; GG: *afferant*.
2   So also L, DN91; P: *uisu*.
3   P: *bibes*
4   DN91: *diceris*.
5   So too DN91; P, P2: Gogmagog capimus, Gogmagog bibimus, Gogmagog uincimus; L p.
     28: Gog magog capimus, gog magog bibimus, gog <u>magor</u> vincimus; GG p. 36: <u>Gomagog</u>
     capimus, <u>gomagog</u> bibimus, <u>gomagog</u> vincimus. W4667: go maggo, Capimus, go maggo
     bibimus, go maggo vincimus.
6   DN91, GG, and L also read *uos*. P originally read uos, ("you") which was written over to
     read *nos* ("we"). W4667 likewise reads *nos*. P2 supports the first person reading: My
     stworzeni na obraz i podobieństwo Boga.
7   DN91: *timore*.

your **Amalthai** servants from whom I may obtain, by your order, that which I desire, and while they are present may you not hinder me, and may they not strike terror into my associates, and may they come and appear in an attractive and pleasing form, and in the shape of a human for example, or any animal, but not ferocious or horrible, but pleasant and sociable.

Having said this invocation, you should sacrifice a rooster, with the sword which you have prepared, in the name of the intelligence which you are invoking, and you should burn up the sacrifice in the exorcised fire, and collect the ashes, and add to some fresh wine, (into which you should mix a little consecrated water), which you and your associates should drink, and while drinking, you should recite these words:

Gog Magog we seize, Gog Magog we drink, Gog Magog we conquer.

With this finished, hold the sword in the left hand covered up, and the pentacle in the right hand, and standing facing east, repeat these words:

Haiah, haiah,[1] we being made after the image and likeness of God the Most High, who has ordered you to obey from eternity, and we have obtained power and authority over you from Him and from your prince. We conjure you through him whose great name is **Tetragrammaton**, and through those princes of whom you are the Amalthai, that you manifest yourselves to us, as visible creatures, without shaking or grumbling, and obey our commands. We conjure you to not delay, through this prayer of great power.

Then you should say the preceding prayer, which contains the seventy-two sacred names, and when that is completed, you should whistle towards

---

1   L: Haiah, haiach. W4669 p. 103: Hahial, haih, qui n'est pas fait à l'Image de Dieu ("... who is *not* made in the image of God")!

quod si nihil tibi, et sociis appareat, coniurationem pręcedentem reiterabis cum hac sequente.

> Coniuro uos Dęmones [+per nomen sanctum **Adonay**,][1] per nomen **Elohim**,[2] per nomen **Ilchios**, et **Eschirioth**,[3] per nomen **Saday**, et **Mattation**, per nomen **Gog**, et **Magog**,[4] per sedem sacram, in qua sedet sanctus, sanctus, sanctus Dominus Deus Sabaoth, et per ineffabilia nomina **On** et **el**, et per hanc orationem, **Ancor, Curmenis, Cachryo, Sateram, Ihuhies, Poliseps, Dozicamy, Lalastai, bacamen, Agiami, Tembul, Darah, faralgar, Mansturas, Bosgurfabalas, Malmar, Delebari, Acham**,[5] ut appareatis[6] nobis uisibiles, pulchra forma dotati.

His dictis tunc subito audies clamores, cantus, uaria instrumenta musica pulsata cum tympanis [36r] et psalteriis, incensos ignes coram te, et sociis uidebis, te et socios firmabis, ne illos inuadat timor. Post quas apparitiones formas complures uisibiles uidebis, uel hominis, uel alicuius animalis domestici, et sociabilis, quibus pentaculum ostendes dicendo.

Ecce uestram conclusionem, et gladium nudum dicendo,[7] Ecce uestram condemnationem, nolite fieri rebelles, et inobedientes, quibus rite peractis tibi respondebunt.

---

1   So L, DN91, P, GG.
2   L omits the rest of the conjuration.
3   DN91: Ischios, et Inchirioth; P: Ischiros, et Ischirioth. GG: Ischiros, et Ischyriot.
4   DN91: *God*[sic], et *magog*.
5   DN91: Ancor, Curmenis cachryo, sateram, Insichies Poliseps, Doricamy, Lalastai, bacamen agiami Tembul, barah faralgar Mansfaras Bofbur fagalas, malmar, Dalebari, Arham; P: Ancor, Carmenis, Cachrio, Suteram, Ilichies, policeps, Dociami, Lalastai, bacamen, Agiami, Tembal, Barah, faralgar, monsfaras, Bofgur, falalas, malmar, Delebaci, Acham . GG: Ancor, Carmenij, Cachrio, Sutiram, Ilichies, Policeps, Dociamij, Lalastai, Bacamen, Agiami, Tembal, Barach, faralgar, Monsfaras, Bofgur, falalas, Chalmar, Dalebaci, Acham; P2: Ancor – Carmenis – Cachrio – Suteram – Illichies, Polliceps, Dociami, - Lalastai – Bacamen – Agiami – Tembal – Barah – Faralgar – Monsforas - Bofgur, Falalas, Malmar – Delebaci – Acham; W4667: A Carminis, Tembal, baraoh, feralgra, Manforas, bofger, falatas, malmar, dalibachi, acham.
6   P adds *mihi*.
7   So also L, DN91. These 7 words are not found in P, GG.

the four parts of the world marked out in your circle. But if nothing appears to you or your associates, repeat the preceding conjuration, with this following:

> I conjure you, O daemones, by the holy name **Adonay**,[1] and by the name **Elohim**, and by the name **Ilchios** [*Ischios*], and **Eschirioth**,[2] and by the name **Saday**, and **Mattation**, and by the name **Gog** and **Magog**, and by the sacred seat on which he sits, Holy, holy, holy, Lord God of hosts, and by the ineffable names **On** and **El**, and by this prayer, **Ancor, Curmenis, Cachryo, Sateram, Ihuhies, Poliseps, Dozicamy, Lalastai, bacamen, Agiami, Tembul, Darah, faralgar, Mansturas, Bosgurfabalas, Malmar, Delebari, Acham**, that you appear visible to us, in a fair form, richly endowed.

This said, you will suddenly hear shouts, song, and the beat of various musical instruments, with drums and psalteries, and you and your associates will see fires burning in front of you. You must encourage your associates to be strong, and not give in to fear of them, after which you will see apparitions of many visible forms, like people or some domestic and tame animals. You should show the pentacle to them saying:

> Behold your conclusion!

Then uncover the sword, saying:

> Behold your condemnation; rebel and disobey no more.[3]

With this duly carried out, they will then answer you:

---

1   L truncates the conjuration at this point. The last 4 words are missing in ASV.
2   DN91: <u>Ischios</u>, et <u>Inchirioth</u>; P: Ischiros, et Ischirioth. GG: Ischiros, et Ischyriot.
3   Compare LIH CXXXIII.57.

Pete, et iube, quia missi summus ad obedientiam, et uoluntatem tuam exigendam, petesque ab illis quidquid[1] uoles, et impetrabis, eosque interrogabis, qui sunt sub ministerio[2] Intelligentię, a qua aliquid tibi concedi exoptas, dabuntque tibi pentacula, characteres, aliaque necessaria ad aquirendas scientias artes, et secreta, quę scire, et habere [36v] desideras, immo semetipsos tibi offerent ut te ducant quo uoles, nunquam te derelinquent, si sit tua uoluntas, ibisque securus[3] sine timore, et periculo, et operaberis per[4] illos uisibiliter, et inuisibiliter, fideliterque mandata tua exequentur. De his hactenus: Sequuntur[5] Experimenta.[6]

De Experimentis. Cap. XVI.

Difficiliorem partem artis nostrę in pręcedentibus capitibus tetigimus, omnesque artes operationes, quas si rite[7] peregeris mirabilia facies, quibus inter mortales immortalis uideberis, deueniesque tandem ad summam illam perfectionem, quam antiqui nostri sapientes habuerunt.[8]

Restat nunc, ut de experimentis loquamur, et doceamus quomodo acquiri possint pentaculis,[9] characteribus, et ui uerborum, primoque [37r] de experimentis,[10] quę ad **Orifielem** pertinent, et quomodo nobis comparare possimus[11] per pentacula, quę debent fieri secundum institutionem nostram in charta uirginea pręparata eo modo, quo superius diximus.

---

1 DN91, P: *quicquid.*
2 So L, DN91, GG. P: *mysterio.*
3 DN91: *illisque secure.*
4 So also L, DN91. P, GG: *post.*
5 P, GG: *sequentur.*
6 DN91 omits this sentence.
7 DN91: *recte.*
8   L omits all the experiments, and instead jumps directly to book 3.
9 P: *pentalis.*
10 DN91 omits the last 3 words.
11 DN91: *possint.*

Ask what you wish, because we are sent to obey and fulfill your wishes.

And you shall obtain from them whatever you wish, and ask them those things which are under the offices of the intelligence of the thing you desire, and they will give you the pentacles, characters, and other things necessary for acquiring knowledge, the arts, and secrets you seek; indeed they themselves will offer to lead you to that which you desire, never leaving you if you wish, and you can go about safely, without fear or danger, and you can work through them visibly or invisibly, and they will faithfully carry out your orders. From these thus far follow the experiments.

Chap. 16. Concerning the experiments.

We have touched on the more difficult part of our art in the preceding chapters, and all the arts and operations, which if you have duly carried through, you will accomplish miracles, and among mortals will seem to be like an immortal, and you will ultimately achieve that highest state of perfection, which our ancient wise men achieved.

Now it remains for us to speak about the experiments, and we will teach how they may be acquired with the pentacles, characters, and with the power of words, and first regarding the experiments which pertain to **Orifiel**, and how we can prove those experiments through the pentacles, which must be made according to our instructions, prepared on virgin paper in the manner spoken of earlier.

De pentaculis Orifielis.

[+Ad Acquirendas scientias - Orifielis][1]

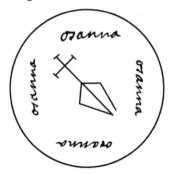

Cantetur supra hoc pentaculum missa die[2] sanctę crucis, et obtinebis amplam cognitionem harum[3] scientiarum **Orifielis**, si dum legis libros talium scientiarum in dextra parte capitis suspendas.

Ad aquirendam prophetiam.

[37v]

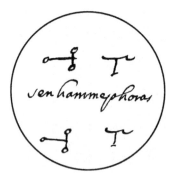

fiat hoc pentaculum die Sancti Ioannis, et fer tecum, et quando uoles prophetizabis.[4]

---

1   So DN91, BNF, P. GG: *Pentacula sequentia Orifielis sunt ad scientias acquirendas.*

2   P, GG omit.

3   DN91 omits.

4   BNF, P: *profitabis*; G: *prophetaueris.*

Concerning the pentacles of Orifiel.

[+For acquiring the knowledge of Orifiel.]

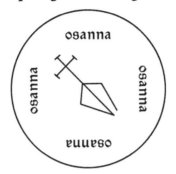

A Mass of the Holy Cross should sung over this pentacle, and you will acquire great knowledge in the science of **Orifiel**, if while reading books on such sciences, you suspend it from the right-hand side of your head.[1]

For acquiring prophecy.[2]

Make this pentacle on the Day of Saint John,[3] and carry it with you, and you will be able to make prophecies when you wish.

---

1   Osanna (hosanna, Heb. הושיעה־נא) is an appeal for divine help,

2   ASV reads "senhammephoras", but other mss all support the more correct "semhammephoras," which I have accordingly used in my version. Shem HaMephorash (Heb. שם המפורש) refers to the "explicit name" of God, as opposed to descriptive names such as "the Almighty."

3   Presumably the feast of St. John the Baptist, June 24.

Ut duo corpora sint in eodem loco.[1]

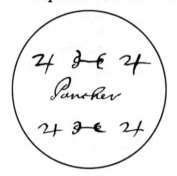

Hoc pentaculum compones die Iouis hora dominationis suę, habebisque semper tecum, quia hominum insidiis auersatur, magnęque est uirtutis, ut te experientia docebit.

Ut homo in instanti reperiatur in multis locis.

[38r]

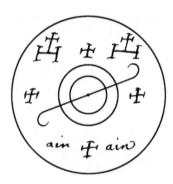

Hoc pentaculum compones die Mercurii hora suę dominationis, [+habebisque semper tecum],[2] et cum uoles[3] operari collocabis sub solea calceamentorum tuorum, et uidebis.

---

1   The figures and headings of this are swapped in P and GG.

2   So P.

3   DN91: *si uelis.*

For two bodies to be in the same place.

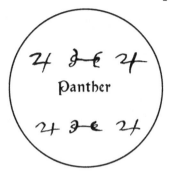

Compose this pentacle on the day and hour ruled by Jupiter, and keep it with you always, because it counters the ambushes of men, and has great virtue, as experimentation will teach you.

In order that the person can be seen in several places.

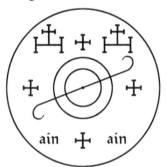

Compose this pentacle on the day and hour when Mercury rules, [+and keep it with you always,][1] and when you wish to perform the experiment, arrange the pentacle under the sole of your shoe, and you will see the result.

---

1   The phrase in brackets is only found in P.

Pentaculum ad inuisibilitatem.

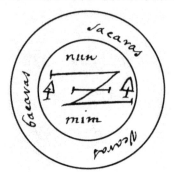

Scribatur hoc pentaculum sanguine noctuę die lunę ante ortum solis, fiesque per illud inuisibilis, modo nudum teneas in manu, (uisibilis uero si illud cooperias) et hęc uerba proferas, In nomine **gog Magog**[1] fio inuisibilis.

[38v]   **Ut scias [+pręsentia,][2] pręterita, et futura.**

Ieiunas[3] spatio trium dierum, dum cubas hoc pentaculum sub tuo puluinari collocabis, et in somno[4] per reuelationem habebis pręsentia, pręterita, et futura, quę desideras.

---

1   DN91: *God* (!) *magog*; P: gog illa *gog.!* GG: In nomine gog et magog, fis inuisibilis ("In the name of Gog and Magog, you become invisible"); P2: Gog, Magog niewidzialny;W4667 p. 63: gomagog fio inuisibilis ("gomagog I become invisible"). The connection of Gog – Magog with invisibility may be evidence of an Arabic influence.

2   So DN91, BNF, P, and to be consistent with description below. GG: Pentaculum ut praesentia futura scias.

3   DN91, P: *ieiunus*; GG: *ieiunes*.

4   So too DN91; P: *sumno*. GG: *somnio*.

For Invisibility.

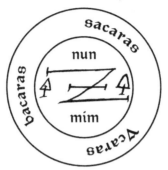

This pentacle should be written with the blood of a small owl on a Monday before sunrise, and through it you will become invisible, if you hold it in your hand uncovered, and become visible if you cover it, and utter these words:

In the name of **Gog Magog**, I become invisible.

In order to know the past, [+present,] and future.

Fast for the space of three days while you lie with this pentacle placed under your pillow, and in sleep you will have the past, present, and future revealed, as desired.[1]

---

1 Written around the circle are the words "Jesus of Nazareth, King of the Jews."

Pentacula Magrielis.

Ad Aquirendas scientias Magrielis.

Hoc pentaculo[1] composito[2] dum luna ecclypsatur sub nostro horizonte scientias omnes et artes [39r] **Magrieli** tributas aquires, si legendo, et studendo illum tecum habeas.

Ut scias quidquid est in intellectu hominum.

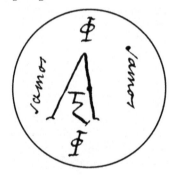

Si tecum feras subdio[3] radiante luna hoc pentaculum, uocem audies, qua scies omnia, quę scire desideras, illius cuius secretum uis patefieri tibi aperietur.

---

1   DN91: *pentaculum.*
2   DN91: *componas.*
3   DN91, P, GG: *subdie.*

The Pentacles of Magriel.

For acquiring the knowledge of Magriel.[1]

Compose this pentacle while the moon is eclipsed under our horizon. You will be granted all sciences and arts of **Magriel**, if you have it with you while reading and studying them.

To know anything that can be comprehended by people.

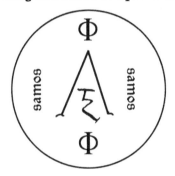

If you bring this pentacle with you under the light of the shining moon, with this pentacle, you will hear a voice, you will know everything which you desire to learn about it, whatever secret you wish to be revealed will be explained to you.

---

1   DN91, BNF, P, and GG all have single circle, but the double circle is also supported by W4667.

Ad aquiras Magnos honores.[1]

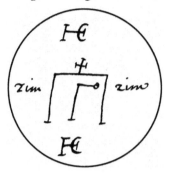

Hoc pentaculum debet fieri sole existente[2] in signo leonis [39v] quod factum inuolues in panno serico, semperque tecum feres,[3] dum scilicet Reges, Principes, et Magnates comitaberis, a quibus sine dubbio magnos honores pręcęteris[4] obtinebis.

Pentacula Vrielis.

Ad aquirendas scientias, et artes Vrielis.

Hoc pentaculum debet fieri die, et hora dominationis Saturni, illudque si tecum habeas scientias, et artes **Vrielis** obtinebis, fiesque uerecundus, uirtuosus, studiosus, et cuilibet personę amabilis.

---

1 DN91 adds: *omnesque quos dessideras* ("and all that you desire").
2 DN91: *radiente.*
3 DN91: *ferto.*
4 DN91: *pręctoris.* P omits. GG: *honores et utilitates ab eis.*

To acquire great honors.

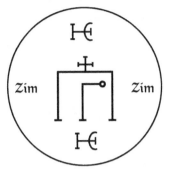

This pentacle must be made when the Sun enters the sign of Leo, and afterwards wrap it in a silk cloth, and carry it with you always, especially when you are in the presence of kings, princes, and other important people, and thereby without doubt you will obtain great honors before others do.

The Pentacles of Uriel.

For acquiring the knowledge and arts of Uriel.[1]

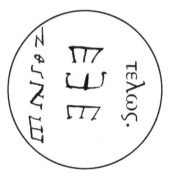

This pentacle must be made in the day and hour ruled by Saturn, and keep it with you, and you will obtain the knowledge and arts of **Uriel**, and you will become modest, virtuous, studious, and likable to everyone.

---

1   Telos Greek τέλος for "end, purpose, goal."

Ut uolare possis per aerem et inuisibiliter si cupis.

[40r]

Hoc pentaculum compones die sanctissimae Trinitatis, et in honorem illius cantabitur missa, et cum uoles operare per illud, hęc uerba pronunciabis,

Chulo losan.[1]

Pentacula Pamechielis.

Ad aquirendas scientias, et artes Pamechielis.

Hoc pentaculum fiat die et hora natiuitatis Christi, tecumque feras, et uidebis operationes mirabiles.[2]

[40v]

---

1   Only ASV and DN91 have multiple words. P: Chalolosam. P2 p. 154 #2: Chalalosam; GG p. 43: Cuculosam; W4667 p. 66: Culolosam.
2   DN91: *uidebis mirabilia.*

To enable you to fly through the air, and invisibly if you wish.

Compose this pentacle on the Day of the most Holy Trinity,[1] and have its Mass sung over it, and when you wish to operate with it, pronounce these words:

Chulo losan.

The Pentacles of Pamechiel.

For acquiring the knowledge and arts of Pamechiel.

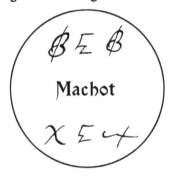

Make this pentacle on the day and hour of the birth of Christ,[2] and carry it with you, and you will see wonderful operations.

---

1   Catholics observe this on the first Sunday after Pentecost, but Orthodox Christians on the Sunday of Pentecost.

2   Traditionally midnight on December 25.

Ut aquiras omnia, quę uoles a Pamechiele, eaque, quę in illius sunt potestate.

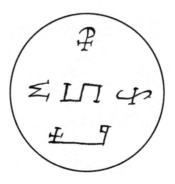

Hoc pentaculum fiat sole intrante in Capricornum, et per illud aquires omnia arcana, quę sunt in potestate **Pamechielis**.

Eiusdem Pamechielis Pentaculum quo animalibus poteris imperare.

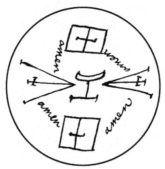

Hoc pentaculum scribes sanguine bufonis[1] tempore ingressionis solis in Sagittarium, illudque sic pręparatum [41r] tecum portabis,[2] dum scilicet operari[3] uoles, omniaque animalia, quę desideras mandato tuo parebunt, et mira per illud super animalia operaberis.

---

1   DN91: *bubonis.*
2   So too DN91; P, GG: *feres.*
3   P: *operare.*

To acquire all that you wish from Pamechiel, and with it, whatever is in his power.

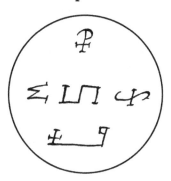

This pentacle should be made when the Sun enters the constellation Capricorn, and through it you can acquire all secrets which are in the power of **Pamechiel**.

Another pentacle of Pamechiel, to be able to command animals.

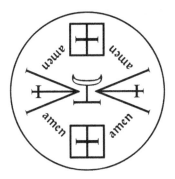

Write this pentacle with the blood of a toad, at the time when the Sun enters Sagittarius, and once it is made, carry it with you, namely when you wish to operate, and all animals which you wish to command will obey you, and thereby you will be able to perform amazing things with animals.

Pentacula Pomerielis.

Ad obtinendas artes Pomerielis.

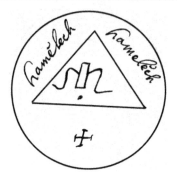

Hoc pentaculum scribes sanguine Upubę die Iouis tempore suę dominationis, tecumque habebis dum artes **Pomerielis** obtinere uoles.

Eiusdem Pentaculum magnę uirtutis.[1]

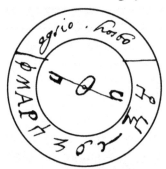

[41v] Hoc pentaculum scribes sanguine Galli tempore coniunctionis Martis cum sole, diligenterque seruabis quia magnę est uirtutis, etenim per illud fies bellicosus, Martialis, et sine timore, fiesque per illud[2] si tecum habeas inuulnerabilis, et hostibus terribilis.

---

1   DN91 omits the last two words.
2   DN91 omits the last 7 words.

The Pentacles of Pomeriel.

For acquiring the arts of Pomeriel.

Write this pentacle with the blood of a hoopoe on the day of Jupiter and the time when Jupiter rules, and carry it with you when you wish to obtain the arts of **Pomeriel**.

Another Pentacle of the same of great virtue.

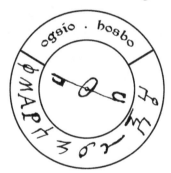

Write this pentacle with the blood of a rooster, when Mars is in conjunction with the Sun, and protect it carefully, because it has great power, and indeed thereby you will become warlike, Martial, and without fear, and thereby you will become invulnerable, if you have it with you, and the enemies will become terrified.

Eiusdem Pentaculum magnę uirtutis.

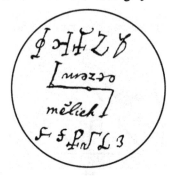

Hoc pentaculum scribes in plenilunio, tecumque, portabis in bello alligatum in bracchio dextro, et quando uoles pugnabis inuisibiliter modo dicas hęc uerba quinquies **Melich et zem**,[1] fiesque per illud fortissimus, ita ut si uelis totum exercitum hostium [+solus][2] nemine iuuante destrues, omnesque hostium [42r] machinationes, et quidquid illis est in animo per illud cognosces, et urbes quas cupis fient oppugnabiles, uel inexpugnabiles.

Pentacula Sabrielis.

Ad obtinendas artes Sabrielis.

---

1   The words "Melich et zem" are also found on the accompanying pentacle. GG also supports this, although slightly reworded: dic*endo* haec verba quinquies <u>Melich</u> et <u>zem</u>. W4667 p. 70 likewise supports this reading: dit cinq fois Melich et Zem ("say this five times: Melich et Zem"). P: *dicas haec uerba. (quinquies millies et zem)*. P2 as usual follows P; it has "Quinquies Millies" in red ink, marking them as words to be spoken.

2   P adds *solus*. DN91 adds *solues*.

Another pentacle of great virtue.

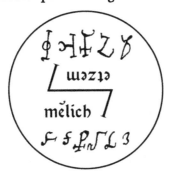

Write this pentacle on the full moon, and carry it with you into war, bound to your right arm, and when you wish to fight invisibly, say these words five times: "**Melich et zem**," and thereby you will become very powerful, such that you could defeat a whole army of enemies if you wished, with nobody helping you, and all of the enemies' war machines, and by it you will understand whatever they are thinking, and whichever cities you wish will become vulnerable or impregnable.

The Pentacles of Sabriel.

For acquiring the arts of Sabriel.

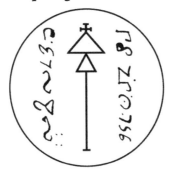

Hoc pentaculum scribes die Veneris hora dominationis suę, illudque serua, quia per illud dum uoles habebis cognitionem omnium artium quę sunt sub **Sabriele.**

Eiusdem pentaculum Ad resurrectionem Mortuorum.[1] [42v]

Hoc pentaculum scribas[2] sanguine upubę, super quo cantetur missa die mortuorum, et dum uoles operari[3] corpora mortua tanges pentaculo, et uidebis mira.[4]

Eiusdem pentaculum Magnę efficacię.

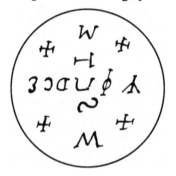

Hoc pentaculum scribes in oppositione solis, et lunę, et dum uoles operari,[5] in uas plenum aquę benedictę iniicito illud, quo facto pete quod

---

1   DN91 adds: *mirabile Pentaculum.*
2   BNF, P, GG: *scribes.*
3   P: *operare.*
4   DN91, GG: *mirabilia.*
5   So also DN91, GG; P: *operare.* The former is more correct Latin.

Write this pentacle on the day and hour ruled by Venus, and protect it, for by it you can acquire the knowledge of all arts which are under **Sabriel**, when you wish.

Another Pentacle of the same (spirit) for resurrecting the dead.[1]

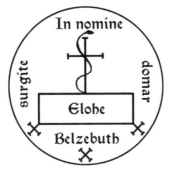

Write this pentacle with the blood of a hoopoe, over which should be sung a Mass for the Day of the Dead, and when you wish to operate, touch the pentacle to the dead body, and you will see amazing things.

Another pentacle of great effectiveness.

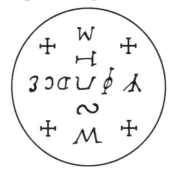

Write this pentacle when the Sun and Moon are in opposition, and when you wish to operate, throw it into a vessel full of holy water. With that done,

---

1   *Surgite in nomine domar*: "Arise in the name of Domar." the central figure is more obviously snake-like in DN91, BNF, and GG, so I have made it a bit more distinct in my version.

uoles, et habebis, miraque per illud facies, cursum solis impedies, si cupis, meteora mittes deorsum et in aere prouocabis.[1]

[43r]　　　　　　　　**Eiusdem ad longęuam uitam.**

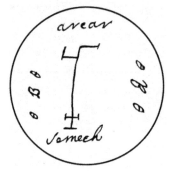

Hoc pentaculum scribes dum sol perlustrat libram, illudque tecum feres, quia[2] per illud longęuam uitam obtinebis.

Pentacula Vcharielis.

Ad obtinendas scientias, et artes Vcharielis.

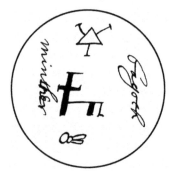

Hoc pentaculum scribes die Martis summo mane ante solis ortum, illudque tecum habebis dum scientias, et artes **Vcharielis** ediscere[3] optabis, easque subito impetrabis.

1　GG p. 44 # 3: in <u>arcum</u> prouocabis ("you can cause it to go in an arc").

2　DN91: *qui.*

3　So too DN91; P, GG: *addiscere.*

pray for what you wish, and you will have it, and through its wonderful shape, you can hinder the course of the sun if you wish, and cause meteors to fall and move around in the air.

Another of the same (spirit) for long life.[1]

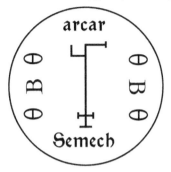

Write this pentacle when the Sun crosses Libra, and carry it with you, because with it you will attain great longevity.

The Pentacles of Uchariel.

For acquiring the knowledge and arts of Uchariel.

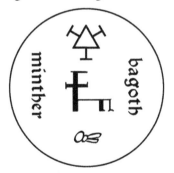

Write this pentacle on the day of Mars, very early in the morning before sunrise, and have it with you when you wish to become more learned in the science and arts of **Uchariel**, and you will suddenly learn it by heart.

---

1   DN91 reads *azcar*, but all other mss read *arcar*.

[43v]   **Eiusdem pentaculum magnę efficacię.**

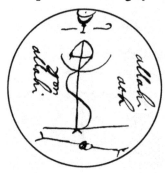

Hoc pentaculum scribes die Mercurii hora suę dominationis,[1] tecumque portabis, quia magnę est uirtutis, mira enim operatur supra hominibus, sanos facit ęgrotosue,[2] si cupis, modo eos dicto pentaculo tangas,[3] et tangendo eorum nomina pronunciabis: dat senectutem, uel iuuentutem cui uoles, dat morbum, uel uitam si cupis.

Pentacula Charielis [*Charariel].[4]

Ad amorem conciliandum.

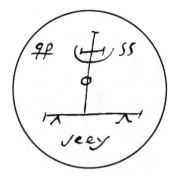

[44r] Hoc pentaculum scribes sanguine Galli sacrificati tempore oppositionis Veneris cum Marte, supra quo cantetur Missa die Sanctę Marię

---

1 So too BNF; P: *hora eius.* DN91: *d. et h.*
2 P, GG: ægrotos. DN91: *ęgrotare.*
3 DN91: *tanges.*
4 BNF and W4667 are the only manuscripts that have the name correct here, although earlier references strongly support it.

A Pentacle of the same (intelligence), of great effectiveness.

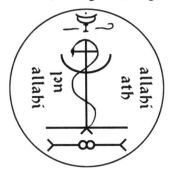

Write this pentacle on the day and hour of Mercury, and carry it with you, for it has great power or effectiveness over people, even miraculous, if you wish it can make them healthy or sick. The method is to touch them with the pentacle, and while touching pronounce those names. It can give old age or youth to whomever you wish, and it can also give sickness or life if you wish.

The Pentacles of Charariel.

Pentacle for winning over love.

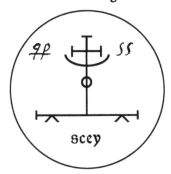

Write this pentacle with the blood of a rooster, sacrificed when Venus is in opposition to Mars, and have a mass of Saint Mary Magdalene sung over it,

Magdalenę, sicque pręparatum seruetur[1] dum opus erit, quia magnę est
uirtutis ad amorem conciliandum, pręcipue foeminarum, et puellarum, et
dum uoles operari[2] tange eo foeminas, uel puellas, quo tacto[3] pete ab illis
quidquid uoles, et obtinebis, neminem pręter te illę amabunt si cupis.

Eiusdem pentaculum ad ligandum.

Hoc pentaculum fiat[4] die uigilię sancti Ioannis Baptistę in occasu solis; sic
pręparatum habet uim [44v] soluendi, et dissoluendi potestatem genitalem
utriusque sexus, modo eo tangas personam quam desideras solui, uel[5]
dissolui, et tangendo dicas, uolo eam[6] solui, uel dissolui in nomine
Middatho,[7] uel aliter si personę sint absentes poteris hoc modo ligare.
Virgam lupi accipias,[8] et ea pentaculum ligabis, et dices: Ut hoc pentaculum
ligo, sic N.[9] ligari cupio, et uidebis effectum.

Pentacula Pantherielis.

Ad ludum, et Mercaturam.

---

1   P: *seruitur.*
2   P: *operare.*
3   DN91, P: *facto.*
4   DN91: *fac.*
5   P: *et.*
6   P: *iam.*
7   So too BNF; GG; W4667: *midadaeo.* P2: *medelatho.*
8   So too DN91; P: *accipies;* GG: *acceperis.*
9   So also GG; DN91, P: *talem.*

and thus prepared it should be protected until needed, for it has great power for winning over the love of someone, especially of women and girls, and when you wish to operate, touch it to those women or whomever you desire, and you will prevail. If you wish, they will love nobody else but you.

Another Pentacle of the same spirit for binding.

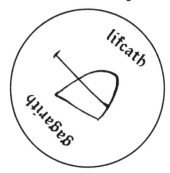

Prepare this pentacle on the day of the vigil of Saint John the Baptist while the sun is setting. It has the power of releasing and unbinding the reproductive power of each sex. The method is to touch the person whom you wish to be released and unbound, and while touching them say, "I wish you to be released or unbound now in the name of **Middathus**," or else if the persons are absent, you can bind them in this manner: Take the penis of a wolf, and bind it to the pentacle, and say, "as I bind this pentacle, so do I wish such-and-such to be bound," and you will see it accomplished.

The Pentacles of Pantheriel.

For gaming and commerce.

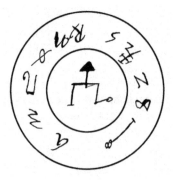

Hoc pentaculum factum sabbato sancto docet omnes artes **Pantherielis** facit hominem lucrosum in ludo, et in mercatura, si tecum feras.

[45r]   **Eiusdem Pentaculum ad liberandum Incarceratos.**

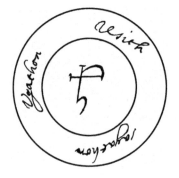

Hoc pentaculum fiat die sancti Claudii, eoque[1] die cantetur missa super eo, seruabisque illud sic prȩparatum, quia magnȩ est uirtutis, uincula incarceratorum dissoluit, si eo tangantur, redditque eos insensibiles ad torturam si secum habeant.[2]

---

1   P: *eaque.*
2   DN91: *habeas.*

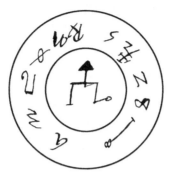

Have this pentacle made on the holy Sabbath. It teaches all arts of Pantheriel, makes one profitable at gaming, and in commerce, if you bring it with you.

Pentacle for freeing one from prison.

Make this pentacle on the day of Saint Claudius,[1] and have a Mass sung over it on that day, and it will protect the one so prepared, because it is of great virtue. It loosens the chains of the imprisoned, if they are touched with it, and makes them insensible to torture, if they have it with them.

---

1 Most likely Saint Claude or Claudius, bishop of Besançon (d. 699), whose feast day is June 6.

Eiusdem pentaculum submersionem impediens.

[45v] Hoc pentaculum fiat in plenilunio, tecumque feras,[1] dum nauigabis, quia impedit non tantum submersionem,[2] sed etiam mare placatum,[3] et tranquillum facit.

Pentacula[4] Araton.

[+Ad deambulans per flammas, et Ignem.]

Fiat hoc pentaculum die Saturni hora suę dominationis, et sic pręparatum omnem ignis lęsionem impedit, si tecum feras, poterisque ire securus sine periculo per flammas, et per ignes[5] non secus ac per aerem, tutusque ibis per omnia incendia.

---

1   DN91, BNF, P, GG: *feras.*
2   P: *submersiones.*
3   P: *paratum.*
4   P, GG: *pentaculum.*
5   P: *ignem.*

Pentacle to prevent sinking.

Make this pentacle on the full Moon, and bring it with you while sailing, because it prevents not only sinking, but also make the sea peaceful and calm.

Pentacles of Araton.

[+For the ability to walk through flames and fire.]

Make this pentacle on the day and hour ruled by Saturn, and thus preparing it will impede harm from fire, if you carry it with you, and you will be able to go carefree without danger through flames and fire, as if you were going through air, and safely pass through all fiery heat.

Aliud pentaculum eiusdem.

[46r]

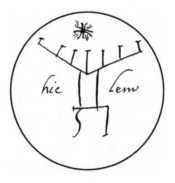

Hoc pentaculum factum dum Sol ingreditur in Leonem incendia prouocat in omni loco, quem comburi desideras, modo eo tangas locum, et hęc uerba recites, (**ortas, orcas, orlas, Gimelec**) nec eo utere nisi tempore necessitatis.

Pentacula Agiaton.

Pentaculum magnę uirtutis.

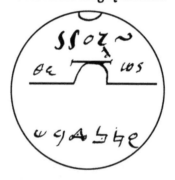

Hoc pentaculum scriptum sanguine scorpionis, dum Sol [46v] scorpionem perlustrat magnam habet uirtutem super aues qui secum illud portabit, auibus imperabit, redditque per illud aerem salubrem, uel insalubrem hominibus, immo pestiferum si cupit.[1]

---

1   DN91: *si cupis*. This pentacle is missing from P. The wording in GG, as always, is slightly different.

Another Pentacle of the same (spirit).

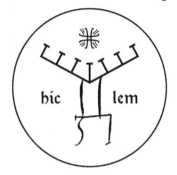

This pentacle should be made when the Sun enters Leo. It can cause fires in any place that you wish. It will burn any place, if you touch it with the pentacle, and recite these words aloud: "**Ortas, Orcas, Orlas, Gimelec,**" but you should not use it except in time of need.[1]

The Pentacles of Agiaton.

A pentacle of great power.

This pentacle is written with the blood of a scorpion, while the Sun traverses Scorpio. It has great power over birds, such that anyone who carries it can command birds, and with it you can make air healthy or unhealthy (or more correctly, pestilential) for people to breathe, if desired.

---

1   So too P2 p. 157 #5. GG pp. 47-48, says the words should be pronounced five times. Also see W4667 p. 78 #1 mentions no repetitions, and the words are slightly different: "oreus, oreas, ortas, gimelet."

Eiusdem pentaculum magnę uirtutis.[1]

Hoc pentaculum fiat die sancti Geruasii, et eo die cantetur missa super eo ante solis ortum, et tecum feras, et hęc uerba proferas. Eo in nomine **argidam, margidam, sturgidam**, et uidebis te subito eleuatum in nubibus, et inuisibiliter si cupis.[2]

Pentacula Begud.

Pentaculum Magnę uirtutis. [47r]

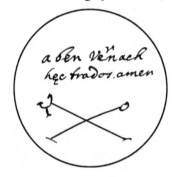

Hoc pentaculum fiat dum luna, et Saturnus se inuicem aspiciunt, et sic pręparatum seruabis, quia magnam habet uirtutem super aquas, per illud enim omnia uidebis in aqua quę desideras tam pręsentia, pręterita, quam

---

1   DN91: *Eiusdem magnę uirtutis*; P: *Pentaculum magnae virtutis.* GG: *Pentaculum ejusdem.*

2   DN91: *... proferas. Et in nomine....* GG p. 48 #1 gives the words as: Argidam, Margidam, *et* Turgidam; W4667 pp. 78-79: argidam, margidam, hargidam, but matching figure is on p. 80 #1.

Another pentacle of great power.

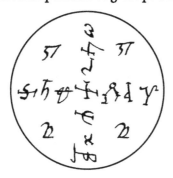

Make this pentacle on the Day of Saint Gervase,[1] and have a Mass sung over it on that day before sunrise, and carry it with you, and utter these words: "I go in the name of **Argidam, Margidam, Sturgidam**,"[2] and you will see yourself suddenly lifted into the clouds, and invisibly if you wish.

The Pentacles of Begud.

A pentacle of great virtue.[3]

Make this pentacle when the Moon and Saturn face each other reciprocally, and thus prepared, preserve it, because it has great power over the waters, and by it you can see whatever you wish in water, whether past,

---

1   June 19.

2   The placement in the text is different in ASV and P. My translation *eo* ("I go") is based on ASV, which has the comma before *eo*. In P, the comma is after *eo*, which would mean "(recite the words) with that object." GG omits the word entirely,

3   ASV has the *r* in Vernach written above the word, but DN91, BNF, and W4667 all show it in line as in my version. GG reads "abeuernach hactrados."

futura, super aquas ambulabis, descendesque in imum maris, si cupis, nullumque aquarum periculum subibis.[1]

Aliud eiusdem pentaculum.

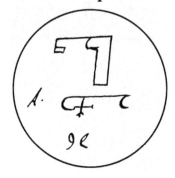

Hoc pentaculum fiat sanguine noctuę, tempus dum erit nubilosum,[2] [47v] eoque ita pręparato nauium nauigationem prouocabis, uel impedies, si cupis, idque celeriter, si tecum illud feras, thesauros in mari reconditos reperies, modo in illud descendas munitus prędicto pentaculo.

Pentaculum [*pentacula][3] Tainor.

Ad obtinendas artes, et secreta Tainor.

Fiat hoc pentaculum hora matutina, diei[4] beatę Virginis ante solis ortum, seruesque sic pręparatum, quia per illud obtinebis omnes fere artes, et secreta

---

1   DN91: *habebis.*
2   So ASV, P, GG; DN91, BNF: *nebulosum.*
3   So DN91, BNF.
4   P: *die.*

present, or future, and you will be able to walk upon water, and descend into the depths of the sea, if you wish, and no danger will come to you from water.

Another pentacle of the same (intelligence).[1]

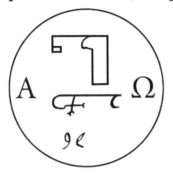

Make this pentacle with the blood of a small owl, at a time when it is cloudy, and with it thus prepared, you can help the progress of sailing ships, or hinder them if you wish, and that quickly. If you carry it with you, you can discover treasures hidden in the sea, and with it you will be able to descend into that water safely.

The pentacles of Tainor.

For acquiring the arts and secrets of Tainor.

Make this pentacle at the hour of matins, on the Day of the Blessed Virgin,[2] before sunrise, and thus prepared, keep it safe, because with it you

---

1   DN91 has an omega (Ω) on the right side of the figure – not seen in other mss, but it seems quite possible it was an original element.

2   January 1.

Tainor, thesauros reconditos in terra reuelat, aliaque permulta quę **Tainor** possidet.

[48r]   **Aliud eiusdem pentaculum.**

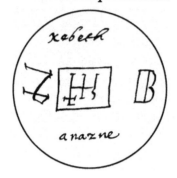

     Hoc pentaculum factum die lunę hora suę dominationis motus omnium [+rerum]¹ artificialium ligat, modo eo illos tangas, et dicas hęc uerba.

     Vos ligo in nomine **soc non, soc non, soc non**. Amen.²

Finis.

---

1   So DN91, BNF, P, GG.
2   GG p. 49 #3: <u>sornon</u>, socnon, <u>soenon</u>; P2 p. 158 #4: soc nie soc nie son nie (*nie* being the Polish equivalent of Latin *non*). W4667 pp. 81-82: sirnon, socnon, socnon, amen.

will be able to obtain nearly all the arts and secrets of **Tainor**. And it reveals treasures hidden in the earth, and many other things which **Tainor** possesses.

Another pentacle of the same.

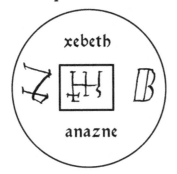

Make this pentacle on the day and hour ruled by the Moon. It binds the movement of all artificial things, if you touch them with the pentacle, and recite these words:

"I bind you in the name **Soc non, Soc non, Soc non.** Amen."

The End.[1]

---

1   The figure appended here seems to be simply ornamental in this instance. See below. BNF uses the blank space between books to insert a table of unlucky days of each month, a table of metals and days of the week associated with each planet, and alchemical symbols for the four elements.

INCIPIT LIBER TERTIUS CLAUICULĘ SALOMONIS,

bi abstrusiora artis magicę pręcepta in compendium redacta sunt in gratiam eorum, qui curiosis Magię[1] operationibus addicti sunt scripta a sapientum omnium sapientissimo [48v] Magosopho Salomone, itemque diuinissimo omnium naturę arcanorum scrutatore. Quantum [*quoniam][2] in nostra arte plus iuuat praxis, quam speculatio, ideo[3] nos tantum pauca de spirituum natura, potestatibus, et[4] ordine pręmittemus,[5] itemque eorum characteres, saltem principalium subiiciemus,[6] deinde totus in praxim me conuertam, hinc[7] nobiliora huius artis experimenta explicabuntur, quorum omnium effectus mirabiles certe, et stupendi non sine magno huius artis honore, et utilitate experienti prodesse ipsumque delectari[8] poterunt omnia autem, quę in hoc libro traduntur, silentio teneas, secreta enim sunt, et rara magni momenti, quę non nisi doctis artis huius admiratoribus philomagis reuelanda sunt.

Scias itaque[9] omnia mundana ab Intelligentiis regi, et illis aliquo modo subdita esse, quin immo, et ipsa res[10] suarum Intelligentiarum [49r] naturam sequi, quippe quę imperium omnium teneant, ut autem melius intelligas[11] quid sint[12] Intelligentię,[13] genii, siue spiritus sui naturam sequi; nota quod totidem sunt[14] species Intelligentiarum, quot rerum, deinde unicuique numero sua quoque numero pręest intelligentia, res autem sunt[15] mortales,

---

1   So also L, DN91, BNF; P: *magis.*
2   L, DN91, BNF, P: *quoniam.*
3   BNF: *intro.*
4   BNF: *ex.*
5   BNF skips ahead to *sunt ergo tres ordines spirituum....*
6   L omits the rest of the paragraph.
7   DN91: *hunc.*
8   P: *delectare.*
9   So also L, DN91; P: *igitur.*
10 P: *quinimo ipsas res*; L: *quin imo et ipsas res*; DN91: *quinimo, et ipsas res.*
11 So also L, P; DN91: *intelligentias.*
12 So too L, but DN91, P read: *sit.*
13 DN91: *intelligentia.*
14 So too L; DN91: *fuere*; P: *sint.*
15 So too L, P; DN91: *fient.*

BOOK THREE

ere begins the third book of the *Key of Solomon*, where the more secret teachings of the magical art have been condensed into a compendium, for the benefit of those who are addicted to the most elaborate magical operations, written by the wisest of all wise men, the Mago-sage Solomon. Likewise, with the most divine scrutinizing of all secrets of Nature, because in our art practice is worth more than speculation, therefore we will set before you the nature of only a few of the spirits, with their powers and ranks, and likewise their characters, at least enough to reveal the principles, then I will convert everything into practice, from here the more noble experiments of this art will be expounded, of which all the wonderful accomplishments, surely and much to the astonishment to be useful when put to the test, not without great honor of this Art, and will be able to delight themselves, therefore all the things which are handed down in this book you must hold in strict silence, for they are indeed secrets and rare, and of great significance, which should only be taught to those revealed to be admirers of this art and Philomagi.

You should know therefore that all worldly things are ruled by intelligences, and furthermore, they have been placed under them in some way, and the things themselves to follow the nature of their own intelligences, in as much as they can hold the authority of them all. But in order for you to better understand the nature of the intelligences, guardian spirits, or spirits to follow, note that there are just as many kinds of intelligences as there are things, then to each and every one has its own intelligence in charge. Therefore, things which are mortal and changeable,

et[1] mutationi, corruptionique subditę, Intelligentię immortales, et a mutatione, corruptioneque alienę, rebus itaque pereuntibus non itidem pereunt, et earum spiritus, mortuo Achille non periit ei[2] genius, remansit, et forte idem postea fuit genius Alexandri Magni.

Intelligentia[3] autem quęlibet in sua specie uariis bonitatis, dignitatis, uirtutis, uitii, et cęterarum qualitatum, quę in ipsas cadere possunt gradibus dignoscuntur.[4] Geniorum V.g. (sunt enim genii intelligentię humanę) quidam sunt sapientes [49v] item,[5] et sapientum quidam plus minusue sapiunt. Sic[6] Socratis genium, Epicuri[7] genium[8] superasse dici poterit, quidam sunt fortes, itemque ex illis hic pluribus, hic paucioribus pollet uiribus, sic Alexandri Magni genius Darii genio fortior, itemque Paridis genius licet superior,[9] tamen ipso Achillis ignobilior fuit. Quidam industrii, pariterque eorum non ęqualis est[10] industria, genius[11] enim Parrhasii Zeuxidis genio[12] peritior fuit &c.

Ipsę autem intelligentię[13] non sorte, nec ad libitum[14] hoc uel illud indiuiduum sibi assumunt, superioribus enim ancillantur inferiores, nihilque nisi cęlestium angelorum decreto moliuntur sublunares intelligentię, quomodo[15] autem superiores intelligentię omnia hęc [16]inferiora gubernant uideas.

Hę intelligentię, de quibus iam diximus sunt particulares, et quę rebus ipsis particularibus adsunt, et quodammodo iungi affectant, itaque omnium infimę.

---

1 DN91, L: *ut.*
2 P: *eius.*
3 P, L: *intelligentiae.*
4 P, L: *distinguntur.* DN91: *distinguuntur.*
5 So also L, DN91; P: *imo.*
6 So too L, P; DN91: *fit.*
7 DN91: *Epicurii.*
8 L and DN91 add: *sapientia.*
9 L: *superiortãm tam ipso.*
10 DN91: *et.*
11 DN91: *genus.*
12 L: *Parthasii Zeuxidii genio;* DN91: *Parcharii Leuclidis genio.* P: *Parrasii Genio Zeuxidis.*
13 DN91: *Ipsa autem Intelligentia.*
14 ASV has what appears to be a crossed-out comma here.
15 L, DN91: *quo.*
16 DN91: *habet.*

are subject to corruption of the subordinate; but the intelligences are immortal, and not subject to change and corruption. Therefore they do not perish in the same way that those things perish, nor do their spirits. When Achilles died, his guardian spirit did not die with him; it remained. And perhaps the same is the case in later times with the guardian spirit of Alexander the Great.

Moreover, intelligences can be distinguished by their various forms, of goodness, dignity, virtue, sin, and of other qualities, which are able to fall into themselves, distinguished by degrees or position. For example, (the position) of the guardian spirits (which also includes guardian spirits of the human intelligence) of some sages are more or less wise than that of other sages.[1]

Thus the guardian spirit of Socrates is said to have overcome the guardian spirit of Epicurus, some have more strength, others exert more influence with fewer strengths, thus the guardian spirit of Alexander the Great was stronger than the guardian spirit of Darius, and likewise the guardian spirit of Paris is judged superior, even though Achilles himself had been more dishonorable, and so on. Certain industrious people are not equally industriousness; indeed the guardian spirit of Parrhasius proved more skilled than that of Zeuxis, etc.[2]

Nevertheless the intelligences themselves are not fated, nor at liberty to take this or that atom upon themselves; indeed the inferiors are subservient to the superiors, but the sublunary intelligences only carry out the decrees of the celestial angels; you can see therefore the way in which the superior intelligences govern all these inferior ones.

These intelligences, concerning which we have now spoken, are particulars, and those which are present in the particular things themselves, are therefore lowest of all.

---

1   This could also mean the degree of a sage's genius, but it is clear a separate intelligence is meant.
2   Pliny the Elder recounted the story of a contest between famous artists Parrhasius and Zeuxis, which the former won, See *The Natural History Book 35,* chap 36.

[50r] Suprema sunt cęlestes illę intelligentię[1] (omnium uidelicet[2] astrorum) quarum potentia immensa est, maximeque pura, et efficax, quippe quę ab illo primo, et immutabili, et indesinente[3] principio Deo immediate profluat,[4] inter autem ipsas supremas, infimasque intelligentias sunt et medię ferme infinitę, quarum maxime usus est in **magia**; suprema enim quęuis intelligentia, uerbi gratia Angelus Mercurii innumeros habet satellites, ipse angelus instar Regis omnibus illis imperat, et pro uaria inferioris materię dispositione modo hoc, modo illo utitur, ut influendas ab ipso facultates in diuersa subiecta diuersarum facultatum capacia respergat.[5]

Nec[6] enim ignoras[7] quomodo ex[8] uariis planetarum aspectibus et diuersa[9] Coeli constitutione uarię[10] oriantur in natura dispositiones tam ad agendum, quam ad patiendum Ipsa igitur[11] naturę energia[12] actuatur per primam, [50v] mediamque intelligentiam. uerbi gratia **Raphael** Angelus Mercurii natum prudentem, et ingeniosum, **Turmiel**[13] Astrologum, posterior[14] tandem genius, qui ex[15] ultima, et infima Intelligentia magis, uel minus doctum in astrologia efficit.

Vides igitur tres[16] esse ordines. infimus ordo est influentiarum particularium, quę corporibus sublunaribus uniuntur per necessitatem naturalem. Secundus est medius ab illa unione naturali alienus, a quo

---

1   P: *Coelestes illa sunt intelligentiae*; L: *Supremae Intelligentiae sunt caelestia illę Intelligentiae*; DN91: *Supremę sunt Cœlestes Intelligentię.*

2   L: *Comunium videlicet*; DN91: *comunium scilicet.*

3   L: *indesignente.* DN91: *indesinenti.*

4   So too L, DN91; P: *profluunt.*

5   So too L, DN91; P: *inspergat.*

6   So too L, DN91; P: *ne.*

7   So too L, DN91; P: *ignores.*

8   P: *et.*

9   So too L, DN91; P: *diutosa* [sic].

10   DN91: *varia.*

11   So too L, DN91; P: *autem.*

12   L: *Enargia*; DN91: *natura actuatur*; P: *inergia.*

13   On Turmiel, see below. L: *Caluel.* DN91: *Caluet*; P omits. On Caluel as an angel associated with Mercury, see *Heptameron* p. 144; Davidson, 1971, p. 80; BoO p. 204.

14   L, DN91: *posterius.*

15   L, DN91, P: *est.*

16   DN91: *omnes.*

The celestial ones are those intelligences, (namely of all stars) whose power is immeasurable, and of greatest purity, and effectiveness, which of course emanate directly from that first, and unchangeable, and endless principle, God. But between the highest and the lowest intelligences there are nearly infinite intermediates, which are especially used in magic. For each supreme intelligence, for example, the angel of Mercury, has innumerable officers. The angel itself commands all those as his representative, according to the various arrangements of the material here below, using them in whatever way suits their diverse abilities.

Nor indeed should you ignore the aspects of the planets and the different arrangements of the heavens, which arrangements may arise in nature, either by acting or permitting; therefore the energy of Nature itself is activated by the primary and the intermediate intelligences. For example **Raphael,** the angel of Mercury a prudent and clever child, and **Turmiel** the astrologer.

Finally, the next genius in order which is the ultimate and lowest intelligence, more or less taught effects in astronomy.

You see therefore that there are three orders. The lowest order is that of particular influences, which are joined with sublunary bodies by a natural necessity. The second is the intermediate, separated from that natural unity

proxime infimus dependet, et tales Intelligentię sunt promptę, agiles, utpote nullam cum corporibus sublunaribus communionem habentes, ipsę tamen dependent[1] a supremis, quę a suis orbibus ne momento quidem absunt, et tali ratione materię illi cęlesti[2] uniuntur, qua inferiores intelligentię sublunari.

Sunt ergo tres ordines spirituum, cęlestes, Medii, qui proprie spiritus, et sublunares siue particulares [51r] influentię.[3] De cęlestibus pauca, de mediis plura, de sublunaribus particularibus nulla fere dicemus, nec enim[4] absolute agunt in sua corpora, sed tantum per obedientiam, item[5] non uniuersales in plura subiecta, sed particulares uni tantum corpori uires imprimunt.

Tot sunt cęlestes intelligentię, quot astra pręcipue sunt planetaria,[6] et ideo terrę proximiores a suo opifice constitutę sunt.

Inter ipsas sol, et luna uaria secundum anni tempestates nomina sortiuntur, quę licet omnibus nota sint, hic tamen pro Tyronibus subscribere placuit.

Nomina Intelligentiarum Solis et Lunę ☉ ☾.

[51v] **Vere:** Sol Abraym. Luna Agusita. ♈ ♉ ♊

aestate: Sol Arthenay. Luna Armatas. ♋ ♌ ♍

Autumno: Sol Abragini. Luna Matasigais. ♎ ♏ ♐

hyeme: Sol Communtas [*Communtaf] - Luna affaterim. ♑ ♒ ♓

Pręter autem suas particulares intelligentias habent ut et reliqui planetę suas ordinarias intelligentias, quarum uirtutes, nomina et characteres tibi subiicio.

---

1   DN91: *dependunt.*
2   L: *illae celesti,* DN91: *illę cœlestes.*
3   L omits the rest of this book, and skips directly to *De Lapide.*
4   P: *etiam.*
5   BNF: *idem.*
6   DN91, BNF, P: *planetariae.*

which the lowest depends on, and such intelligences are willing, energetic, but have no communion with the sublunary bodies themselves, yet they are dependent on the highest, which indeed never deviate for a moment from the orbits of their superiors, and for the same reason, the materials can be united to the celestial, which are inferior to the sublunar intelligences.

There are therefore three orders of spirits, the celestials, the intermediate ones, who are more properly referred to as spirits, and the sublunary or those of a particular influence.[1] We will speak about the celestial spirits only a little, but more about the intermediate ones, and almost nothing about particular sublunary spirits, nor indeed do they act completely in their bodies, but only through obedience, likewise they are not universal in more subjects, but they imprint powers to only one particular body.

There are as many celestial intelligences as there are stars, and especially the planets, and therefore have been set up nearer to the earth from their maker.

Of them, the Sun and the Moon are assigned names according to the different seasons of the year, which although they are well known, yet we will write this below for the benefit of beginners.

The names of the Intelligences of the Sun and the Moon.[2]

Spring: Sun – Abraym; Moon - Agusita. ♈ ♉ ♊

Summer: Sun – Arthenay; Moon – Armatas. ♋ ♌ ♍

Autumn: Sun – Abragini; Moon – Matasigais. ♎ ♏ ♐

Winter: Sun – Communtas [*Communtaf]; Moon - Affaterim. ♑ ♒ ♓

Moreover, in addition to their particular intelligences, they have those such as the regular intelligences of the remaining planets, whose powers, names, and characters I will provide to you.

---

1 L omits the rest of this book, and skips directly to *De Lapide*.

2 Compare *Heptameron*, pp. 103-104: Abraym Agusita Athemay/ Atbemay Armatus/ Armatas Abragini Matasignais Commutaff Affaterim. Note GG follows H more closely than P here: Abraym Agusita Artenii Armatas Abragini Matasigais Communtaf Affaterim. It is evident that GG manuscript is also informed by H directly as well as his *de secretis* original, as seen by the fact that he gives two versions of some of the material below. P2 diverges further, e.g. Abragini Matasigais Comuntal Affaterim....

De intelligentia Solis ☉ Nomen Michael.

Character.

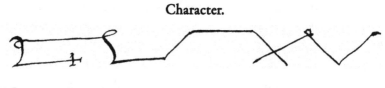

[52r]   **Virtutes.**

Habet uim maximam in reliquas intelligentias, est enim Princeps omnium quotquot sunt spirituum, facit homines magnanimos, prudentes, fortes honorum, et dignitatum appetentissimos,[1] iustitię obseruantissimos,[2] amicitię custodes, fidei incorruptę, religioni addictos, pręter omnia magnum in diuitias imperium habet.

Imploratur ad aurum, gemmas, diuitias nummos, gratiam, et bene-uolentiam apud Magnates impetrandam,[3] honores assequendos, amicitias[4] apud inimicos stabiliendas, infirmitates abigendas.

Tandem ab hoc spiritu nihil mali, alexiacus[5] enim est, et bonus bonis, et bonus malis, De spiritibus qui illi subsunt postea uidebimus.[6]

De Intelligentia Lunę ☾ Nomen Gabriel.

Character.

---

1   BNF: *appetissimos* (!)
2   BNF: *obseruatissimos.*
3   BNF skips ahead to *De Intelligentia Lunae.*
4   DN91: *Amicitiam.*
5   P: *alisiamus.* DN91: *Tandem ab hoc spiritu nihil mali habetur, est bonus cum bonis, et cum malis.*
6   DN91: *Tandem ab hoc spiritum nihil mali habetur, est bonus cum bonis, et cum malis.*

Concerning the Intelligence of the Sun, named Michael.

Character.[1]

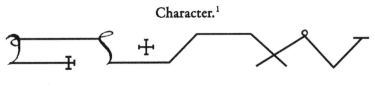

Virtues.

He has the greatest strength over the remaining intelligences; he is indeed the prince of all spirits, however many there are. He makes men noble in spirit, foreseeing, strong of honors, and of the strongest longing for dignities, most watchful for justice, custodians of friendship, unwavering faith, and devoted to worship. Besides everything great, he has command of riches.

He is appealed to for gold, jewels, wealth, coins, grace, and for obtaining the good will of magnates, procuring honors, firming up friendships among enemies, and expelling infirmities.

Finally, nothing evil is had from this spirit; he is even a remedy,[2] and good with the good, as well as good with the bad. We will see later about the spirits which are under him.

Concerning the Intelligence of the Moon, named Gabriel.

Character.[3]

---

1   Compare H sigil of Michael.
2   ASV: *alexiacus*: meaning uncertain.
3   Compare H sigil of Gabriel.

[52v]   **Virtutes.**

Nemo est qui ignoret maxime humidam esse lunam, eius Intelligentia in
humida quoque imperium habet, reddit homines contumaces, uanitatibus[1]
addictos, obtusi ingenii, pusillanimes, uilisque, et humilis animi, tardos in
negotiis, et super[2] omnia phlegmaticos, Zephirus subditus est Intelligentię
lunę.

Imploratur ad argentum, ad hęc inferiora humiditatem influendam.[3] Ista
intelligentia cum Angelo Mercurii concurrens, et implorata Metamorphosin,[4]
quamcunque molitur,[5] modo nos inuisibiles, modo in leonem, modo in
lupum, modo in ignem, arborem, uel alius simile transformans,[6] quin et res,
quę non sunt tibi, uel quibusue adstantibus[7] non sine magna omnium
admiratione proponet,[8] conuiuium uerbi gratia puellam, amicum absentem,
nummos, [53r] superbum palatium etc. Sed omnia erunt delusio, et falsa
apparentia per lunę satellites, de quibus postea dicemus, molitę.

De Intelligentia Martis ♂ nomen Samael.

Character.

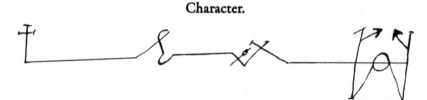

Virtutes.

Per **Samael** omnia prompte,[9] et sine timore peraguntur, efficit animos[10]
generosos confortando, et calefaciendo Cor, sępius iracundos, et sibi minime

---

1   BNF: *varietatibus.*
2   P: *supra.*
3   DN91, BNF, P: *imploratur ad argentum assequendum, ad humiditatem in haec inferiora
    influendam.* BNF skips ahead again.
4   DN91: *metmorphesim;* P: *metamorphosim.*
5   DN91: *melior.*
6   DN91: *transformatur.*
7   DN91: *astantibus.*
8   P: *propones.*
9   DN91: *prompta.*
10 So too BNF; DN91: *afficit omnes;* P: *efficit omnes.*

Virtues.

Nobody is ignorant of the fact that the Moon is especially humid; its Intelligence likewise has rule over all things which are humid. He makes men insolent, prone to vanity, of a blunt nature, cowardly, and cheap, and feeble minded, and slow working. All phlegmatics, and the West Wind (Zephyr) are subject to the Intelligence of the Moon.

He can be petitioned for silver, and for causing moisture to flow in these lower levels. This same Intelligence, similar to the angel of Mercury, can be invoked for undertaking any kind of metamorphosis, such as making us invisible, or changing shapes into the form of a lion, wolf, fire, a tree, or other similar things. He can also make things other than you appear nearby, much to the great wonder of all who see it, for example, a feast, a girl, an absent friend, coins, a lofty palace, etc. But it will all be an illusion, and false apparitions from the officers of the Moon, which we will endeavor to speak about later.

Concerning the Intelligence of Mars, named Samael.

Character.[1]

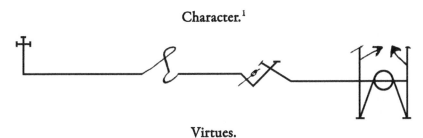

Virtues.

By means of **Samael**, all things are carried out readily, and without fear. He effects noble souls with courage, and by warming the heart, frequently

---

1   Compare H sigil of Samael.

imperantes[1] homines reddit, uindictę cupidos, uehementes manu, Temerarios, si plus decet calefaciat,[2] sine metu in pericula quęque sese pręcipitant Martiales, et differunt gratiosi Solares a gratiosis Martialibus [53v] in eo quod solarium gratiositas sic[3] cum iudicio contemperata, et cum quadam grauitate;

Martialium uero ab omni iudicio[4] aliena, immo et rationi aduersatur, huic comes est leuitas, temeritas, impatientia, iactantia, passionumque omnium fere[5] penitus emersa ęconomia; si uero Intelligentia Martis debiliter influat, id est remisse calefaciat,[6] tunc facit truculentos,[7] rixosos, effusores sanguinis, aliena, suaque destruentes, latrones, erga Deum irreuerendos discordiarum authores,[8] arrogantes,[9] seditiosos, maleque[10] legibus obtemperantes.

Subsolanus uentus, quo[11] plurimum gaudet **Samael**.

Imploratur ad rixas inter Amicos, Ciues, domesticos, fratres, filios, et parentes excitandas, discordiam inter Principes, grassandam mortalitatem, bella, Combustiones, et caetera hostilia acta in prouinciam quamlibet iniicienda, numerum quemlibet militum inuocatus dabit, inimici per illum occumbunt, galli sacrificio[12] plurimum gaudet, gallique cor mense martio nati pluribus Magię usibus,[13] et pręcipue ad inimicos occidendos inseruit, apparet[14] aliquando sub hac figura.

---

1   So too BNF; DN91, P: *temperantes*.
2   DN91 omits the last 4 words. P: *si plus decet calefaciat*. BNF skips to *imploratur ad rixas....*
3   DN91: *fit*; P: *sit*.
4   DN91: *iudicium*.
5   P: *ferme*.
6   DN91: *remissue calefacit*.
7   DN91 adds "Thraso, non Tyrannos, Turbulentos" ("Thracian, not tyrants, unruly"). but P reads *turbulentos*. vs. ASV *truculentos*.
8   P: *auctores*.
9   DN91 omites the last 3 words.
10 P: *malisque*.
11 P: *subsolanus uenter est quo....*
12 DN91: *sacrificium*. DN91 has this sentence underscored, and a large asterisk in the margin.
13 P: *magis artibus*.
14 DN91 omits *apparet*.

angry, with little self control, eager for vengeance, very eager with the hand, and careless. If the influence is more, they may become heated, throwing themselves headlong into martial danger without fear, and the favorable Martials differ from the favorable Solars, in that the favorability of the Solars may be moderated by judgment, and with certain gravitas.

To Mars also belongs all contrary judgments, contradicting and against reason. Devotees to it are shallow, rash, impatient, boastful, and tolerant of nearly all suffering. If however, the Intelligence of Mars should flow weakly, so that it heats gently, then it makes one ferocious, quarrelsome, wasteful of blood, and demolishing the property of others, and their own, robbers, irreverent towards God, in conflict with authorities, arrogant, mutinous, and obeying the law poorly.

The eastern wind is what **Samael** uses most.

He can be petitioned to provoke brawls between friends, neighbors, household members, brothers, sons, and parents, disagreement among princes, rioting, plague, wars, burnings, and other hostile acts in the region, however caused. He is invoked to give any number of soldiers; enemies die through him; he enjoys the sacrifice of a cock the most, and there are more magic uses for the heart of a cock born in the month of March, and it is especially used for ruining enemies. He appears sometimes in the following shape:

[54r]

De Intelligentia Mercurii ☿ Nomen Raphael.

Character.

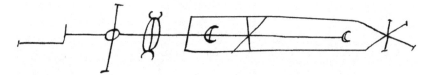

Virtutes.

Per **Raphael** omnia ingeniosa, dolosa, docta, et artificii plena, reddet[1] homines ingenii acumine excellentes, omnium artium, et scientiarum capaces, [+sagaces,][2] solertes, studiosos, cum dexteritate omnia peragentes, Poetas, Mathematicos, astronomos,[3] eloquentes, pictores, sculptores, Inuentores nouarum artium,

si minus influat,[4] cautos, et nimis dolosos reddet, malis artibus addictos, malitiosos, mendaces, de fallendo proximo perpetuo cogitantes, dissimulatores, perfidos, et cum quadam agilitate [54v] fraudes suas in usum

---

1 DN91, BNF, P: *reddit.*
2 BNF, P add.
3 BNF jumps to *imploratur ad guauis....*
4 DN91: *influet.*

Concerning the Intelligence of Mercury, named Raphael.

Character.[1]

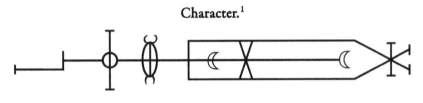

Virtues.

Through **Raphael** is everything ingenious, crafty, learned, and artistic. He restores talent, cunning, distinguished in all arts and great knowledge, sharp senses, clever, studious, with dexterity to accomplish everything, poets, mathematicians, astronomers, eloquent, painters, sculptors, and inventors of new arts.

If his influence is less, he makes one cautious and very deceitful, addicted to evil arts, wicked, lying, always thinking about deceiving his neighbor, dissemblers, faithless, and drawing them into his frauds with certain agility,

---

1   Compare H sigil of Raphael.

reducentes, falsarios, insidias struentes,[1] aleatores, in qua arte uafri euadunt, modo ergo potenter[2] in hęc inferiora agit,[3] optatos producit effectus, immo corpori agilitatem ad fallendum, et deludendum[4] influit, ab illo Circulatores, Pręstigiatores, schęnobantes,[5] Petauristę, saltatores, Pantomimi,[6] Vesticulatores [*gesticulatores],[7] histriones Comedi[8] adiuuantur, omnesque suas subtilitates solo[9] Raphael et suis subditis debent.

Imploratur ad quęuis metalla assequenda, pręterita, et futura reuelanda, omnes scientias, artes, industrias nobis infundendas,[10] unum in aliud transmutandum, ut[11] bouem in equum, hominem[12] in asinum, lupum, porcum, aquilam etc.[13] Illius tandem ope in rei cuiusuis cognitionem deuenimus, exoticorum[14] regnorum acta cognoscimus, in speculo Magica ratione pręparato, cuiusuis rei ueritatem[15] oculis proponet,[16] si uxor sit adultera, ipsam cum adultero latentem aspicies, si pręlium inter duos [55r] exercitus sit committendum ita[17] bene omnia uidebis, ac si in ipsa pugna esses, puellę cuiusuis, puta Dominę tuę effigiem tibi proponet.

Subtilior, et agilior est[18] reliquis cęlestibus Intelligentiis Raphael, ipsi sacrificia ex uulpe placent, item apum, formicarumque[19] oblatione, (sunt enim mercurialia[20] ista animalia[21]) delectatur.

1 DN91: *subruentes.*
2 DN91: *potentes.*
3 DN91: *agant.*
4 P: *dedendum.*
5 i.e. *scanobata.* DN91: *schanobantes*; P: *schoenobantes.*
6 P: *pantomemi.*
7 DN91, P: *gesticulatores.*
8 P: *comredi.*
9 P: *soli.*
10 BNF: *insinuendas.*
11 P omits.
12 P: *homines.*
13 BNF skips ahead to *de intelligentia Iouis.*
14 P: *exeticorum.*
15 DN91: *uirtutem.*
16 DN91: *occultis sponet.*
17 DN91 omits.
18 DN91: *es.*
19 P: *formicarum.*
20 DN91 adds *omnia.*
21 P: *omnia.*

forgers, concocting ambushes, dice players, those skilled in the art of escape, performing these in a competent manner into these inferior things, he produces the desired effects, or rather deceiving by the agility of the body, and he influences by deception, thereby itinerant performers, jugglers, tightrope walkers,[1] acrobats, dancers, pantomimes, gymnasts, comic actors are helped, and all their subtleties, due solely to Raphael and his subordinates.

He is invoked for attaining any metals you desire, revealing the past and future, instilling all learning, arts, and skills into us, transmuting one thing into another, such as an ox into a horse, a man into an ass, wolf, pig, eagle etc. Finally, with power from him, we can achieve knowledge of whatever you please; we can know the actions of foreign powers, in a mirror prepared with magical methods; it will display the truth about anything you can imagine. If your wife has been unfaithful, you can observe the one who was secretly with the adulterer. And if a battle between two armies is to occur, you can see if it will go well, or if the battle itself will even happen, and he can display for you the image of any girl you wish, for example, your wife.

Raphael is more subtle and more agile than the other celestial intelligences; he is placated with the sacrifice of a fox, likewise he delights in an offering of bees and ants, (which are indeed animals associated with Mercury).

---

1   The word *scenobata* is used for a ropewalker, or alternatively, a slapstick or physical comedian. See Du Cange vol. VI: Paris, 1736, p. 212.

De Intelligentia Iouis ♃ Nomen Sachiel.

Character.

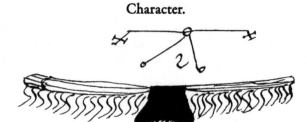

Virtutes.

Sanguineus est **Sachiel**, ideoque naturę humanę maxime consentaneus, facit honestos, religiosos, in superstitionem uergentes, boni temperamenti [55v] et consequenter bonę indolis, et animi, moderatos in omnibus animi pathematis, beneuolos, liberales,[1] fidos, amicos, facętos, uel potius facętiarum amantes: Iouialibus ergo tranquilla, et serena frons est.[2]

Si minus influat Iuppiter superstitiosos omnino facit animos, et timidę naturę prodigos, superbos, negligentes, simulatos, amicos, facetos sed stultos reddit homines, tandem remissa eius influentia ignobilis est.

In medio summę, remissęque influentię consistit medium quoddam,[3] quibus taliter influit **Sachiel**, Magię plurimum addicti sunt, ut et[4] astrologię diuinatrici Negromantię,[5] phisionomię, Chyromantię, et reliquis artibus, quibus futura prędicuntur.

Antequam ergo te Magicis[6] artibus initieris, huic te deuoueas, magnum enim in his rebus progressum facies, [56r] si te Iuppiter media uirtute suę influentię inspexerit.

1　BNF skips to *imploratur ad laetos....*
2　DN91: *... et serena fronte.*
3　P adds *hi.*
4　P: *V.G.*
5　DN91: *necromantię.*
6　These 4 words are underscored in DN91, with another large asterisk in the margin.

Concerning the Intelligence of Jupiter, named Sachiel.

Character.[1]

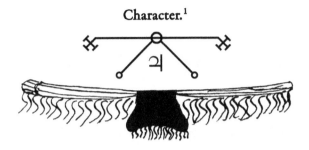

Virtues.

Sachiel is sanguineous, and therefore greatly in harmony with human nature, he makes one honored, devout, inclined to superstition, of good temperament, and consequently innately good of character and mind, controlling all mental passions, benevolent, generous, faithful, friendly, witty, or rather a lover of wit: With the influence of Jupiter, therefore, one's appearance is tranquil and serene.

If the influence of Jupiter is less, he makes the minds entirely superstitious, and of a timid nature, wasteful, arrogant, negligent, phony, loving, witty but can make people foolish; finally, his decreased influence is ignoble.

If the influence which flows from **Sachiel** is somewhat above average, those affected by it are most frequently addicted to magic, such as of astrology, nigramantic divination, physiognomy, chiromancy, and all other arts which predict the future.

Therefore, before you can be initiated into the magical arts, you should devote yourself to this (intelligence), for you will make great progress in these matters, if Jupiter inspires you with the intermediate virtue of his influence.

---

1   This does not much resemble the sigil of Sachiel in H.

Imploratur ad laetos, hilaresque animos[1] reddendos, lites pacificandas,[2] item huius[3] ope inimici mitigantur, ualet etiam ad mulierum amorem conciliandum, sed plus Venus, quam Iuppiter in his rebus potest, per Venerem enim concubitum, per Iouem autem id solum consequimur, quod nostrę consuetudinis dulcedine pellecta,[4] perpetuo nostri consortii desiderio[5] teneantur.

De intelligentia Veneris ♀ Nomen Anael.

Character.

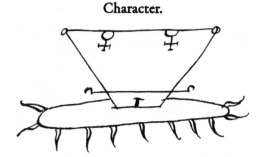

Virtutes.

Spiritus **Anael** gratissimus est, et omnium fere dulcior,[6] reddit homines uenustos, laetos, formosos, misericordes, suauibus moribus imbutos,[7] beneficos, pręcipue autem pronos, addictosque omnibus gradibus[8] uoluptatum, mulieribus, genio, musicę, choreis, comędiis, tandem delitiarum[9] omnium amantes reddit, ipsa autem propensitas ad libidinem est pręcipuus[10] anaelis effectus.[11]

---

1   DN91: *honores*; BNF, P: *homines.*
2   BNF skips to *De intelligentia Veneris.*
3   P: *eius.*
4   DN91, P: *pellectae.*
5   P: *desiderii consortio.*
6   DN91: *pulchrior.*
7   BNF: *indutos.*
8   DN91, BNF, P: *generibus.*
9   BNF, P: *deliciarum.*
10 DN91: *et pręcipue.*
11 DN91: *effectas.*

He is invoked to make one's spirit happy and cheerful, settling lawsuits, likewise the power of enemies is mitigated. He also has power to win over the love of women, but sexual attraction is more under Venus than Jupiter, especially sexual acts, nevertheless through Jupiter we pursue it uniquely, because having attracted through the sweetness of our intimacy, they may be held to our partnership everlastingly with continuous desire.

Concerning the Intelligence of Venus, named Anael.

Character.[1]

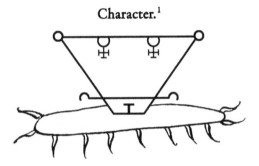

Virtues.

The spirit **Anael** is most pleasing and is the most sweet of them all. He renders people attractive, happy, beautiful, merciful, imbued with agreeable manners, beneficent, however especially prone and addicted to all types of pleasures – to women, to good taste, to music, to dances, to meals, finally makes them lovers of all pleasures; moreover an inclination toward lust is a particular effect of Anael.

---

1   Does not much resemble the sigil of Anael in H.

Imploratur autem ad mulieres ad concubitum alliciendas, ipsas enim adeo[1] in luxuriam excitat, ut uix priori atrestamento[2] resistere possint,[3] imploratur etiam pariter ad matrimonia facienda.

Delectatur potissimum sacrificio columbarum, passerum, reliquorumque animalium Venereorum, quorum[4] ad eroticas partes[5] plurimum iuuat.

[57r]   **De intelligentia Saturni ♄ Nomen Cassiel.**

Character.

Virtutes.

Inquibus[6] **Cassiel** dominatur sunt graues profundi ingenii arcanorum naturę scrutatores, frigidi, melanconici [*melancholici],[7] taciturni, solitarii, męstitię addictę,[8] laborum patientissimi, ut et asinus,[9] qui inter bruta patientissimus, et saturninus[10] est, frigidique temperamenti, timidique sunt saturnini homines, auari, liuidi, maligni, et insidiatores, pręcipue dum minus influit, pigri, deceptores, Inculti.[11]

---

1   P: *ita.*
2   DN91, BNF, P: *attrectamento.*
3   BNF skips ahead to *De intelliga Saturni.*
4   P: *cor eorum.*
5   P: *passiones.* DN91 omits.
6   P: *Hi quibus.*
7   BNF: *melancolici;* DN91: *Malancolici;* P: *melancholici.*
8   DN91, BNF, P: *addicti.*
9   BNF reads *asimes* (!), then skips to *Imploratur ad discordias....*
10 DN91: *Saturnissimus.*
11 DN91: *Iniusti.*

He is invoked moreover for enticing women towards sexual acts, indeed for making them so aroused in wantonness, that they can scarcely resist, where earlier they had been able to resist. He is also equally invoked for making marriages.

He delights chiefly with the sacrifice of pigeons, sparrows, and of other animals associated with Venus, and the erotic parts[1] of which helps the most.

Concerning the Intelligence of Saturn, named Cassiel.

Character.[2]

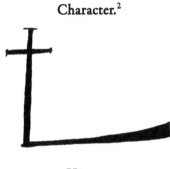

Virtues.

Those over whom **Cassiel** has dominion are serious, of deep character, searching deeply into the secrets of nature, cold, melancholic, silent, solitary, addicted to sadness, working very patiently like a mule, which among beasts is the most patient and Saturn-like. Saturnians also have a cold temperament, and are timid, miserly, livid, spiteful, and ambushers. When the influx is especially low, they are lazy, deceivers, and uncultivated.

---

1   P seems to have misread *quorum* ("of which") as *cor eorum* ("their heart"), which may have influenced the French text of W4667: *Il a le coeur ardent pour les passion heroyique.*

2   Compare H sigil of Cassiel.

Imploratur ad discordias seminandos, odia, mentisque[1] [57v] cogitationes, quemlibet interficiendum, et quodlibet mutilandum membrum etc[a].

Et hęc de spiritibus planetariis dictę[2] sufficiant, nunc ad medios, eorumque satellites me conuertam.

De spiritibus mediis siue Satellitibus Supremorum.[3]

Characteres sunt signa latentia diuinitatis alicuius, quę ab ipsis spiritibus per reuelationem traduntur,[4] et exinde uim habent ab ipso spiritu tradente impressam ad tales effectus producendos sub nomine characterem comprehendo et sigilla, et imagines, licet ea potius dici possint[5] characteres compositi: spiritus autem primam uim ipsis characteribus imprimunt.

Nota autem quod operatio quęuis per Characteres nulla est nisi prius inito foedere aut promissa fide uel obedientia spiritibus [58r] characteribus autem adhibendę[6] sunt suffumigationes,[7] oblationes, sacrificia, ut earum[8] ueritas occulta in actum, usumque reducatur.

Pentacula sunt etiam characteres oppositi [*appositi],[9] et signa, quę nos a malis euentibus[10] pręseruant, de quibus postea ample tractabimus.

Habes[11] itaque in sequentibus pręcipuos supremarum[12] septem intelligentiarum satellites, et in quibusdam locis subqua figura se se uisibiliter reddunt, et nobis apparent, quando inuocantur, notabis etiam quod spiritus superiores figuram accipiunt humanam, satellites raro, sed sub bestiarum imaginibus se pandunt.

---

1 P: *mentis.* DN91: *odiamentisque.*
2 BNF, P: *dicta.*
3 BNF skips to *Spiritus Solares.*
4 DN91: *traduuntur.*
5 DN91: *possent.*
6 P: *adhibenda.*
7 P: *fumigationes.*
8 DN91, P: *eorum.*
9 DN91, P: *appositi.* W4667 (Fr): *oppose.*
10 P: *ruentibus.*
11 DN91 has this underscored, and a large asterisk in the margin.
12 DN91: *supręmorum.*

He is invoked for sowing discord, hatred, and thoughts of killing and mutilating limbs, etc.

And these sayings of the astrologers about the spirits should suffice; now I will turn towards the intermediate spirits, and their officers.

Concerning the intermediate spirits or the officers of the highest.

The characters are hidden signs of some divinity, which are bequeathed by the spirits themselves through revelation, and from thence they have power given by the spirit itself imprinted for producing such effects, which I am including under the name of "character," and the seals and images, although those might rather be called "compound characters." Moreover the spirits imprint the foremost strength onto the characters themselves.

Note however that whatever operation you wish through the characters will be ineffectual unless you have previously entered into an agreement[1] or have promised loyalty or obedience to the spirits with the characters. Moreover, suffumigations, offerings, and sacrifices are to be employed, so that the hidden truth of them may be drawn out in action and use.

The pentacles are also assigned characters and signs, which preserve us from bad consequences, concerning which we will discuss later at length.

Therefore you have in the following the particular officers of the seven highest intelligences, and in which places and in what forms they will become visible and appear to us, when they are invoked. You will also note that the superior spirits take human shape, but the attendants seldom do, but display themselves in the likenesses of beasts.

---

1   Or "pact," but the term pact I think has misleading connotations in this context, given all the literature codifying a "pact with the devil."

Spiritus Solares.

Spiritus Solares tunc aderunt tibi in inuocatione, quando te aliquantulum sudore consperseris.

fabriel, et **Vstael** pręcipui sunt omnium. **Fabriel** diuitiarum directionem,[1] **Vstael** uero beneuolentiam, et apud Magnates gubernationem habet. **Tumel**[2] officium est gemmas dare.

[58v]   fabriel

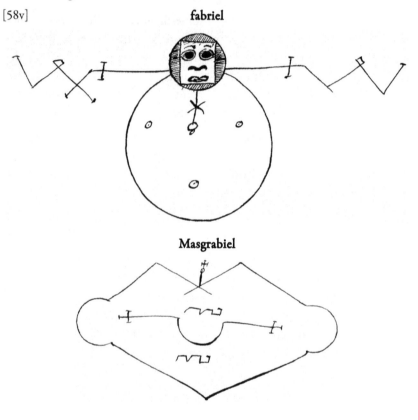

Masgrabiel

---

1   BNF: *diuersionem.*
2   Spelled Tumael below. P: Turnel. Not found in *Heptameron.*

The Solar Spirits.

You will know the Solar spirits are present before you in the invocation, when you feel yourself breaking out in a light sweat.[1]

Fabriel and **Ustael** are the foremost of them all. **Fabriel** shows how to obtain wealth, **Ustael** however has benevolence, and controlling important persons. The office of **Tumel**[2] is to give jewels.

Fabriel

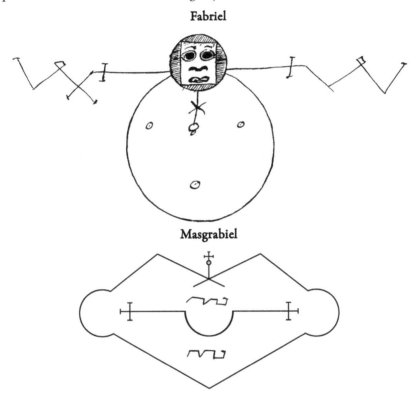

Masgrabiel

---

1   Compare LIH CXIX.4, and OP4 p. 22.
2   Spelled Tumael below.

Ustael

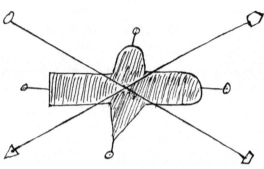

[59r]   Aiel

Sapiel

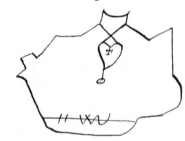

Tumael

Vstael

Aiel

Sapiel

Tumael

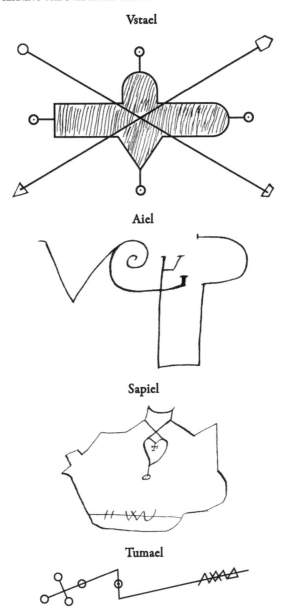

Capabali

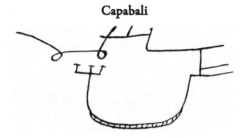

Spiritus Lunares.

Spiritus lunares molli ut plurimum apparent corpore, colore instar argenti, signum erit eos adesse, quando madidus erit circulus. **Madiel** argentum tenet. **Ianael** pluuiam, grandinem, niuem; In hęc inferiora effundit[1]. **Anayl** metamorphosem[2] spiritus est, et cum nos inuisibiles reddere uolumus inuocandus. **Vetael** conuiuiorum, festorumque superbo[3] apparatu adstantes[4] deludet.

Madiel.   [60r] **Ianael**

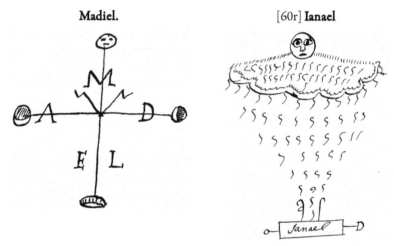

---

1 P: *infundit.*
2 DN91: *methamorfesen*; BNF, P: *metamorphosen.*
3 BNF: *suporborem.*
4 DN91: *astantes.*

Capabali

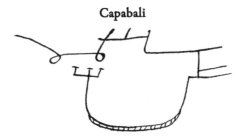

The Lunar Spirits.

The lunar spirits for the most part appear with soft bodies, colored like silver. The sign that they have appeared is that the circle will become wet.[1] **Madiel** has silver. **Ianael** pours rain, hail, and snow into these lower realms. **Anayl** is the spirit of metamorphoses, and is to be invoked when we wish to become invisible. **Vetael** can make the illusion of haughty feasts and banquets appear.

Madiel.[2]   Ianael

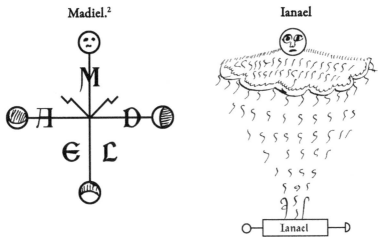

---

1 Compare LIH CXX.5, with parallels in OP4 p. 24.
2 Seems to represent the phases of the Moon.

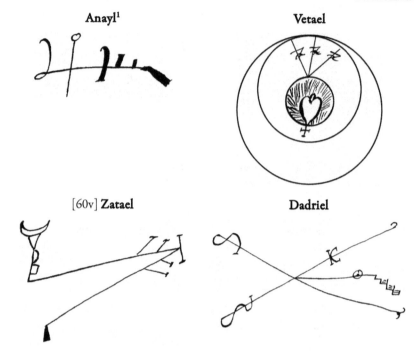

Anayl[1]   Vetael

[60v] Zatael   Dadriel

Spiritus Martiales.

Turpissimi sunt omnium Martiales spiritus, nemo est qui ab ipsis non terreatur, uen[i]unt cum fragore,[2] et strepitu, et sępe instar flammę collucent, **Amabiel** combustiones Prouinciarum, mortalitatem etcetera exequitur. **Iaxel** officium est rixas inter fratres, bellum inter populos, odium inter amicos excitare. **Galdel** tot spiritus pro [61r] militibus tibi dabit, quot desideraueris. **Vianuel** quodlibet homicidium perpetrabit.

---

1   Looks like Anail with an extra stroke added to make the 'i' into a 'y.'
2   BNF: *stragore* (!).

Anayl   Vetael

Zatael   Dadriel

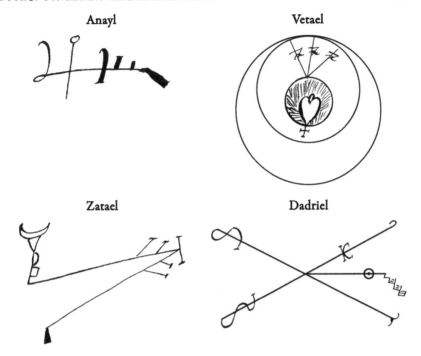

The Martial Spirits.

Martial spirits are the most ugly of all spirits; everyone will be terrified of them when they come, with noise and roaring, and often they shine like bright flames.[1]

Amabiel carries out the burnings of provinces, mortality, and the like.

Iaxel's office is to incite violent quarrels between brothers, war between peoples, and hatred among friends.

Galdel will give you many spirits as soldiers, as many as you desire.

Vianuel perpetrates the murder of anyone.

---

1   Compare LIH CXXI.5, with parallel in OP4 p. 21..

Amabiel   **Iaxel**

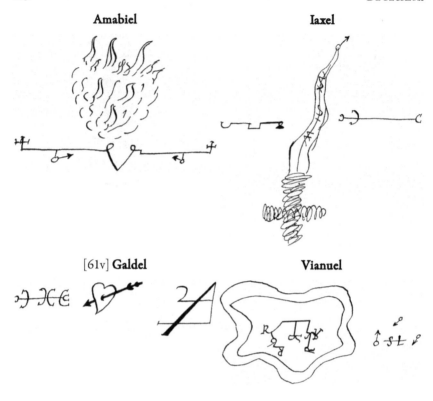

[61v] **Galdel**   **Vianuel**

Spiritus Mercurii.

Spiritus hi apparent, ut plurimum figura humana, tunc eos adesse sis securus, cum te horrore tremescere[1] persenseris.[2]

Mielis officium est aleatoribus adesse, ut uel perpetuo lucrentur, uel perdant. **Turmiel** omnes scientias, artesque nobis infundit. **Ruduel,** quęcunque dicuntur, et [62r] peraguntur in locis dissitis[3] reuelat. **Iarihael**[4] in speculo omnia quae fiunt in tua familia representat.

---

1   P: *fremescere.*
2   BNF: *senseris*; DN91: *...cum te horrore tremore.*
3   P: *remotis.*
4   DN91 has this name underscored, and an asterisk in the margin.

Amabiel   Iaxel

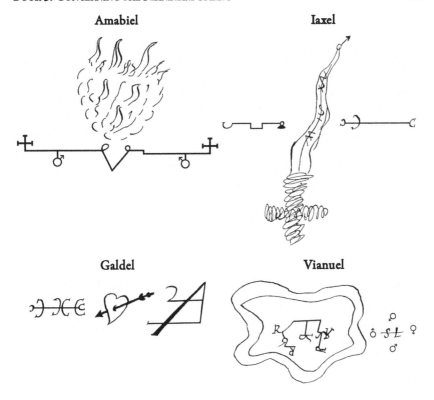

Galdel   Vianuel

Mercurial spirits.

These spirits appear for the most part in human form. You know them to be present when you strongly feel a shivering growling.[1]

Miel's office is to assist dice players, so that they constantly win or lose. **Turmiel** can infuse you with all arts and sciences. **Ruduel** can reveal anything that is said or done in remote places. **Iarihael** can show all things that are happening in your family.

---

1   Compare LIH CXXVI.10: The sign is that your hair will start to bristle when they are invoked. Compare also OP4 p. 24.

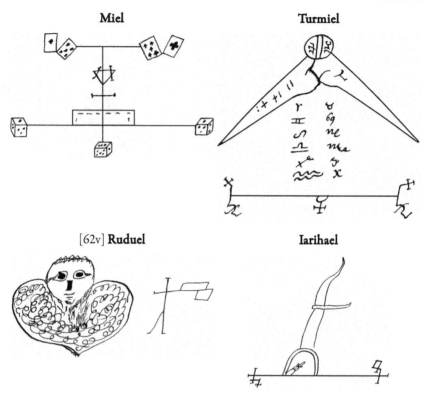

Miel

Turmiel

[62v] **Ruduel**

Iarihael

Spiritus Iouis.

Iouis spiritus sunt placidi, pulchri, aureoque colore micantes, adueniunt cum harmonico[1] quodam susurro.[2]

[63r] **Castiel** spiritus est ab omnibus, qui diuinatricibus artibus student inuocandus,[3] **Assasiel** inuocatur ad lites compescendas. **Gutriel** ad mulierum amorem conciliandum.

---

1 So too BNF; DN91: *armoniaco*; P: *harmoniaco*.
2 BNF: *susarro* (!).
3 DN91 omits this word.

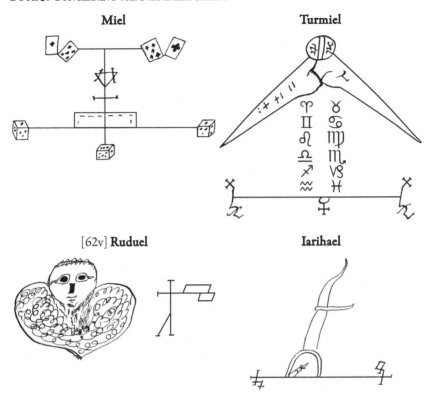

Miel · Turmiel · [62v] Ruduel · Iarihael

Spirits of Jupiter.

The spirits of Jupiter are gentle, pretty, and they arrive with a glittering golden colour, and arrive with a certain harmonious whispering sound.[1]

The spirit **Castiel** is invoked by all who desire the divinatory arts; **Assasiel** is invoked for blocking lawsuits; **Gutriel** can win over the love of women.[2]

---

1 Compare LIH CXXIV.5 and OP4 p. 20.
2 Note missing are Maganth and Salkariel, whose sigils are given with the others below.

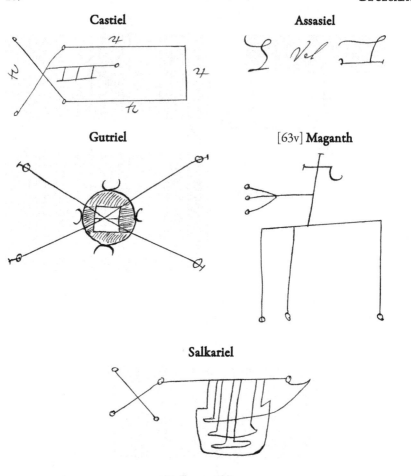

Castiel

Assasiel

Gutriel

[63v] Maganth

Salkariel

Spiritus Veneris.

Nulli formosiores Veneris, uisui iucundiores, cum inuocabis uidebis circa circulum[1] puellas ludentes, choreasque ducentes, uestibus albis indutas.

Guadoliel, et **Sagum** sunt illi, qui foeminas ad [64r] concubitum excitant. **Tamael** ad matrimonium[2] inuocatur. **Mustalfiel** ad puellam tuam uidendam, ac si presens esset. **Doromiel** te cuilibet puellę gratum reddet.

---

1 BNF *in circulo* (corrected frrom *in circulum*).
2 DN91, BNF: *matrimonia*.

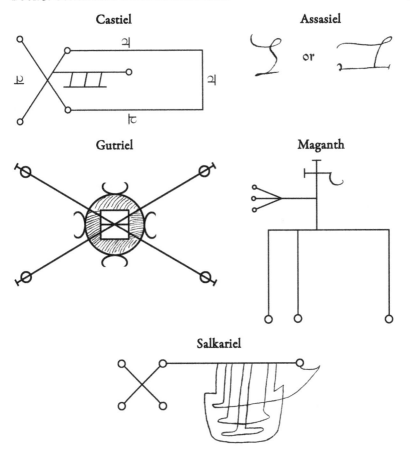

Castiel

Assasiel

Gutriel

Maganth

Salkariel

The Spirits of Venus.

No spirits are more beautiful than those of Venus, or more pleasant to the sight; when you invoke them you will see girls playing around the circle, and leading circle dances, wearing white garments.[1]

Guadoliel and **Sagum** are those which arouse women to amorous activity. **Tamael** should be invoked for purposes of marriage. **Mustalfiel** can let you see a young woman as clearly as if she is present.[2] **Doromiel** will restore the good graces of young women to anyone.

---

1 Compare LIH CXXV.6 and OP4 p. 23.

2 GG: ludendam ("playing"), which calls to mind the statement in the *Sworn Book of Honorius* that the sign that the spirits of Venus are present, is that "a girl will be seen playing outside the circle." Peterson 2016 p. 237.

Guadoliel

Sagum

Tamael

[64v] Mustalfiel

Doromiel

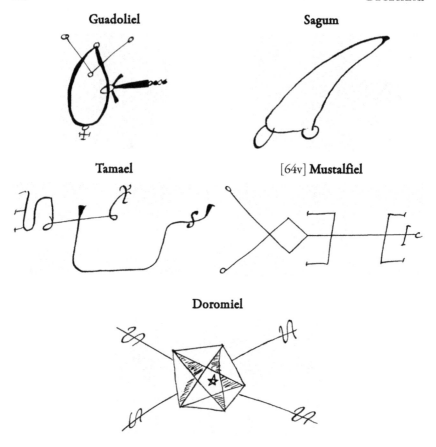

Spiritus Saturni.

Cani sunt Saturni spiritus, longaque barba uenerandi, baculoque inni-
tuntur, senes enim sunt omnes. Tunc aderunt cum te modico frigore horrere
persenseris.[1]

Vriel imploratur ad discordias seminandas. **Periel** quemcunque [+turpi
morte interimet. **Abumalith** quemcunque][2] subita morte occidit. **Assaibi**
membra quęuis mutilabit.

---

1 DN91, P: *senseris.* BNF: *horrore senseris.*
2 The words in [] are found in DN91, BNF, and GG.

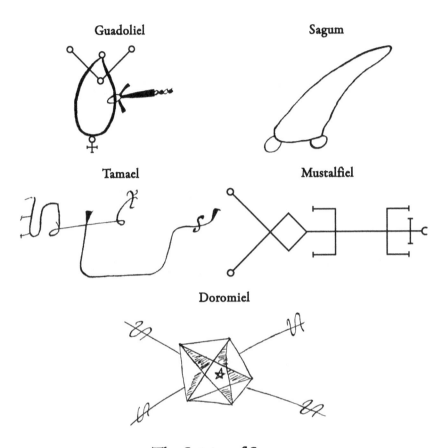

Guadoliel

Sagum

Tamael

Mustalfiel

Doromiel

The Spirits of Saturn.

The spirits of Saturn are gray-white, and have long venerable beards, and they lean on canes. They all appear as old men. When they are present, you will shiver, and feel moderate cold.[1]

Uriel will sow discord when requested.

Periel will do away with anyone, [+with an ugly death.

Abumalith kills whomever] with a sudden death.

Assaibi will maim the limbs of anyone that you wish.

---

1   Compare LIH CXXII.6 and OP4 p. 20. Note the offices of Sidrigol are omitted.

[65r] **Vriel**   **Abumalith**

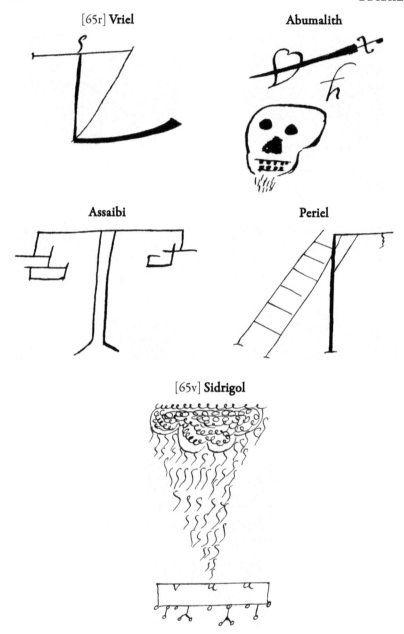

Assaibi   **Periel**

[65v] **Sidrigol**

Finis Characterismorum Magicorum.

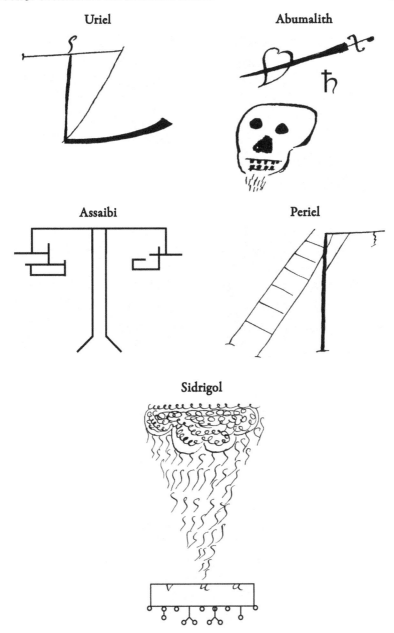

Uriel

Abumalith

Assaibi

Periel

Sidrigol

End of the magical characters or marks.

DE LAPIDE.

d omnes operationes Magicas opus est fide, et animo alacri[1] parato ad omnia peragenda, quoniam [66r] enim Magia est ars[2] rerum, quę sunt[3] pręternaturam, multa accidunt stupenda, quęque omnibus aliis pręterquam iis,[4] qui in arte initiati sunt timorem simul, et[5] stuporem excitare possent: ad firmandos itaque nostros[6] animos, fiduciamque augendam hoc lapide utimur nos, cuius pręparationem in sequentibus uidebis.

Ad lapidem autem 4[7] potissimum requirantur, Confectio[8], purgatio, consecratio, et Baptismus, hoc enim esto instar axiomatis, omnia, quę consecranda sunt prius purganda esse, insuper baptizatur lapis, id est nomen ei secundum cerimonias inferius expositas imponimus, ipsum autem nomen debet esse[9] spiritus Dominantis[10] in tali hora diei, in qua ipse lapis baptizatur.

De confectione lapidis.

Ad ipsius [66v] autem lapidis confectionem habeas calicem, uel cuppam ex stamno siue quouis alio metallo, et in eius[11] fundo tale effinge character.

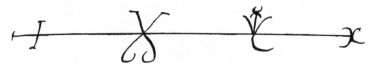

Mox cape argillam in pauca quantitate, et in fundo cuppę calicisue[12] reponito, deinde ipsam argillam sale cooperito, supra sal oleum, post oleum

---

1 P omits.
2 P omits.
3 P: *si.*
4 DN91 omits the last 2 words.
5 P adds *tremorem* ("of trembling"), but this word is not found in ASV, L, DN91, or BNF.
6 So L, DN91. BNF: *vestros*; P omits.
7 L: *tria* (!).
8 BNF adds: *scilicet.*
9 BNF, P add: *illud.*
10 DN91: *nominantis.*
11 BNF: *cujus.*
12 P: *calicitus.*

CONCERNING THE STONE.

or all magic operations there is need for faith, and for the soul to be prepared with zeal for everything which must be accomplished. Because indeed magic is the art of things which are preternatural, which causes many to be astonished, but is able to simultaneously awaken fear and astonishment in those who have been initiated into the Art. In order to strengthen our souls, therefore, and increase our faith, we use this stone, the preparation of which you will see in the following.

Therefore, chiefly four things are required for the stone: The preparation, purification, consecration, and baptism, indeed this is the counterpart of the axiom: all things which are to be consecrated, are to be purified beforehand, and additionally the stone is to be baptised, that is, its name declared following the ceremonies we are setting down. Moreover, it must be the name of the spirit which is dominant in the hour of the day in which the stone itself is baptized.

Concerning the preparation of the stone.

And so, for preparing the stone itself, you should have a cup or chalice made of tin, or any other metal, and on its base fashion this character:

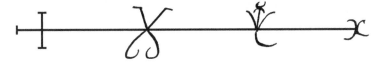

Next, take a small amount of clay, and put it in the bottom of the chalice or cup, then cover the clay itself with salt, pour oil over the salt, and wine

174

uinum infundito;[1] prius autem quam ultra progrediamur notandum est,
quod in nostro lapide quattuor elementa repręsentantur; per argillam intellige terram; per sal mare, per oleum aerem, perque uinum ignem: sic noster
lapis uere Microcosmus dici poterit,[2] representatio quippe erit magni mundi.
Terra, quę ex natura sua arridissima est, infertilis protinus, et hominum habi-
tationi inepta fuisset, nisi extremam eius siccitatem [67r] contemperasset
maris consortium, quod salso suo humore[3] per insensibiles porros se insin-
uans illam ad omnes rerum generationes secundum uarias Cęli[4] dispositiones,
et superiorum ordinum influentias aptam efficiat:[5] per oleum aer reprę-
sentatur, quippe oleum est aereę naturę, per uinum ignis, quod igneum est.

Iam confectionem persequamur. hęc quattuor in calice[6] congesta
permiscebis, et in pastam reduces, postea calicem super altare ponito, et
super[7] calicem hęc uerba proferto. fiat homo. mox pastam manibus accipies,
et ex ea hominem melius quam fieri poterit efformabis, et igne desiccabis,[8] et
hęc erit lapidis nostri magici confectio.

De purgatione lapidis.

Lapis autem purgatur orationibus, et ieiuniis, orationes sunt pręcipua
purgationis omnis instrumenta:[9] sine ieiuniis autem nihil operantur,[10] [67v]
quippe animum disponunt ieiunia ad melius orandum. gula enim est mater
omnium malarum cogitationum, et a bonis studiis animum aufert.

Ieiunus ergo orationi te accinges, tuoque potissimum genio te uouebis,
inde altari flexis genibus te apropinquans lapidem tuum iam desiccatum[11]
manu sinistra tenens pectus ter [+dextra][12] concuties dicens.[13]

---

1   BNF skips ahead to *haec quatuor in calice congesta....*
2   P: *potest.*
3   So also DN91; L: *sale suo humore*; P: *salso humore.*
4   L: *sui.*
5   P: *efficit*; DN91: *efficies*; L: *efficiet.*
6   P: *calicem.*
7   P: *supra.*
8   P: *descicabis* (!).
9   BNF: *instituta.*
10 So too L, BNF; DN91: *nihil* operatur; P: *nil operamur.*
11 P: *descicatum* (!).
12 So L, DN91, BNF, P.
13 DN91: *dextra ter concutiens dicens*; P: *ter dextra concutiens dices*; L: ter dextra
    concutiens dicens.

over the oil. But before we can continue, it should be noted that there are four elements which are represented in our stone. By the clay you recognize the earth; by salt, the sea; by the oil, the air; by the wine, the fire; thus our stone can truly be called the microcosm – a manifest representation of the great Universe. The earth, by its nature is very dry, constantly infertile, and unfit for human habitation, unless its extreme dryness is moderated by a partnership with the sea; because with its salty humor penetrating through imperceptible pores, for all generations of things, according to the various arrangements of the heavens, it can produce the appropriate influences of the superior orders. The air is represented by oil, because oil has an airy nature; fire by wine, because it is fiery.

Now we can proceed with the composition. Mix these four together in the chalice, and reduce them to a paste. Afterwards, put the cup on the altar, and over the chalice recite these words: "Let there be man." Next take the paste in your hands, and from it form a man, as accurately shaped as possible, and dry it with a fire, and this will be the completion of our magic stone.

Concerning the purification of the stone.

Moreover, the stone is to be purified with prayers and fasting, the prayers are particularly for purifying all instruments, however, we cannot work without fasting, since fasting prepares the soul for better praying. For indeed gluttony is the mother of all bad thoughts, and from good practice it is removed from the soul.

Fasting therefore will prepare you for prayer, and chiefly you should vow to your guardian spirit. Then kneel before an altar, holding the stone, now dried, in your left hand. Beat your chest three times with your [+right] hand, saying:

Abhamali nexor helain abriel,[1]

Deinde talem proferes[2] orationem.

> God Voose name Is terrible to all the Vvorlde teake array all the
> corruption of this stone and meake to exercice all the
> supernaturall Wortks stat one secret science theachos us todoer
> that no euill phantosmos thoued [*should] enter Intoit by
> ouelourd Iesus Christ.[3]

His dictis asperges tuum lapidem [+aqua benedicta],[4] deinde[5] insculpes
tale character in bracchio sinistro.

[68r]   ## De consecratione lapidis.

Lapide benedicto ad consecrationem te accinges;[6] habe ergo gallum
gallinaceum, et cultro per cor transfixo occides, et eius sanguine lapidem
asperges, mox aqua benedicta ipsum optime lauabis dicens[7]

Ancor anacor hedroin blemith hemaleir.[8]

Hęc autem fieri debent cum cęrimoniis requisitis in talibus operibus, id
est uestibus, stola, bacculo ornatus esse debes, hęc autem omnia fusius in
sequentibus explicabuntur.

---

1   DN91, BNF, L: Abhamali nexor helahim abriel; P: Athumali nexor helatim abriel. BNF
     skip from here to *his dictis asperges....*
2   So also DN91, L; P: *proferas.*
3   L has only the first several words: God vuose name is; P: Gad Vuosse name is terrible to
     allthe Vuorlde teake avvay allthe corruption of this stone and meake to exercice allthe
     supernaturall Vuolks thac one scret science theates ue (?) todoc thac no euill phantosmes
     should enter intoit byour Lard Iesus christ. P2: Gad-Vuosse-Name Is terribile-to althe-
     Vuerdle-Teake-arraj athe Corruptionem Ofihistone-andmeake-To exercice-Althe-Super
     Natural Vuolks. Thaoseret-Sciena Theates-Vętodve-Thacno-Evill-Phantames-Should-
     Enter-Into it-Byour-Lard-Jesus-Christus.
4   BNF, P, and DN91 add. L omit the sentence entirely.
5   Instead of *deinde,* P and DN91 read *et in ipso.*
6   P: *accinge.*
7   L omits the rest of this chapter.
8   P: *œnter anacor hedroin blemith hemalico*; DN91: *ancor, anacor, hedroin, blemith,
     hemalico*; BNF: ancoo anacor hedroin cleinth hemaleir; L omits.

Abhamali nexor helain abriel.

Then you should offer a prayer thus:

> God woose name is terrible to all the worlde teake away all the
> corruption of this stone and meake to exercice all the
> supernaturall works that one secret science teaches us to doe
> that no euill phantosmes should enter intoit by our Lord Jesus
> Christ.[1]

Having said this, sprinkle your stone [+with consecrated water], and
engrave this character on the left arm:

Concerning the consecration of the stone.

With the stone blessed you should prepare for the consecration. You
should have a rooster, and kill it by piercing its heart with the knife, and
sprinkle the stone with its blood, then wash it thoroughly with holy water,
saying:

Ancor anacor hedroin blemith hemaleir.

However, these things must be done with the proper ceremonies, and
equipped with the requisites for such operations, such as the garments, stole,
and wand, which will be set forth in more detail in the following.

---

1   I.e. God whose name is terrible to all the world, take away all this corruption of this stone,
    and make to exercise all the supernatural works that one secret science teaches us to do,
    that no evil phantasms should enter into it, by our Lord Jesus Christ. Note the unusual use
    of English for *voces magicae* (magic words of power).

Baptismus lapidis.

Nomen lapidis ad libitum accipies, modo terminetur in **el**, et non incipiat per aleph. nomen insculpe fronti lapidis, cultro deinde magico tale character ei insculpes in bracchio dextro.

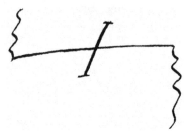

[68v] Postea tuum lapidem sinistra accipies,[1] dextra infundes aquam benedictam super ipsius caput, et tandem dices **Abacadrin, Sumerrath, Rechin,**[2] et sic baptizatus erit tuus lapis.[3]

Praxis, et ordo consecrationis, et primo de Pentaculis.

Pentaculum est signum quoddam sacrum a malis euentibus[4] nos prę̨seruans, et ad malorum dę̨moniorum constrictionem et exterminationem, per ipsa boni spiritus nobis conciliantur, et pelliciuntur.[5]

Constant[6] autem ipsa pentacula characteribus, et nominibus bonorum spirituum superioris ordinis, uel ex[7] sacris picturis sacrarum litterarum, seu[8] reuelationum uersiculis adaptis, uel ex geometricis figuris, sacrisque Dei nominibus secundum multorum rationem inuicem compositis, uel ex omnibus iis, aut eorum pluribus in unum compositis.[9] Characteres autem, qui

---

1   P, DN91: *accipiens*. L abbreviates this paragraph.
2   P: *Abacadrim, Sumerach, rechin*. DN91: *Abacadrin, Sumerach nechin*. BNF: <u>Abacadrin</u> <u>fumerrach</u> rechin.
3   BNF concludes with *Finis praxis consecrandi totiusque claviculae*, and appends a French translation of OP4, also written in a different handwriting.
4   P: *accidentibus*.
5   DN91: *pellicientur*; P: *polliciuntur*.
6   So OP4 and DN91, and needed for noun agreement. P: Constat.
7   So also OP4 and DN91. P omits.
8   So OP4, and DN91; P: *uel*.
9   P omits *uel ex omnibus .. compositis*.

The baptism of the stone.

Choose a name for the stone as you please, except it should end with "-el",
and it should not start with an *aleph*. Carve the name on the face of the
stone with the knife, then carve this magical character on its right arm:

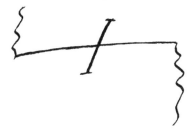

Afterwards take your stone with the left hand, pour the holy water over
its head/top with your right hand, and finally you should say: "**Abacadrin,
Sumerrath, Rechin**." And thus your stone will have been baptized.[1]

The practice and procedure of consecration, and first concerning the Pentacle.[2]

A pentacle is a certain sacred sign preserving us from evil things
happening, and for constraining evil demons and destruction. Through them
the good spirits may be drawn to us and won over.

Moreover, the pentacles themselves depend on the characters, and the
names of the good spirits of the superior order, or on sacred depictions, or
sacred letters, or from Revelations, with verses you can adapt, or from
geometric shapes and sacred names of God, or following the methods of
many combined together. Moreover, the characters, which are useful for us

---

1   L ends at this point.
2   This section is adapted from Agrippa von Nettesheim (pseudo-), 1559, pp. 25 ff. I will
     abbreviate this OP4.

ad pentacula nobis constituenda utiles sunt,[1] ipsi [69r], sunt characteres
bonorum dęmonum primi, et secundi ordinis, et nonnunquam tertii, et ex
ipso characterum genere, quod potentissimum appellatur sacrum: quocunque
igitur huiusmodi charactere instituto circunducemus illum[2] dupplici circulo,
inquo circunscribemus nomen sui angeli, et si uolumus ei addere no men
aliquod diuinum sibi congruum maioris erit efficacię, et si secundum
numerorum[3] rationem circumducere uolumus ei angularem aliquam figuram,
id fieri quoque licebit. Sacrę autem picturę, quę pentacula constituunt, ipsę
sunt, quę passim in sacris litteris, et prophętis tam ueteris, quam noui
testamenti traduntur, utpote figura serpentis in cruce suspensi, et consimiles,[4]
quarum[5] multa copia ex prophętarum <uersiculis, et>[6] uisionibus, ut Isaię,
Danielis, et aliorum, tum ex reuelatione apocalypsis inueniuntur, ut nos de
illis loquuti[7] sumus in alio libro.

[69v] Posita itaque aliqua sacrorum librorum imagine[8] circundetur
dupplici circulo, cui inscribatur nomen aliquod diuinum ipsi figurę
effectuique aptatum,[9] et conforme, uel circunscribatur ei uersiculus ex parte
corporis sacrę[10] scripturę sumptus, qui desideratum effectum polliceatur, uel
deprecetur, ut puta si fiat pentaculum ad uictoriam, et uindictam contra
inimicos tam uisibiles quam inuisibiles, figura sumi potest ex secundo libro
Mars [*Machabeorum].[11] Videlicet Manus tenens aureum ensem euaginatum,
cui circunscribatur uersiculus ibidem contentus, scilicet "accipe, gladium
sanctum a Deo inquo occides aduersarios populi mei Israel," uel et
circunscribatur ei uersiculus psalmi 3[i]. In spe fortitudo brachii tui ante faciem
tuam,[12] uel aliquis alius consimilis uersiculus.

---

1   So OP4, DN91. P: *scilicet* (!).
2   So OP4, DN91. P: *illud.*
3   So OP4, DN91. P: *numero rerum.*
4   So OP4, DN91. P: *consimilia.*
5   So OP4, DN91. P: *quorum.*
6   OP4, DN91, and P all read *ex Prophetarum visionibus.*
7   OP4, DN91, P: *locuti.*
8   So too DN91; OP4: *Posita itaque aliqua huiusmodi sacrarum imaginum pictura.* P:
    Posita itaque sacrorum librorum imagine.
9   So OP4; DN91: *effectuique optatum;* P: *effectui optatum.*
10 So OP4, DN91; P omits.
11 (!) OP4, P, and DN91 all read *Machabeorum.*
12 So too DN91; OP4: *psalmi quinti (!): In hoc fortitudo brachii tui, ante faciem tuam, ibi*
    Mors. This verse is not from Psalm 5 (or 3). A similar phrase, *cornua in manibus eius: ibi*
    absconda est fortitudo eius. Ante faciem eius ibit mors ("horns are in his hands; there is

making the pentacles, are themselves characters of the good daemons[1] of the first and second orders, and sometimes the third, and of the characters of this type, the most powerful are said to be sacred. Then, whatever character of this kind that is being prepared, we should draw around it a double circle, wherein we must circumscribe the name of their angels. And if we wish to add to it a divine name that is harmonious, it will be the more effective. And if we wish we can draw around it some angular shape, following the reckoning of its numbers, that likewise will be of value. But the sacred depictions which make the pentacles themselves, are handed down to us everywhere in the sacred literature and prophecies, both in the Old and New Testaments, such as with the figure of a serpent suspended on a cross, and similar things which can be found in great abundance in the visions of the prophets, as of Isaiah, of Daniel, and of others, moreover they can be discovered in the revelation of the Apocalypse, as we have mentioned in another book.[2]

Therefore when any sacred images are depicted in this way, it should be surrounded with a double circle, between which some divine name should be written, that is chosen and adapted to the effect and the figure itself. Or a verse may be circumscribed there from some part of holy scripture, which may promise or plead for the desired result. For example, if the pentacle is for victory and vengeance against enemies, whether visible or invisible, a figure may be taken from the Second book of *Maccabees, namely, a hand holding a golden sword, unsheathed, and a verse may be written around that from the same, namely, "take this holy sword from God, wherewith you shall overthrow the enemies of my people Israel,"[3] or you may write around it a verse from the third Psalm: "in hope, the strength of your arm, before your face," or some similar verse.

---

his strength hidden. Death shall go before his face") occurs in Hab. 3:4-5. P: *psal. 32 (!)*. *in spe fortitudo brachii tui ante faciem tuam.*

1 OP4: bonorum spirituum ("of the good spirits"), i.e. the Angels, Archangels, and Principalities.

2 OP4 is specifically referencing *de occulta phil. Lib. III* (OP3.62 to be precise).

3 2Mac15.16.

Si uero nomen diuinum ei circunscribere libuerit, accipiatur nomen aliquod timorem, iram, uindictam Dei, uel aliquod simile nomen desiderato effectui congruum, et si figuram angularem circunscribere [70r] libuerit, accipiatur secundum numerorum rationem, numerus Martialis, uel saturninus, tales sunt congruentes desiderato effectui, et talia pentacula sunt maximę potentię, et sublimis uirtutis, et ad consecrationem spirituum necessaria, ex iis[1] unum est quod habetur Apocalip. Cap. 1° scilicet figura Maiestatis Dei sedentis in trono habentis in ore gladium, cui circumscribitur. Ego sum **alpha, et omega,** principium, et finis, qui est, qui erat, et qui uenturus est, omnipotens ego sum primus, et nouissimus uiuus, et fui mortuus, et ecce[2] sum uiuens in caecula caeculorum, et habe claues mortis et inferni." deinde circunscribantur hi tres uersiculi. "Manda Deus uirtuti tuę", "Confirma hoc Deus quod operatus[3] est [*es] in nobis",[4] "fiant tanquam puluis a facie uenti, et Angelus Domini coarctans eos, fiant uiae illorum tenebrae, et lubricum, et Angelus Domini persequens uos",[5] pręterea circunscribantur hęc nomina, quę sunt **El, Elohin, elooe, Zebooth, Elion, Elcheresis, Adonay Ial Tetragrammaton Saday.**[6]

[70v] Alterum pentaculum, cuius figura similis est agno occiso cui cornua, et oculi 7. et sub pedibus liber 7 sigillis obsignatus sicut habetur Apocalypis quinto capite, cui circunscribatur uersiculus iste. "Ecce uicit leo de Tribu Iuda radix Dauid, aperiam librum, et soluam 7 signacula eius;" Et alter uersiculus, "Vidi Satanam sicut fulgur de coelo cadentem, ecce dedi uobis potestatem calcandi super serpentes, et scorpiones, et super omnem uirtutem Inimici, et nihil uobis nocebit," et circunscribantur ei 10[7] generalia, ut supra.

---

1   So too OP4; P: *his.* DN91: *...ad consecrationem spirituum nostram est Iis unum....*
2   P omits.
3   So Ps. 67, OP4, DN91. P: *operaturus.*
4   Compare Ps. 67:29 (KJV 68): Manda Deus virtutem tuam confirma Deus hoc quod operatus es nobis.
5   Ps. 34:5. Curiously, ASV and DN91 change the original wording *persequens eos* ("pursue them") to *persequens uos* ("pursue you"), while OP4 and P preserve the original third person of the Psalm.
6   OP4: El, Elohim, Elohe, Zebaoth, Elion, Escerchie, Adonay, Iah, Tetragrammaton, Saday. Here DN91 is closest: el, eloym eloe Zebooth, elion, escheresis Adonai, Ial Tetragrammaton, Sadai. P: El, Elohin, Zebooth, Elion, Elchenesis, Adonay, Ial, Tetragrammaton, Saday.
7   So OP4; ASV: *ei* nomina; P: *ei conomina.* (!)

But if you wish to circumscribe some divine name around such a figure, then some name may be taken signifying the fear of God, the wrath, or the vengeance of God, or some similar name consistent with the desired effect, and if an angular shape is used, it may be chosen according to the reckoning of the numbers, the number of Mars, or of Saturn,[1] such that they agree with the desired effect. And such pentacles have great power and sublime virtue, and are necessary for the consecration of (when dealing with) the spirits. Of these, one is that which is found in the first chapter of the Apocalypse, namely the figure of the greatness of God sitting on a throne, having a sword in his mouth, designated the **Alpha and the Omega**. "I am the First and the Last, who is, was, and shall be, I am almighty, First and Newest, alive and was dead, and behold, I am living forever and ever, and have the keys of death and of hell."[2] Then write these three verses around the edge: "Command, O God, your strength; confirm, O God, what you have wrought in us."[3] "Let them be like dust in the wind, and let the angel of the Lord hem them in; Let their paths become dark and slippery, and may the angel of the Lord pursue them."[4] In addition, these names should be circumscribed: **El, Elohin, Zebooth, Elion, Elchenesis, Adonay, Ial, Tetragrammaton, Saday.**

Another pentacle, of similar shape is with a lamb killed, which has seven horns and seven eyes, and under its feet a book sealed with seven seals, as described in Rev. 5, which has this verse written around the edge: "behold the lion from the tribe of Judah, the root of David, has conquered; I will open the book and break its seven seals;"[5] and another verse: "I have seen Satan falling from the sky like lightning, behold I have given to you the power to tread upon serpents and scorpions, and over all the power of the enemy, and nothing shall harm you,"[6] and circumscribe those ten general as above.

---

1   OP2.20 associates eight with Saturn, and nine with Mars.
2   Rev. 1:17-18.
3   Ps. 68:29.
4   Ps. 35:5-6.
5   Rev. 5:5.
6   Luke 10:18-19.

Quę uero pentacula constituuntur ex figuris, et nominibus hunc ordinem obseruant, nam posita aliqua figura conformi alicui numero ad aliquem certum effectum inscribatur ei in singulis angulis nomen aliquod diuinum desideratę rei uim obtinens, ita tamen quod nomen totidem litteris constet, quot unitatibus numerus constat. Tale uero nomen intensum [*inuentum][1] unum, uel plura, uel diuersa in singulis [71r] angulis figurę inscribatur, in medio uero figurę ipsius nominis reuolutio tota, uel saltem principalis collocetur.

Sępe etiam pentaculum constituimus facta reuolutione aliqua alicuius nominis in tabella quadrata circulo simplici circunducto, uel dupplici inscribendo uersiculum aliquem sacrum nomini huic congruentem,[2] uel ex quo hoc nomen extractum sit, et hęc est ratio[3] pentaculorum, quę ad libitum ad maiorem efficaciam, et uirtutem intentiorem[4] possumus sese [*et se] inuicem,[5] tum aliis multiplicare, et commiscere:

Ut si fiat deprecatio pro destructione inimicorum recordemur quomodo Deus destruxerit faciem terrę in diluuio aquarum uniuersali Sodomam, et Gomorrham per pluuiam sulphuris, et ignis, exercitum Pharaonis in mari rubro, et [+deprecando contra pericula][6] meminerimus, Christum[7] siccis pedibus[8] ambulare super aquas, uel eundem seruisse [*seruasse][9] nauiculam periclitantem, uentisque et fluctibus imperasse, et Petrum Mergentem eduxisse[10] ex aquis, et sic de similibus.

Denique cum iis [71v] inuocamus sacra quędam nomina Dei, ea uidelicet quę desiderii nostri sunt significatiua, et ad effectum operandum

---

1   OP4: *inuentum.*
2   So too DN91, but OP4: *competentem*; P: *congruum.*
3   So OP4; P and DN91 read *reuolutio.*
4   So too DN91, but OP4: *intentionem*; P: *intensionem.*
5   OP4, DN91: *in se inuicem*; P: *et in sese inuicem.*
6   The manuscripts skip some text from OP4, but this at least is implied by context.
7   OP4: *exercitum Pharaonis, in Mari rubro: {& si quae alia maledictio in sacris literis reperitur, et sic de similibus. Ita deprecando contra pericula Aquarum, recordemur salutis Noe, in Diluuio: Transitus filiorum Israel, in mari rubro:}* & *meminerimus Christum, siccis pedibus.* At some point a common ancestor of all these manuscripts dropped a line or 2 from OP4, due to homeoteleuton.
8   P: *Exercitum Pharaonis siccis pedibus.*
9   So OP4, which clearly makes more sense. DN91: *eumdem seruisse*; P: *eandem si uis.*
10 So also OP4, P; DN91: *aduxisse.*

But those pentacles which are thus constructed with figures and names, should follow this arrangement, with any number conforming with it, for any specific effect, some divine name should be written in each angle, containing the power of the thing that is desired, in such a way that the number of letters in the name should agree with the number of units it contains.

With such a name or names being discovered, it should be written in the various angles of the figure. But in the middle of the figure itself, there should be arranged the whole revolution of the name, or at least the main part.

Often too we construct a pentacle made with the revolution of some name in a square table, with a single or double circle drawn around it, inscribed with some sacred verse consistent with this name, or from which that name has been extracted, and this is the method of making pentacles which we can in turn multiply and combine as desired, for greater effectiveness and intensity of power.

If for instance the supplication is for the destruction of enemies, we may commemorate how God demolished the face of the earth in the Great Flood, or how he destroyed Sodom and Gomorrah with a rain of fire and brimstone, or the army of Pharaoh in the Red Sea. And [+for protection from dangers],[1] we may commemorate how Christ walked upon the waters with dry feet, or in the same incident protected the ship in danger, by commanding the winds and the waves, and how he pulled Peter out of the water when he was drowning, and so on.

Finally, with these we call upon certain sacred certain names of God, namely, those which have significance with what we desire, and which

---

1   The text skips some of the text found in OP4.

accommodata, ut ad destructionem inimicorum inuocamus nomina irę, uindictę, iustitię, et fortitudinis Dei: ad euitandum uero aliquod malum, uel periculum inuocamus nomina misericordię, defensionis, salutis, fortitudinis, bonitatis, et similia Dei nomina:

Quandoque etiam Deum precamur largiri ad id, quod desideramus executorem aliquem spiritum bonus unum, uel plures, quorum id quod desideramus officium est, illius nomen interserentes;[1] sępe etiam malum spiritum aliquem ad homines cogendos obtestamur, cuius nomen scilicet [*similiter][2] inserimus, et hoc iuste si ad malum tendit operatio, ut ad uindictam, uel destructionem.

Pręterea si quis uersiculus in psalmis, uel aliqua parte sacratum litterarum desiderio nostro congruens habetur, illum orationibus inserimus: facta autem oratione ad Deum quandoque post ipsam conuenit facere orationem ad exe-cutorum illum, quem nobis ministraturum optauimus in oratione pręcedenti, siue unus sit, [72r] siue plures, siue angelus siue stella, siue influentia.

[+De consecratione.]

Iam conuenit ut tractemus de consecratione, quę fit per instrumenta huic arti necessaria, et huius uirtus duobus potissimum perficitur, scilicet uirtute ipsius personę consecrantis, et uirtute ipsius orationis, per quam fit consecratio. Nam in persona requiruntur [*requiritur] uitę sanctimonia, et sanctificandi potestas, quę[3] utraque per dignificationem, et initiationem aquiruntur; deinde quod ipsa persona habeat [*hanc][4] uirtutem, et potestatem firma et indubia fide in se ipsa cognoscat. Ex parte autem ipsius orationis, per quam fit consecratio desideratur quoque consimilis sanctimonia, quę per se inest ipsi orationi, ut si sit diuinitus ad hoc ordinata, quales habemus in plerisque sacris bibliorum eloquiis, uel quod sit uirtute spiritus sancti ex ordinatione Ecclesię ad hoc instituta, aut inest sanctimonia orationi non per se, sed per commemorationem rerum sacrarum, ut puta sacrarum litterarum [72v] hystoriarum, operum, miraculorum, effectum,

---

1   So also OP4; P, DN91: *intercedentes*.
2   DN91 also reads *scilicet*, but OP4, P: *similiter*.
3   So also OP4; P, DN91: *qua*.
4   OP4, DN91, and P all read *hanc*.

adapted to the desired effect, such as, for the destruction of enemies, we invoke names of wrath, vengeance, justice, and of the strength of God. For avoiding some evil or danger, we invoke names of mercy, defense, health, strength, goodness, and similar names of God.

And when we plead with God to grant us what we desire, the executor should interject the name of one or more good spirits, whose office corresponds with that which we desire. And sometimes we even conjure some evil spirit in order to compel persons, similarly we interject that spirit's name; and this justly, if the operation strives for something bad, such as vengeance or destruction.

Moreover, if there is some verse in the Psalms, or any part of holy scripture, that is suited to our desire, we can insert that into our prayers. And having completed our prayers to God, when appropriate, we should add a speech to that one who carries out or administers what we have requested in the preceding prayer, whether it is one or more, or whether it is an angel, or a star, or an influence.[1]

[+Concerning the consecrations.]

Now it is appropriate to speak about consecrations which are necessary for the instruments of this Art, and the virtue of this is achieved chiefly by two things, namely, by the virtue of the person doing the consecrating, and by the virtue of the prayer through which the consecration occurs. For in the person, the sanctity of life is required, and the power of sanctifying, each of which are acquired through dignification and initiation. Then that person must recognize this virtue and power, with firm and undoubting faith in himself. Then there is the part from the prayer itself, through which the desired consecration is made; it requires a similar sanctification, which either belongs to the prayer itself, for instance if it had been divinely arranged for this purpose, we can find many such instances spoken of in the holy Bible; or it may be instituted for this purpose, through the power of the Holy Spirit, according to the ordination of the Church, or the sanctity doesn't belong to the prayer itself, but through the commemoration of holy things, such as the commemoration of sacred literature, histories, works, miracles, achievements,

---

1   OP4 includes a paragraph on bonds at this point, which the present text omits.

gratiarum, promissionum,[1] sacramentorum, rerumque sacramentalium, et consimilium quę rei consecrandę proprie uel improprie per similitudinem aliquam attinere uidebuntur.

Adhibita etiam sacrorum,[2] diuinorumque nominum impositione[3] cum sacrorum[4] signaculorum consignatione, et eiusdem [*huiusmodi][5] similibus, quę ad sanctificationem, et expiationem conferunt, ut sunt aquę benedictę inspersiones, sacri olei inunctiones, odoriferę suffumigationes ad cultum religiosum adhibitę, atque inde est quod in omni consecratione pręcedunt benedictiones, et consecrationes aquę, olei, ignis, et suffumigiorum, adhibitis undique cereis uel lampadibus benedictis lucentibus, nam sine lumine nullum sacramentum rite perficitur; illud est sciendum, et firmiter obseruandum quod si res consecranda sit ex rebus profanioribus, in quam[6] potuit incidisse aliqua coinquinatio, tunc earum rerum excoriatio,[7] et expiatio pręcedere debet consecrationem. [73r] Res enim uirgines, et purę aptiores sunt ad recipiendos influxus diuinos;

obseruandum etiam est quod in fine cuiuslibet consecrationis post orationem debite prolatam, debet ipse consecrans per uerba de pręsenti in uirtute, et potestate diuina rem ipsam consecrandam inhalando benedicere cum commemoratione uirtutis, atque autoritatis suę, prout illud magis rite, lubentique[8] animo id fieri poterit.

Horum nunc tibi exempla quędam ponemus, per quę facile tibi patebit uis ad totam hanc considerationem; sic in consecratione aquę commemoramus[9] quomodo Deus locauerit firmamentum in medio aquarum, quomodo in Paradiso terrestri locauit fontem aquarum, ex quo per quattuor flumina sacra rigatur uniuersus orbis terrarum. Item quod fecit aquas iustitię suę

1 P: *promissionem.*
2 DN91: *fauorum.*
3 OP4: *inuocatione.*
4 P accidentally omits the line *diuinorumque nominum impositione cum sacrorum,* through homeoteleuton.
5 OP4, DN91, P: *huiusmodi.*
6 So too P, but OP4: *in quas.* DN91: *in qua.*
7 OP4: *exorcizatio.*
8 OP4: *intentoque.* DN91: *libentique.*
9 So OP4, DN91; P: *commemorans.*

grace, promises, of sacraments, and of sacramental things, and of similar things, which things, through some similarity, will be considered to properly or improperly belong to the thing consecrated.

Also the application of sacred and divine names, are sometimes employed, with sacred seals affixed, and similar things, which unite sanctification and atonement, such as the sprinkling of holy water, the applications of consecrated oil, and the use of fragrant suffumigations used in religious worship, and so blessings precede all consecrations, and the consecrations of water, oil, fire, and suffumigations, and consecrated wax candles or lamps should be shining on every side, for without light no sacrament can be duly completed. This must be known and firmly observed, that if a profane thing must be consecrated, which has somehow gotten polluted, then a flaying [*exorcising][1] and atonement must precede the consecration. But things that are virgin and pure are more suitable for receiving the divine influx.

It should also be observed, that in the end of any consecration, after the prayer has been duly offered, the one doing the consecrating, using the present words, with virtue and divine power, must bless the thing that is to be consecrated, by breathing on it, while mentioning his power and authority: as it may be more practicable with a solemn and willing (or intent) mind.

Of these now we will give you some examples, by which you may easily know the whole purpose of this. Thus in the consecration of the water we should commemorate how God placed the water in the midst of the firmament, how he placed a spring in the earthly Paradise, from which sprang four sacred rivers, moistening the whole earth. Likewise that he made the

---

1   So OP4, but perhaps the sentence was intentionally reworked to suggest that self-flagellation is needed to effect the purification.

instrumentum[1] in destructione [73v] gigantum[2] per diluuium generale super omnem terram, et in destructione exercitus Pharaonis in mari rubro. Item quod[3] eduxit Populum suum siccis pedibus per medium maris, et per medium Iordani, & quomodo miraculose eduxit aquam de petra in deserto, et eduxit fontem aquę uiuę a dente molari maxillę asininę ad pręces Sansonis, et inuocanda insuper sunt diuina nomina ad hoc conformia, Vt puta quod Deus sit fons uiuus, aqua uiua, flumen misericordię.

Sic in consecratione ignis commemoramus quomodo Deus creauit ignem iustitię suę instrumentum in peccatorum uindictam, et expiationem. Item quomodo iudicium pręcedere debet uniuersa mundi conflagratio.[4] Item quomodo Deus apparuit Moisi in rubo[5] ignis ardentis, Item quomodo pręcessit filiis Israel in columna ignis, et quomodo nil offerri, neque sacrificari sine igne potest etcetera.

[74r] Inuocabuntur etiam nomina Dei ad hoc conformia sicut legitur in lege, et prophetis, quia Deus ignis consumens est, et si quod nomen in diuinis nominibus ignem sonans, aut nomina consimilia, ut splendor Dei, lux Dei, lumen mundi.

Iam ueniamus ad consecrationes locorum, instrumentorum, et similium.

Consecraturus igitur locum aliquem siue circulum transumere poteris orationem Salomonis in dedicatione templi: pręterea benedices locum cum aspersione aquę benedictę, et suffumigatione commemorando in suffumigatione mysteria qualia sunt sanctificatio Throni Dei, Montis Sinay, Tabernaculi foederis, Sancti Sanctorum Templi Ierusalem etcetera.

Inuocabis nomina Dei ad hoc conformia, ut locus Dei, Thronus Dei, Cathedra Dei, Tabernaculum Dei, ara Dei, habitaculum Dei, et huiusmodi [74v] diuina nomina, quę circulo, uel loco scribenda occurrunt.

1　So also OP4, DN91; P: *instrumenta.*
2　So also OP4, DN91; P: *gigantium.*
3　So also DN91, but OP4: *quomodo*; P: *quot.*
4　So also DN91. OP4: *item, quomodo iudicaturus mundum, ignis conflagrationem praecedere iubebit.* P: *item quomodo Iudicium praecedere debet uniuersa conflagratione.*
5　*Rubo* ("bush"): so too OP4, but P, DN91 misread *rubro* ("red"). See Exod. 3:2: *apparuitque ei Dominus in flamma ignis de medio rubi.*

waters tools of his justice in the destruction of the giants through the great Deluge over all land,[1] and in the destruction of the army of Pharaoh in the Red Sea, likewise how he led his people through the middle of that sea with dry feet, and through the middle of the Jordan, and how he miraculously caused water to issue forth from a rock in the desert, and he caused a stream of running water to issue forth from a great tooth in the jaw of the ass at the praying of Samson,[2] and moreover, the divine names are to be similarly invoked, as for example that God is the fountain of life, the water of life, the river of mercy.

Thus in the consecration of the fire we recall how God created fire as the instrument of his justice in the punishment and atonement of sins, likewise how a universal conflagration must precede the Day of Judgment. Likewise how God appeared to Moses in a bush of burning fire, likewise how a column of fire led the children of Israel, and how nothing is to be offered, nor sacrificed without fire, etc.

They also call upon the names of God which are in harmony with this purpose, such as can be read in the law and the prophets,[3] "because God is a consuming fire,"[4] and if such name sounding like fire, or similar names, such as the splendor of God, the light of God, the light of the world.

Now we come to the consecration of the place, the tools, and the like.

And so, when consecrating any place, or a circle, you should adopt the prayer that Solomon used when he dedicated the Temple.[5] Moreover, you should bless the place with the sprinkling of holy water, and with the suffumigations by commemorating the mysteries, such as the sanctification of the throne of God, of Mount Sinai, of the Ark of the Covenant, of the Holy of Holies , of the Temple in Jerusalem, etc.

You should call upon such names as are in harmony with this purpose, as the place of God, the throne of God, the seat of God, the tabernacle of God, the altar of God, the home of God, and divine names of this kind which are to be written about the circle, or place.

---

1   Namely the Nephilim. See Gen. 6:1-4.
2   Jud. 15:17-19.
3   A common expression for what Christians call the Old Testament of the Bible.
4   Deut. 4:24.
5   2-Chron. 6:14.

In consecratione autem instrumentorum, et quaruncunque rerum artis [*arti][1] seruientium simili uia procedas aspergendo illa aqua benedicta, et suffumigando suffumigio sacrato, ungendo oleo sancto, consignando aliquo signaculo[2] sacro, benedicendo cum oratione sacra, commemorando ex sacris litteris, et religione, et diuinis nominibus, quę[3] rei consecrandę conformia uidebuntur, Vt uerbi gratia in consecrando gladio commemorauimus [*commemoremus][4] illud Euangelii; "qui habet duas Tunicas," etcetera, et illud Prophetę: "Accipite uobis gladios peracutes."

Consimili omnino uia consecrabis libros, et quidquid uolueris aspergendo, suffumigando, inungendo, signando, et benedicendo commemorationibus sanctis commemorando, sanctificationes ex mysteriis, ut sanctificatio [75r] tabularum decem pręceptorum, quę data sunt Moysi a Deo; item sanctificatio testamenti Dei etcetera.

Finis Praxis, et ordinis consecrandi totiusque Clauiculę.

1　So too DN91, but OP4, P: *arti.*
2　So too OP4, DN91; P: *sigillo.*
3　So too OP4, DN91; P: *nominibusque.*
4　So too DN91, but OP4, P: *commemoremus.*

Moreover, whenever consecrating instruments or whatever else may be used in the Art, you should proceed in the same way, by sprinkling it with holy water, and suffumigating with consecrated suffumigations, anointed with consecrated oil, sealing with some holy seal, blessing with a sacred prayer, by commemorating things taken from sacred literature and religion, and with divine names, which are considered in harmony with the thing being consecrated, so for example, when consecrating the sword, we should recall the one in the Gospel, where it says, "He that has two coats," etc.[1] And from the prophets, "take your sharpest swords with you."[2]

In exactly the same way you must consecrate the books, and whatever else you wish, with sprinkling, suffumigating, anointing, marking with a seal, and with a blessing which commemorates sacred memorials, the sanctifications from the mysteries, such as the sanctification of the Table of the Ten Commandments, which were given to Moses by God, likewise the sanctification of the testaments of God, and so on.

End of the practice and order of consecration, and of the whole Key.

---

1   Luke 3:11. This quote has nothing to do with swords; perhaps Luke 22:36 was intended: "let him sell his coat and buy a sword."

2   I have not found a close match to this, although reminiscent of some biblical quotes, such as 1Sam 25:13.

Appendix. Additional Spirits, from W983 pp. 20-21.

Concerning their powers.

Serguty [*Sergurth] has power over women and girls, and makes you have knowledge and pleasure of them, provided it is a good opportunity.

Heramuel [*Heramael] teaches the art of medicine, the virtue of all kinds of plants and herbs, and gives secrets to curing all types of diseases.

Trmael [*Irmasliel] teaches chemistry and gives the true secret of making projection powder, and the transmutation of metals.

Sustugriel [*Suffugrel] teaches magical art, gives familiar spirits for all that you want, and can give mandrakes.

[Their characters:][1]

1. Serguthy [Sergurth]   2. Heramuel [*Heramael]

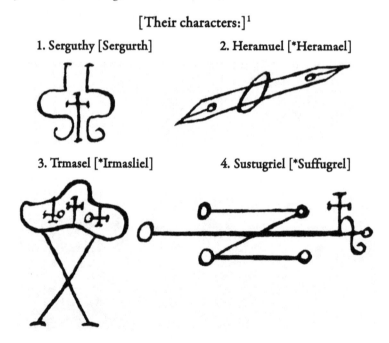

3. Trmasel [*Irmasliel]   4. Sustugriel [*Suffugrel]

[Information on Agateraptarchimath through Sergulath, similar to CSDS, omitted here.]

---

1 In the ms these are all drawn with green ink.

There are still others that depend on those dukes [i.e. Hael and Sergulaf] that have great power; they are eight in number:

The 1st is **Poculo**, 2. **Hariston**. 3. **Aglasis**. 4. **Pantagnon**. 5. **Brurlefer** 6. **Sidragosum**. 7. **Minotous**. 8. **Bucon**.

[Concerning their Powers.]

1. **Poculo** causes one to sleep for 24 hours, [and gives knowledge of the spheres of sleep, etc.][1]

2. **Hariston** lets you walk among flames without burning.

3. **Aglasis** can transport you anywhere in the world.

4. **Pantagnon** makes you invisible, and makes you beloved by great lords.

5. **Bruslefer** makes you loved by women.

6. **Sidragosum** makes young women dance, entirely naked.

7. **Minotous** makes you win at all games.

8. **Bucon** provokes hatred and jealousy.

Their characters are as follows:[2]

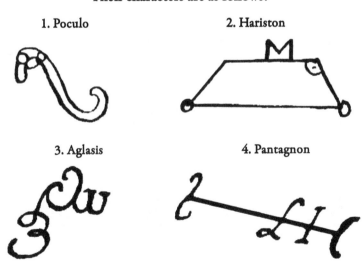

1. Poculo   2. Hariston

3. Aglasis   4. Pantagnon

---

1   So GV.

2   In the ms the first two are drawn with red ink, and the rest with green ink. Note how the seal of Bucon resembles that of Hepath.

5. Bruslefer

6. Sidragosum

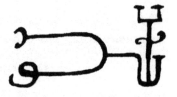

7. Minotous

8. Bucon

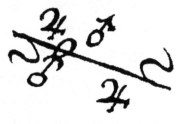

BIBLIOGRAPHY

Manuscripts, primary sources

ASV	Archivio di Stato di Venezia *Sant'Uffizio*, b.93. 76 unnumbered folios, 160 x 250 mm. Bound in thin cardboard, sewn together. Figured in a 1630s trial. The title page reads, "Clauicula Salomonis / Ad / Sciendum Secreta Secretorum". Incipit: "Clauicula Salomonis / de secretis. / In nomine Adonai Tetragrammaton / Apyruch Exbranor." Described by Federico Barbierato in 'Magical Literature of the Venice Inquisition from the Sixteenth to the Eighteenth Centuries' in Gilly, Carlos, and Cis van Heertum. *Magia, alchimia, scienza dal '400 al '700: l'influsso di Ermete Trismegisto = Magic, alchemy and science, 15th-18th centuries: the influence of Hermes Trismegistus*, Vol. I, Firenze: Centro Di, 2002, pp. 166, 175 n28. Unlike P and P2, All figures are complete. Very minimal use of Latin abbreviations. Unlike P, it uses a cursive script. Shows a tendency to use e-caudata (ę,) where P and BNF use æ or e, even to the point of crossing out -ae that he had originally written, and superimposing ę (e.g. folio 73v line 10). ASV makes more use of punctuation, and separates text into more paragraphs.	Ca 1630
BNF	Paris: Bibliothèque nationale de France, Département des manuscrits, Latin ms 18511. 48 folios. Omits many passages, many of them key, such as magic words, and even whole chapters found in other manuscripts. Artwork very closely matches ASV. Includes some marginal notes. The title reads "Salomonis Clavicula."	Ca 1701-1800
DN91	Dresden: The Saxon State and University Library Dresden (SLUB) Dres. N.91 Brown calf binding with gold tooling and lettering on the spine and covers. Carefully written in block script, and complete, but names vary from sentence to sentence (e.g. Frimodth, firmodth – several times, and Frimoth). This is the same manuscript quoted by Adelung. The frontispiece has "6 6 6," seemingly by the original scribe. This leaf is followed by one (numbered: "iii") with the words "Clauicula Salomonis." These are followed by 152 non-blank pages. The actual title reads "De Secretis Sapientissimi Salomonis Clauicula." This is	Ca 1650-1700.

	followed by the usual incipit: "In nomine Adonay / Tetragrammaton, Apyruch / Exbranor. Clauicula Salomonis, quam olim composuit ...." Like ASV, it also uses e-caudata (ę).	
L	Leipzig: Cod. mag. 136. Johann Christoph Wagenseil, circa 1700. 20 folios, 4°. Much of the text is omitted, and nearly all the drawings. Like P, writing is in block script, not cursive. Uses more Latin abbreviations, such as *ht* = *habet.* Title reads "Clavicula Salomonis de secretis." Incipit: "In nomine Adonai Tetragrammaton Appruch, Exbranor."	Ca 1700
GG	Gerald Gardner's library includes another Latin manuscript, catalog number B134, now owned by Richard and Tamarra James in Toronto. Title: "Clavicula Salomonis de Secretis Secretorum." 317 non-blank pages, includes CSDS and a version of Clavicula Salomonis. 158 x 232 mm. They acquired it from Ripley's, and it also has a sticker on the back cover which is labelled "London / Wax Museum / 0986". Writing is cursive but careful; drawings are complete. Text is often simplified or paraphrased. Because of the wide differences, I have not attempted to record here all the alternate readings from this manuscript, but only when they seem to shed light on the urtext. The CSDS text is on pp. 1-68, to which is appended a variant of the *Clavicula Salomonis* in the same hand, paginated separately, as well as some other texts.	Ca 1720
P	Warsaw, Poland, National Library of Poland (Biblioteka Narodowa), Catalog number Rps 3352 II. *Sans loc.* Ca 1600-1700; Physical description: 56 folios; 130 x 195 mm. Text is very carefully written in block script, and drawings carefully executed, but many were left incomplete. Title and incipit reads: *Clauicula Salomonis / De Secretis / In nomine Adonay, Tetragrammaton, Apyruch, Ekbranor. Incipit clauicula Salomonis, quam olim composuit ipse sapientissimus Salomon filius Davidis, ut filios suos institueret in arte Rabidmaclar.* http://www.polona.pl/item/8078413/6/, accessed September 22, 2017	Ca 1600-1700
P2	Warsaw, Poland, National Library of Poland, Rps 6698 II: Salomonowe dziela zabrane : [Kabala] 135 folios; 185 x 225 mm. "Collected (magic) works of Solomon;" includes *De*	Ca 1758-1800

	Secretis starting on p. 127. Manuscript in Polish and Latin. Drawings are very carefully drawn, but many were never completed. Post 1758, because it contains internal references to that date on p. 222. https://polona.pl/item/salomonowe-dziela-zabrane-kabala,ODAzODg2NA/4/#info:metadata, accessed July 2, 2017	
W4667	London: Wellcome Library, manuscript 4667. French. Described by Adam MacLean as follows: "Les Secret misterieux que dieu a Revellez au sage et sauvent Salomon fils de david. Traduit de l'Hebreux en françois. i + 435 pp +2 folios. 124 x 181 mm (8vo). Original brown calf Jansenist binding. Premie Livre. Tey Commence la clavicule Du Très Sauvant Salomon fils de David. Dans laquelle Le Secret de secrets sont ouverts et descovert au Nom d'adonay, Tetragrammaton, aspiruche Exbranor." This manuscript has much of the text of the Latin exemplars, some of which is rearranged, and supplemented with material from other texts. Some of the conjurations are in Latin. This ms. omits or abstracts many passages that are more complicated grammatically, or have obscure vocabulary. Some of the text is disguised with ciphers and abbreviations, and some of the pentacles are mismatched with their descriptions, when compared with other manuscripts. Nevertheless, it is an important witness, since the text and drawings support elements from some of the others.	Mid 1700's
SJ	A Radical's Books: The Library Catalogue of Samuel Jeake of Rye, 1623-90, edited by Michael Cyril William Hunter, lists ms titled "Clavicula Salomonis de Secretis" as "M 1.4° l."	1623-1690
Ar	http://de.wikisource.org/wiki/Beim_Goldmacher_in_Arabien (accessed June 18, 2016) describes another manuscript as follows: "das heißt das Zauberbuch. Es war ein lateinisches Manuscript, auf dessen breitem Rande eine arabische Uebersetzung in ziemlich schlechter Schrift beigefügt war. Der Titel war (deutsch wiedergegeben) „Geheimniß des Schlüssels des hochweisen Salomon, Sohnes des David, Unterweisung in der Kunst ‚Rabidenadaar'. Im Namen von Adonai, Tetragrammaton, Abiruch und Exbranor".	

Manuscripts, secondary sources

AUB24	Oxford, Bodleian Library: Aubrey 24. Titled: Zecorbeni sive Claviculae Salomonis libri IV in quibus I De Praeparementis, II De Experimentis, III De Pentaculis, IV De Artibus. Written by John Aubrey	1674
BNF 24245	Paris: Bibliothèque nationale de France, Département des manuscrits, ms. 24245: French, 1701-1800. Contains some excerpts on fol. 60r-60v.	1701-1800
L1202	London: British Library, Lansdowne MS 1202 has a very abbreviated version of some of the text, also in French.	
W983	London, Wellcome Library, MS 993. L'ART magique: (1) Grimoire. Ou livre 1 des Clavicules de Salomon ou Rabin hébreu contenant les secrets surnaturels qu'y s'opèrent par la puissance des démons.	1709 ?
W4669	London, Wellcome Library, MS 4669 p. 77 ff. *Traité Universel des Clavicules de Salomon*. Also has a highly abbreviated version of some of the text, likewise in French.	1796

Printed sources

Adelung, Johann Christoph. *Geschichte der menschlichen Narrheit oder Lebensbeschreibungen berühmter Schwarzkünstler, Goldmacher, Teufelsbanner ... und anderer philosophischer Unholden 6. 6.* Leipzig: Weygand, 1788. Although Adelung made some errors in his transcription, it can be established that his source manuscript was Dresden N91 (see DN91 above), since it has consistent unique deviations from other exemplars, and matches his description, including number of pages. Adelung was appointed principal librarian to the Elector of Saxony at Dresden in 1787.

Agrippa, Heinrich, *De occulta philosophia Libri Tres,* [Koln,] 1533. Critical edition V. Perrone Compagni. Leiden. Leiden and London: Brill, 1992. English translation: *Three Books of Occult Philosophy,* translated by J[ohn] F[rench], London, 1641.

Agrippa von Nettesheim (pseudo-), Heinrich Cornelius: Henrici Cornelii Agrippae *Liber quartus de Occulta Philosophia, seu de Cerimonijs Magicis,* Bd.: 4, , Marpurgum, 1559, pp. 25 ff.

Alibeck, *Grimorium Verum,* "Memphis," "1517" i.e. probably 1817. The Alibeck edition is largely in French, with a few Latin passages included. See Peterson, 2007.

Barbierato, Federico. *Inquisitor in the Hat Shop: Inquisition, Forbidden Books and Unbelief in Early Modern Venice*. [S.l.]: ROUTLEDGE, 2017.

----, 'Magical Literature of the Venice Inquisition from the Sixteenth to the Eighteenth Centuries' in Gilly, Carlos, and Cis van Heertum. *Magia, alchimia, scienza dal '400 al '700: l'influsso di Ermete Trismegisto = Magic, alchemy and science, 15th-18th centuries: the influence of Hermes Trismegistus*, Vol. I, Firenze: Centro Di, 2002.

----, *Nella stanza dei circoli Chiave di Salomone e libri di magia a Venezia nei secoli 17 e 18*. Milano: Bonnard, 2009.

Brouwer, H. H. J. *Bona Dea: The Sources and a Description of the Cult*. Etudes préliminaires aux religions orientales dans l'Empire romain, t. 110. Leiden: E.J. Brill, 1989.

Cecchetelli, Michael. *Crossed Keys*. n. p.: Scarlet Imprint, 2011.

Damigeron, Patricia Tahil, and Joel Radcliffe. *De Virtutibus Lapidum = The Virtues of Stones*. Seattle: Ars Obscura Press, 2005.

Davidson, Gustav. *A Dictionary of Angels: Including the Fallen Angels*. New York: Free Press, 1971.

Du Cange, *Glossarium ad Scriptores Mediae et Infimae Latinitatis*, vol. VI: Paris: Olmont, 1736.

Duggan, Anne J. *Queens and Queenship in Medieval Europe: Proceedings of a Conference Held at King's College London, April 1995*. Woodbridge: Boydell Press, 2002.

Ficino, Marsilio, and Carol V. Kaske. *Three Books on Life*. Tempe, Ariz: Arizona Center for Medieval and Renaissance Studies, 2006.

Harms, Daniel, James R. Clark, and Joseph H. Peterson. *The Book of Oberon: A Sourcebook of Elizabethan Magic*. Woodbury, Minnesota: Llewellyn Publications, 2015.

Kieckhefer, Richard. *Forbidden Rites: A Necromancer's Manual of the Fifteenth Century*. University Park, Pa. [u.a.]: Pennsylvania State Univ. Press, 1998.

Kiesewetter, Karl. *Faust in der Geschichte und Tradition; mit besonderer Berücksichtigung des occulten Phänomenalismus und des mittelalterlichen Zauberwesens*. Zweiter Teil, Zweite Auflage (= 2nd edition) Berlin: Hermann Barsdorf Verlag, 1921.

Keith, William, and S. L. MacGregor Mathers. *The Grimoire of Armadel*. York Beach, ME: Red Wheel/Weiser, 2001.

Klaassen, Frank. *The Transformations of Magic: Illicit Learned Magic in the Later*

Middle Ages and Renaissance. University Park, PA: The Pennsylvania State University Press, 2013.

Mathers, S. L. MacGregor, ed. *The Key of Solomon the King (Clavicula Salomonis)*. London: Redway, 1889; Reprinted with new artwork: Newburyport, MA: Weiser Books, 2016.

Mathiesen, Robert, "The Key of Solomon: Toward a Typology of Manuscripts", *Societas Magica Newsletter*, Issue 17, 2007.

Peterson, Joseph H. *Grimorium Verum: a handbook of black magic*. Scotts Valley, CA: CreateSpace, 2007.

----, *The Sixth and Seventh Books of Moses, or, Moses, Magical Spirits-Art: Known As the Wonderful Arts of the Old Wise Hebrews, Taken from the Mosaic Books of the Cabala and the Talmud, for the Good of Mankind*. Lake Worth, Fla: Ibis Press, 2008.

----, *Arbatel -- Concerning the Magic of the Ancients: Original Sourcebook of Angel Magic*. Lake Worth, FL: Ibis Press, 2009.

----, *The Sworn Book of Honorius = Liber Iuratus Honorii / by Honorius of Thebes; with text, translation, and commentary by Joseph Peterson*. Lake Worth, FL: Ibis Press, 2016.

Reuchlin, Johann, *On the Art of the Kabbalah*, translated by Martin and Sarah Goodman. Latin text included in facsimile, from Anselm: 1517 edition. Lincoln and London: University of Nebraska Press, 1983.

Shah, Idries, *The Secret Lore of Magic*, New York: Citadel Press, 1970.

Skinner, Stephen. *The Complete Magician's Tables: The Most Complete Set of Magic, Kabbalistic, Angelic, Astrologic, Alchemic, Demonic, Geomantic, Grimoire, Gematria, I Ching, Tarot, Planetary, Pagan Pantheon, Plant, Perfume, Emblem and Character Correspondences in More Than 800 Tables*. Woodbury, Minn: Llewellyn Publications, 2012.

----, *Techniques of Solomonic Magic*, Singapore: Golden Hoard, 2015,

Skinner, Stephen and David Rankine, *The Veritable Key of Solomon*, Singapore: Golden Hoard, 2008.

Stratton-Kent, Jake. *The Trve Grimoire*. Dover: Scarlet Imprint/Bibliothèque Rouge, 2010.

Waite, Arthur Edward. *The Book of Ceremonial Magic*. Secaucus: Citadel, 1911.

Wilby, Emma. *Cunning Folk and Familiar Spirits Shamanistic Visionary Traditions in Early Modern British Witchcraft and Magic*. Brighton [u.a.]: Sussex Academic Press, 2010.

INDEX OF SPIRITS

Abragini: Magical name of the Sun in Autumn, 136

Abraym: Magical name of the Sun in Spring, 136

Abumalith: Spirit of Saturn, kills whomever with a sudden death, 170

Affaterim: Magical name of the Moon in Winter, 136

Agaleraptarkimath: One of Belzebuth's dukes. (var. Agaleraptarkymath, Agaleraptarchimath, Agateraptarkimath), 24

Agiaton: One of the Superior Intelligences, associated with the element Air, clouds, birds, invisibility, commands 130 spirits, 54-58, 64, 122

Aglasis: Invoked for transporting you anywhere, 196

Agusita: Magical name of the Moon in Spring, 136

Aiel: Solar spirit, 158

Amabiel: Martial spirit, can cause burnings, 164

Amalthai: A class of spiritual beings or intelligences, which can include both good and evil spirits. I have not seen these referred to elsewhere, except in the derivative Wellcome manuscript. Perhaps related to Amalthea (Greek "tender goddess"), a mythological nymph, ii, vi, xi, xviii, 54-58, 70, 74, 86

Anael: Intelligence of Venus, described as most pleasing, and can make people more attractive, but addicted to pleasures, 150

Anayl: Lunar spirit, associated with metamorphoses and invisibility, 160, 162

Araton: One of the Superior Intelligences, associated with the element Fire, commands 150 spirits, associated with firearms, 54-58, 64, 120-122

Armatas: Magical name of the Moon in Summer, 136

Arthenay: Magical name of the Sun in Summer, 136

Assaibi: Spirit of Saturn, who can maim anyone, 170-172

Assasiel: Spirit of Jupiter, invoked for blocking lawsuits, 166-168

Begud: One of the Superior Intelligences, associated with the element Water, commands 105 spirits, teaches divination by water, and other arts and sciences associated with water, 54-58, 64, 124

Belzebuth: One of the three infernal Emperors, named as the Prince of Hell, whose subordinates inhabit Africa, ii, xix, 6, 8, 10, 12

Beschard: Daemon said to be a Count, under the command of duke Syrach. Used in weather spells, or moving stones, x, 14, 20, 28, 32

Bruslefer (var. GV Brulefer): Makes you loved by women, 196-197

Bucon (var. GV Bucons): Provokes hatred and jealousy, 196-197

Caluet: Angel of Mercury (var. Caluel), 133n

Capabali: Solar spirit. (var. in H: Capabili), 160

Cassiel: Primary Intelligence of Saturn, invoked to sow discord, 152

Castiel: Spirit of Jupiter, invoked for divination, 166-168

Charariel: One of the Superior Intelligences (or Amalthai), associated with Mercury (var. Chariel), commands 500 spirits, invoked for love and fertility spells, 54-58, 62, 114

Clauneck: *See* Claunth

Claunth: Daemon under the command of duke Syrach. Used in spell for wealth (var. Claunt, Clahunt, and in GV: Clauneck), x, 14, 20, 40

Clepoth: *See* Klepoth

Clistheret: *See* Glithrel

Communtaf (var. Communtas): Magical name of the Sun in Winter, 136

Dadriel: Lunar spirit, 162

Doromiel: Spirit of Venus, invoked to restore the good graces of women, 168-170

Elelogap: *See* Elelographatel

Elelogaphatel: One of the chiefs under Agaleraptarkymath. Used in spells for rain and snow, and commanding water. (var. Elelogafatel, and in GV: Elelogap), ix-x, 24, 28-30

Elestor: One of the three infernal powers or Emperors, named as the Count of Hell, whose subordinates inhabit America, (in GV he is named Astaroth), invoked in a spell against an enemy, 6-12, 42

Fabriel: One of the foremost Solar spirits, invoked for wealth, 156

Frimodth: Daemon under the command of duke Syrach. Used in spells to be impregnable to cold or heat, and love and fertility spells (var. Fremodth, Frimoth, and in GV: Frimost), x, xix, 14-16, 20, 32-38, 198

Frimost: *See* Frimodth

Frucissiere: *See* Frulthiel

Frulthiel: Daemon under the command of duke Syrach. (var. Fructhiel, Fraltiel, Feruothiel, Feruthiel, and in GV: Frucissiere), can bring to you anyone, living or dead, 14, 18, 22, 50

Fruthmerl: Daemon under the command of duke Syrach (var. Frutmerl, Fruthmel, and in GV: Frutimiere), can produce feasts, 14, 18, 22

Frutimiere: *See* Fruthmerl

Ftheruthi: One of Belzebuth's dukes. (var. Fteruthi), 12

Gabriel: Primary Intelligence of the Moon (or sometimes Mercury), petitioned for visions, silver, moisture, metamorphosis, invisibility, 138

Galand: Daemon under the command of duke Syrach. Used in cure or cause disease, and a spell to curse an enemy. (var. in GV: Guland), 14, 18, 22, 42

Galdel: Martial spirit, can provide spirit soldiers, 162-164

Gogmagog: Biblical enemy, invoked for invisibility, v, xiii, 86-88, 95n, 96

Glithrel: Daemon under the command of duke Syrach (var. Glithert, and in GV: Clistheret), can make appearance of daytime or darkness, 14-16, 20

Guadoliel: Spirit of Venus, can arouse lust, invoked for purposes of marriage, 168-170

Guland: See Galand

Gutriel: Spirit of Jupiter, invoked for love, 166-168

Hael: One of the chiefs under duke Resbiroth, teaches languages and secret writing, 24, 26n, 196

Hariston (var. GV Haristum): Invoked for protection from flames, 196

Hepath (var. in GV: Hicpacth, Hiepacth): Daemon under the command of duke Syrach, can make people appear to you, 14, 18, 20, 195n

Heramael (var. GV Heramuel): Daemon under duke Satanachi, 22, 195

Hicpacth, Hiepacth: See Hepath

Huictiigaras: See Hurchetmigarot

Humeth (var. in GV: Humots): Daemon under the command of duke Syrach, can bring any books desired, vii, 14, 18, 22

Humots: See Humeth

Hurchetmigarot (var. Hurchetmigaroth, Hurchet Migaroth, and in GV: Huictiigaras, Huictugaras, Huictiigara): Daemon under the command of duke Syrach, can induce sleep or alertness, 14, 18, 22

Ianael: Lunar spirit, can produce rain, hail, and snow, 160

Iarihael: Spirit of Mercury, can reveal things happening in your family, 164-166

Iaxel: Martial spirit, incites hate and quarrels, 162-164

Irmasliel (var. Hirmasliel, and in GV: Trmael, Trimasel): One of four principal daemons under duke Satanachi, 22, 195

Khil: See Klio

Klepoth (var. Klepot, Clepoth): Daemon under the command of duke Syrach. Produces music, revelry, or hecklers; can also inflict blows invisibly, and can assist card players, 14-16, 20, 44, 45n, 46

Klio (var. Khlio, and in GV: Khil): Daemon under the command of duke Syrach, can cause earthquakes, 14-16, 20

Lucifer: One of the three infernal powers, named as the Emperor of Hell, whose subordinates inhabit Europe and Asia, invoked in spells for causing lightning, and also for invisibility, ii, x, xix-xx, 6-12, 30-32, 44

Madiel: Lunar spirit, invoked for silver, vii, 160

Maganth: Spirit of Jupiter, 168

Magriel: One of the Superior Intelligences, or Amalthai spirits, associated with the Firmament, rules over 9100 spirits, can teach astronomy, divination, politics, and composition of sigils, 54-60, 98-100

Masgrabiel (var. Masgabiel, and in H: Masgabriel): Solar spirit, 156

Matasigais: Magical name of the Moon in Autumn, 136

Menail (var. in GV: Morail): Daemon under the command of duke Syrach, can provide invisibility, 14, 18, 22, 26, 34, 44

Merfiel (var. in GV: Merfilde, Merfide): Daemon under the command of duke Syrach, can transport you, or anything else, anywhere, 14-16, 20

Merfilde, Merfide: See Merfiel

Michael: Primary archangel or Intelligence of the Sun, appealed to for wealth, honors, and curing infirmities, vi, xxii, 138; one of the 72 *Shem ha-Mephoras* angels, 84

Miel: Spirit of Mercury, can help you win at dice, vii, 164-166

Minotous (var. GV Minosons, Minoson): Makes you win at all games, 196-197

Morail: See Menail

Mustalfiel: Spirit of Venus, can let you see a woman from afar, 168-170

Nesbiroth: See Resbiroth

Orifiel: One of the Superior Intelligences, or Amalthai spirits, associated with the Primum Mobile, commands 10000 spirits, can be invoked for knowledge of divinity, theology, metaphysics, religion, knowledge of past, present, and future, and the ability to appear in multiple places at once, 54-58, 72, 90-96

Pamechiel: One of the Superior Intelligences, or Amalthai spirits, associated with Jupiter, commands 4040 spirits, teaches natural philosophy, divination, command over animals, and can transform animals, 54-60, 102-104

Pantagnon (var. GV Pentagnon, Pentagnony): Invoked for invisibility, and to make you beloved of great lords, 196

Pantheriel (var. Panteriel): One of the Superior Intelligences, or Amalthai spirits, associated with the Moon, commands 200 spirits, can teach juggling, commerce, navigation, gaming, can free one from prison, and not feel torture, 54-58, 64,

116-120

Periel: Spirit of Saturn, who can do away with anyone, with an ugly death, 170-172

Poculo (var. GV Proculo): Invoked for sleep and dreams, 196

Pomeriel: One of the Superior Intelligences, or Amalthai spirits, associated with Mars, commands 3100 spirits, invoked for pyrotechnics, metallurgy, martial arts, and invisibility, 54-60, 106-108

Rabidmadar (var. Rabid Madar): Secretary of Sigambach, 2-6

Raphael: Primary Intelligence of Mercury, appealed to for knowledge of arts and crafts, poetics, mathematics, astronomy, performance arts, for metals, knowledge of past and future, transmutation, and a magic mirror, vi, 134, 144-146

Reschin: Daemon under duke Syrach, invoked for knowledge 14, 20

Resbiroth (var. in GV: Nesbiroth): One of Elestor's dukes, 12, 24

Ruduel: Spirit of Mercury, can reveal anything said or done in remote places, 164-166

Sabriel (var. Tabriel): One of the Superior Intelligences, or Amalthai spirits, associated with the Sun, commanding 2000 spirits, invoked for longevity, teaches alchemy, lapidary art, sculpture, can call forth meteors, weapons, spectres, and can resurrect the dead, 54-58, 62, 108-112

Sachiel: Primary archangel, or Intelligence of Jupiter, invoked for help acquiring the magical arts, love, sexual attraction, lawsuits, xii, 148

Sagum: Spirit of Venus, can arouse amorous activity, 168-170

Salkariel: Spirit of Jupiter, 166n, 168

Samael: Archangel, or primary Intelligence of Mars, petitioned to provoke discord, and can provide soldiers, 140-142

Sapiel: Solar spirit, 158

Satanachi: One of Lucifer's dukes, viii, 12, 22

Scyrach: See Syrach

Segol (var. in GV: Segal): Daemon under the command of duke Syrach, can fashion monsters and chimeras, 14, 18, 22

Sergulaf (var. Sergulas, Sergulat, and in GV: Sergulath): Daemon serving under duke Resbiroth, supplies tools, and teaches the workings of machines, 24, 196

Sergulath: See Sergulaf

Sergurth (var. in GV: Serguty, Sergutthy): One of four principal daemons serving under duke Satanachi, viii, 22, 195

Serphgathana: One of Elestor's dukes, 18

Sidragosum: Makes women dance, 196-197

Sidrigol: Spirit of Saturn, 170n, 172

Sigambach: Spirit who supplies specific characters for the agreement or pact. Only mentioned once, 2n, 4

Silcharde: *See* Sirchael

Sirkael (var. Syrchael, Sirchael, and in GV: Silcharde): Daemon under the command of duke Syrach, can display any kind of animal, 14-16, 20

Suffugruel (var. Suffumuguel, Suffugrel, Saffugrel, and in GV: Sustugriel): One of 4 primcipal daemons under duke Satanachi, 22, 195

Surgath (var. in GV: Surgat): Demon under the command of duke Syrach. Used in spell to open locks, x, xiii, 14, 18, 22, 34

Sustugriel: *See* Suffugruel

Syrach (var. Scyrach, Scirach): One of the two dukes under Lucifer, invoked during spell to cause lightning, and another for invisibility, x, 12, 32, 44

Tabriel: *See* Sabriel

Tainor (var. Tainer): One of the Superior Intelligences, or Amalthai spirits, associated with the element Earth, commands 100 spirits, teaches agriculture, reveals treasure, cause or prevents floods, and control gravity, 54-58, 64, 126-128

Tamael: Spirit of Venus, invoked for purposes of marriage, 168

Trimasel. Trmael, Trmasel: *See* Irmasliel

Tumael (var. Tumel): Solar spirit, can give jewels, 156-158

Turmiel: Angel or spirit of Mercury, invoked for having all arts and sciences, and for a prudent or clever child, 134, 164-166

Uriel: (1) Spirit invoked for producing sweet music, 46; (2) One of the Superior Intelligences, or Amalthai spirits, associated with Saturn, commanding 5000 spirits, teaches mathematics, optics, natural magic, invisibility, and ability to fly, and make one more likeable, 46, 54-60, 100-102; (3) Spirit of Saturn, can sow discord, 170-172

Ustael: Solar spirit, invoked for benevolence, and control of important persons, 156-158

Uchariel: One of the Superior Intelligences, or Amalthai spirits, associated with Venus, invoked for longevity and health, learning grammar, rhetoric, logic, medicine, herbs, 54-58, 62, 112-114

Vetael (var. in H: Vetuel): Lunar spirit, can make banquets appear, 160-162

Vetuel: *See* Vetael

Vianuel: Martial spirit, causes death, 162-164

Zatael: Lunar spirit, 162

GENERAL INDEX

Abenarach, Isaac, 52

Abognazar, iii-iv

abortion, 16

Abramelin, Sacred Magic of, ii, 82n

abstinence, 52

Achilles, v, 132

active use, xix

adder's tongue, 50

Adelung, Johann Christoph, iii

Africa, 6, 8, 10, 12, 14

agnocasto wood, v, 36

agreement:. See pact

agriculture, 64

Agrippa, Heinrich, viii, xvi-xviii, xxi, 84n, 184n

Agrippa, pseudo- (OP4), iv, vi, xii-xiii, xvi, xviii, 180n

air, 176; healthy or pestilential, 64, 122

alchemy, 62, 195

Alexander the Great, 132-134

Alibeck, xi

almond oil, 42

aloe, 78

altar, ix-x, 38, 176

alum, 34

Amalthai spirits, ii, vi, xi, xviii, 54-58, 70, 74, 86

Amalthea (goddess), ii, vi

ambushes, protection from, 94

America, 6-14

angels, 188

anger, 142

animal science, 60; controlling, 60, 104; to make appear, 16, 62

ants, 146

apparel, xii, xviii, 76

apparitions, 52

appear, to make one appear in several places at once, 94

Arabic influence, v

Arbatel, 52n

Archivio de Stati di Venezia (ASV), i, iv, xx

arm, 178

armies, 62

artavus, xx

artistry, 144-146; skill in, 164

ashes, 86

Asia, 6, 10, 12, 14

assistants, xi

astrologers, vi, 154; astrology, xviii, 60, 148

astronomy, 60, 136

athame, xix

atonement, 190

attractiveness, 62-64, 150

balsam, 78

baptism of stone, vi, 174, 180

Barbierato, Federico, i-ii, iv-v, xxi

Barrett, Francis, xi

Barron, Paul Harry, xix

basset, i

beating the chest, xii

beauty, 62-64

bed, 96

bees, 146

beginners, 136

benevolence, 156

Bible, vii, 182, 188

Biblioteka Narodowa, iii

birds, 64, 152; power over, 122

bitumen, 50

Black Pullet (*Le Poule Noire*), ii

blood, xi, 4, 6, 46, 66, 76, 80, 96, 104-106, 110, 114, 122, 126, 178

bloodstone, viii-ix, 4, 28

bodies, to make two ~ appear in the same place, 94

Bona Dea (goddess), ii

bond, 6

Book of Oberon, xviii, 82, 133

books, 18, 92; consecrating, 194

brawls, provoke, 142

breathing, 192

bronze, 80n

Brouwer, H. H. J., ii

Bruno, Giordano, ii

burning, to cause, 162

Caesar, 18

camphor, 30

Cancer (constellation), 72

candles, 38, 44, 192; black, ix-x

Capricorn, 104

Cardanus, Gerolamo, vi

cardinal directions, 68, 70, 88

cards, games of, vii, 16

Catholicism, xviii

Cecchetelli, Michael, xviii-xix

celestial influences, 54

chalice, xii, 174-176; copper, 38

chameleon, xi, 44

chant, x

characters (or emblems) of spirits, viii, 4, 18, 154, 182

charms (aka incantations, chants. Latin: *carmina*), ii

chemistry, 195

chimeras, 18

chiromancy, 148

Christ, 186

Christian, xviii

Christmas, 102

chrysolite, x, 36

chthonic spirits, v, vii, xx. See also spirits

Church, 188

Cicero, ii, v, 18

circle, magic, i, vi, ix-xi, xviii, 28, 32-38, 42-46, 50, 66-68, 76, 82, 88, 168, 182, 192; of Lucifer, xx

Clark, James, xviii

Clavicula Salomonis: See *Key of Solomon*

clay image, vi, xii, 28, 174

clientele, iv

cloudy, 126

cold, x

comedy, 146

commerce, 118

companions, vii

conduct, vii

conjurations, xi-xii, 32, 66, 70, 71n, 82, 86-88, 188

consecration, 180-190; of the stone, 174, 178

control of important persons, 156

copper, ix, 80; vessel, x

copyists, ii; for hire, xiii-xiv

courage, 140

cow, 48

craftsmanship, 144

cross, 34

crystal, 76

cup, 174

cuttlefish, xi, 44

Damigeron, viii-ix

damnation, 54

dancing, 196

danger, 184; from practicing magic, 54; from spirits, v

Darius, 132

darkness, to make it appear, 16

date, iv

Davidson, Gustav, 133n

day of Mars, 4

Day of the Dead, 110

daytime, to make it appear, 16

dead, 110; to speak with the, 18, 46-50; death, v, 62

deception, viii

Dee, John, 82n

deer, row, skin, 80

demonology, xviii

destruction, 188

devil, 154n

dignities, 138

directions, cardinal, 88

discord, creating, 154, 170

diseases, curing, 18, 62, 114, 122, 195

dismissing the goal from your mind, xi

divination, 58-60, 64, 148, 166; by water, 124

dog, 46-48

Dominican Order, ii

dreams, 60

Duggan, Anne, ii

earth, 176

earthquakes, 16

east, facing, 86

eclipses, xi, 98

education, v

egg white, 34

elemental spirits, v; elements, vi, 54, 56, 176

emanations, 134

Enchiridion of Pope Leo, xviii

encouragement, 88

enemies, 182-184; against, 62, 106-108, 142, 150, 170

energy of Nature, xii

English, iv, xii-xiii

engraving, 178

Epicurus, 132

escape artistry, 146

Europe, 6, 10, 12, 14

evil, protection from, 180

excavation, 64

Exodus, xi, xvi, 84n

exorcism, xi, 66

experiments, 90

fairies, ix

faith, vii; in oneself, 188; need for, 174

familiar spirits, 195

fasting, xi, 82, 176

Faust, iii

fertility, ii, 62-64, 116

Ficino, Marsilio, viii, xxi

fire, xi, 34, 38, 72, 76, 176; consecrating, 190-192; exorcised, 86; protection from or destruction by, 64, 120-122, 196; causing, 122

firearms, 64

Firmament, 56

fish, 64

flying, 60, 64, 102, 124

folk magic, xviii

folklore, ii, ix

food offerings, viii

Fortuna (goddess), ii

fox, 146

frankincense, 6, 32, 50

French, xx

friendship, 138

fulgurite, x, 32

gaming or gambling, i, 16, 64, 116, 164, 196

Gardner, Gerald, i, iii, xix

garments, ix, xi, 32, 82, 84, 168. See also apparel

gender, ii, iv, vii, 4

genii, xii

genitalia, 38

geography, v

gluttony, 176

God, names of, vii; pleading with, 176

Gog Magog, v, 86-88, 96

gold, 6

Governess Intelligences, 84

Graham, George, xix

grammar, 62

Great Chain of Being, v

grimoires, i, x-xi, xix; *of Armadel*, xix; *of Pope Honorius*, xix

Grimorium Verum, iii, v-vi, ix, xi, xix-xx

guardian spirit(s) (*genius, genii*), 130-132, 176

gymnastics, 146

hail, 160

Harms, Daniel, xviii

hatred, provoking, 164, 162, 196

head, uncovered, 84

healing, 62, 114, 122, 195

heart, 42

heat, x

heavens, 176

Hebrew, xii, xvi-xvii, 52; characters, 36

heliotrope (plant), 72; (gem): See bloodstone

Heptameron, vi-vii, xi, xviii, 136n

herbs, i, ix, 62; virtues of, 195

heterodoxy, xviii

hierarchy of spirits, viii

Holy Spirit, 188

homeoteleuton, xv-xvi, 7n, 63n, 185n, 189n

honors, 100

hoopoe, 80, 106, 110

humors, theory, v, 80n, 176

hunting, 60

ice, 34; to make, 30

illusions, 140; illusory feasts, 18, 160

imprisonment, release from, 118

incantation, viii, 32, 36, 40-42; to be sung, 42

incense, viii, x-xi, 6, 50, 66, 76, 82

industriousness, 132

initiation, xii, 52

injury, cause, 170

ink, xi, 66, 80

Inquisition, Venetian, i

insects, 64

instruments, 188; of the art, 176; consecrating, 192

intelligences, 54, 58, 66, 130-132

intent, 192

intimacy, 150

invisibility, v, xi-xii, 18, 44, 58, 60, 64, 90, 96, 102, 108, 124, 140, 160, 196

invocation, vii, ix-xii, xvii, 6, 30, 36n, 66, 70, 82-86, 156

invulnerability, 106-108

iron filings, x, 36

Isis (goddess), ii

Italian, v

James, Tamarra and Richard, xxi

jasper, green, 4

jealousy, provoking, 196

Jesus, ii

jewels, 156

Jews, 76

juggling, 64

Jupiter, xii, 94, 106, 148-150

justice, 138

Kaske, Carol, viii

Key of Solomon, i-ii, iv, vi, viii-ix, xi, xviii, xx, 80n, 130n

Kieckhefer, Richard, vii, ix

Kiesewetter, Karl, iii

Klaassen, Frank, iv

kneeling, 84, 176

knife, xii, 38, 180

knots, love, x, 36

knowledge, 14, 82, 98; acquiring, 90

Kr, Paweł, xxi

ladle, 36

lamen, vi, viii, xi, 2-4

lamp, x, 34, 192; oil, 32, 34, 42

languages, learning, 24

lapidary, viii; arts, 62

Latin, xiii-xiv, xx

lawsuits, 150, 166

leather, 48

Leipzig, University, iii

Leo, 100, 122

Liber Iuratus Honorii: See *Sworn Book of Honorius*

liberal arts, 62

libido, 150-152, 168

Libra, 112

light, 192

lightning, viii; lightning stone, x, 32

likable, 100

linen, xi, 84

Litany of Saints, xi, xviii, 68, 82

location: See place

locks, x, 18

lodestone, x, 34

logic, 62

longevity, 62, 112

Longo, Leonardo, i, xxi

Lord's Prayer, 82

love, iv-v,x, 16, 62, 114-116, 150, 166-168, 196

loyalty to spirits, xii

lunaria, x, 30-32, 72

lyre, ix-x, 42

Maccabees, 182

machines, understanding, 24

macrocosm, vi

mandrake, x, 36, 195

March, 142

marital fidelity, 146

marranos, 76

marriage, 152, 168

Mars, viii, 106, 112, 114, 140-142, 184

martial arts, 60, 106

Mary, mother of Jesus, ii, 126

mass (ceremony), xii, 76, 110, 124; of Saint Claudius, 118; of Saint Mary Magdalene, 114; of the Holy Cross, 92; of the Nativity, 80; of the Trinity, 102

mathematics, 60, 144

Mathers, Samuel L., iv, viii, xix, 76n

Mathiesen, Robert, iv

matins, 126

McLean, Adam, iii

medicine, 62, 195

memorization, 112

Mercury, 94, 114, 144; angel of, 134

metal chalice, 174

metallurgy, 60

metals, xi; attaining, 146; seven, 72

metamorphoses, 140, 160

meteors, 62, 112

microcosm, vi, 176

milk, ix-x, 36

mirror, magic, 146

moans or sighs (Lat. *gemitus*), x, 44

moderation, vii

monasteries, ii, v

money, v, x, 40-42

monkey, 38

monsters, 18, 60

Moon, 36, 80, 110, 124, 128, 136-140; day of the, 96; eclipse, 98; full, 72, 76, 108; phases, 160n

morning, 82

motivating the spirits, viii

motor intelligences, cosmic, v, 84

mountains, 80

Munich manual of Necromancy, ix

music, ix, 16, 88; to hear, 44-46

musk, 78

myrrh, 32-34, 50, 78

name of person, 36; of stone, 174; names of God, vii, ix, 52, 68, 84, 180-190; of spirits, 180

Naples, i

natural ingredients, ii, viii, xviii

Nature, 130; energy of, xii

navigation, 64. See also sailing

necromancy, 46

needle, 42

neighbors, helping, 52

neo-Platonists, v

nigramantic divination, 148

North, ix, 84; facing, ix, 80

ocre, red, 38

octopus, 44

offerings to spirits, viii, xii, xviii, 6, 10, 154

oil, xii, 174-176; almond, 42; consecrated, 190, 194

onobrychis, 50

optics, 60

owl *(bubo)*, 80, 96, 103n, 126

ox, 30

pact, viii, xii, 4-6, 154

Padua, ii

paper, 90; virgin, 66, 74, 80; see also parchment

parchment, 4, 32, 38, 44, 48, 80; virgin, xi

Paris (mythology), 132

Parrhasius, 132

past and future, revealing, 146; past, present, and future, 96, 124-126

pentacle, "great," xi, 66, 70-76, 84-88; (lesser) pentacles, viii, xii, xix, 2, 22, 52, 70, 74, 180-184; given by spirits, 90

performance arts, 146

periapt, 4

peridot, x, 36

pestilence, 122

Peterson, Joseph, iii, vi, ix, xi, xviii

phantoms, 178

philosophy, natural, 60

phlegmatics, 140

physics, 60

physiognomy, 148

pigeons, 152

pillow, 96

pitch, 44

place for operations, 2, 66, 80; consecrating, 192

planetary hours, i, xi; intelligences, xii; planets, vi, xi, 56, 136; planetary aspects, 136

plants, virtues of, 195

Plato, v

pleading with God, 188

pleasure, 150

Pliny the Elder, 132n

poetry, 144

politics, 60

Poule Noire, Le, ii

practice of magic, 130

prayer, xi-xii, xviii; prayers, 176, 188

pregnancy, 16

priestly apparel, xi

Primum Mobile, vi, 56

prison, 64

prophecy, xii, 58, 92, 96, 124

protection, 118, 184

provoking spirits, 10

Psalms, x-xi, xiv, 76-78, 82, 181n, 182, 184n, 188

Pseudomonarchia Daemonum, viii-ix

pumice, 28

purification, 174

pyrotechnics, 60

QiRui Huo, xxi

quarrels, provoke, 162

rain, ix, 14, 28, 160; of blood, 14; of toads, 14

Rankine, David, iv, xix

Raziel, vi

Red Dragon (*Le Dragon Rouge*), xix

religion, 60

remote viewing, 164, 168

renunciation of God, viii

reproduction, 116

resin, 44

resurrecting the dead, 62, 110

Reuchlin, Johann, xvi-xviii, 84n

revelations, 182

rhetoric, 62

ring for carrying spirits, v, 26

rituals, Catholic, xviii

Roman Gradual, xi

rooster, xii, 42, 80, 86, 106, 114, 142, 178

Sabbath, 118

sacrifice, xii, 10, 38, 86, 154

safety from danger, 90

Sagittarius, 104

sailing, 64, 120, 126, 186

saints, xi; feast days, xii, Saint Andrew's cross, 34; Claudius, 118; Gervase, 124; John the Baptist, 116; John [the Baptist], Day of, 92; Litany of, xi, xviii

salt, xii, 28, 174

sand, 32

Santoro, Raffaele, xxi

Satan, 184

Saturn, 100, 120, 124, 152, 184

sciences, knowledge of, 164

Scorpio, 122

scorpion, 80

Scotus, Michael, vi

sculpture, 62

sea, 176

seals of spirits, vi, 194

seasons of the year, 136

seclusion, vii, 52, 80

secrecy, vii, 52; secrets, 82

self-flagellation, 190n

serpent, 46

sex, iv, x, 16, 38, 195; sexual acts, 150-152, 168

Shah, Idries, xix

Shem ha-Mephorash, xii, 84, 92; angels, xvi

shoe, 94

sickness, 18, 62; cause, 114

sigil of protection, viii; sigils, 60

silence, observing, x-xi, 32

silk cloth, 100

singing incantations, ii, viii-x, 42

skin, 46

Skinner, Stephen, iv, xix, xxi

slapstick, 146n

sleep, xi, 18, 36, 40-42, 50, 96; causing, 196; spheres of, 196

snake, 110n

snow, ix, 14, 30, 160

Socrates, 132

Sodom and Gomorrah, 186

soldiers, 142, 162

Solomon, biblical king, vii, 2, 130, 192

soul, vi-vii; strengthening, 174

sparrows, 152

spectators, 16

specters, 62

spirits of each hour, 174; solar, 156; of Jupiter, 166; of Saturn, 170; of the East, 6; of Venus, 168; Amalthai, xi; anger, 8; sounds, 8; causing injuries, 8, 10, 16; earthly (terrestrial), 8; appearance of, v, 86-88, 168; spirits, chthonic, v, vii, xx, 4-50; infernal, v; constraining or binding, 180; danger from, v; dukes, 6, 12, 14, 22, 24, 32, 196; elemental, iv; emperors, 6, 8; princes, 6; counts, 6; familiarity with, 66, 82; friendship with, 6; intermediate, 154; loyalty to, xii, 154; lunar, 160; martial, 142, 162; Mercurial, 164; names, 188; of the air (aerial), 26; of the fire, 26; visible appearance, 26; terrestrial, 26; Solar, 4, 142. See also Amalthai

sprinkling, 68, 76, 178, 190

star, 46; Starry Heavens, vi; stars, 134, 188

stemma, xvii

stick, 38

stole, xii, 168

stone, ix, magical, vi, xii, 174

storms, ix, 14

Stratton-Kent, Jake, iii, xxi

studious, 60, 100

suffumigating, viii, x, xii, 50, 82, 154, 190-194

Sun, viii-x, 72, 100, 104, 110-112, 122, 136-138; altering the course of the, 112

sunrise, 82, 96, 112, 124, 126

sunset, 82, 116

superstition, 66

sword, vi, xi, xviii, 66, 74-76, 80, 84-88, 194

Sworn Book of Honorius, ii, v, ix, xi, 166n, 168n, 170n

symbolism, vii

sympathetic magic, ii, vii, ix, xviii, 66

Syriac characters, 36

table, 40

Tahil, Patricia, viii

talismans, xix

theology, 60

time for operations, xi-xii, 66, 80

tin, 174

toads, 14, 80, 104

tools, 24

tortoise, 4

torture, insensibility to, 64, 118

Toscano, Salvatore, xxi

trade, 64

trance, xi

transmutation, 60, 146; of metals, 62, 195

transporting, 16, 196

treasure, in the earth, 64, 128; in the sea, 64, 126-128

triangle, 36, 44

Turner, Robert, xi

Universals and Particulars, v

Universe, 176

unlocking, x

use, evidence of, i, xiii

vellum, xi, 80

venereal disease, 18

Venice, Venetian Inquisition, i, xxi

Venus, x, 110, 114, 150-152

verses, 36

vessel, 110; copper, ix-x, 38, 80; mixing, 78

victory, 182

vigilant, to make one, 18

Viola, Francesco, i, xiii, xxi

violence, 162

visible appearance, 154

visions of people, to make appear, 18

voces magicae, iv, xii-xiii

vowing to your guardian spirit, 176

Waite, A. E., iii

wand, ix, xii, xviii, 28, 32, 34, 50, 168

war, 108; art of, 60; provoke, 162

water, 64; artificial sea, 28; consecrated (or holy), xi-xii, 66, 76, 80, 86, 110, 178-180, 190, 192; consecrating, 192; traveling under, 126-128;

control of, 24, 124-126

wealth, 14, 138, 156

weapons, 62-64

weather, 82

Wellcome Library, iii

whistle, ix, xi, 86

Wicca, ii-iii, xix; Wiccan Church of Canada, xxi

Wilby, Emma, ix, xii

will, 192

William of Auvergne, viii

willow, 50

winds, 14; Wind, East, 142; West, 140

wine, xii, 86, 174-176; wine offerings, viii-ix

witchcraft, i-ii, xix, 64n

wolf, 116

womb, xii

women, 16, 116; power over, 195

wood, 50; as spirit offering, viii

Yorke, Gerald, xix

youth, 114

zeal, vii, 174

Zeuxis, 132

Also by Joseph H. Peterson

Arbatel: concerning the Magic of the Ancients, an original sourcebook of angel magic. Lake Worth, FL: Ibis Press, 2009.

The Book of Oberon: A Sourcebook of Elizabethan Magic. Woodbury, MN: Llewellyn Publications, 2015. (With Daniel Harms and James R. Clark)

The Clavis or Key to the Magic of Solomon. Lake Worth, FL: Ibis Press, 2009.

Esoteric Archives CD. Kasson, MN, 2001. http://www.esotericarchives.com. Includes Mathers/Peterson edition of *Key of Solomon the King,* and fifty other rare esoteric books.

Grimorium Verum, Scotts Valley, CA: CreateSpace, 2007.

John Dee's Five Books of Mystery: Original Sourcebook of Enochian Magic : from the Collected Works Known As Mysteriorum Libri Quinque. Boston, MA: Weiser Books, 2003.

The Lesser Key of Solomon: Lemegeton Clavicula Salomonis : Detailing the Ceremonial Art of Commanding Spirits Both Good and Evil. York Beach, ME: Weiser Books, 2001.

Noblet Tarot – Restoration of the oldest Tarot de Marseille deck, 85 cards. 2016.

The Sixth and Seventh Books of Moses. A new edition, corrected and expanded. Lake Worth, FL: Ibis Press, 2008.

The Sworn Book of Honorius = Liber Iuratus Honorii / by Honorius of Thebes; with text, translation, and commentary by Joseph Peterson. Lake Worth, FL: Ibis Press, 2016.

True Black Magic (La véritable magie noire). Kasson, MN: Twilit Grotto Press, 2017.

As contributor:

Document-Based Questions (World History/Ancient Civilizations). Harcourt School Publishers, 2006.

Fieser, James, and John Powers, *Scriptures of the World's Religions.* Boston: McGraw Hill, 1998.

Fisher, Mary P, and Lee W. Bailey. *Anthology of Living Religions.* Upper Saddle River, N.J: Pearson Education, 2011.

CPSIA information can be obtained
at www.ICGtesting.com
Printed in the USA
LVHW11*0328021018
592104LV00008BA/121/P